THE 5 ESSENTIALS OF LIFE

Developing a plan for personal growth in the areas that matter most

Given to

_____

by

_____

because I care about you excelling in the areas that matter most for your future impact and success.

ALSO BY BRANDON PARK

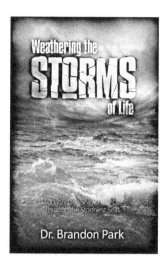

Weathering the Storms of Life
Sometimes life doesn't go the way we planned. All we can see are the storms. We try so hard to escape. We wonder if there's a reason for all of this. But in the midst of the storm, God is working. He is healing. He is cleansing. In this book, Dr. Park shares key biblical principles coupled with powerful stories that illustrate how God offers to us His strength, His presence, and His supply when we find ourselves in life's darkest moments. What difficulty do you find yourself in today? As you explore the truths of Scripture presented in this book, allow those problems to draw you closer to Jesus Christ and to enable you to sense His presence in a powerful way.

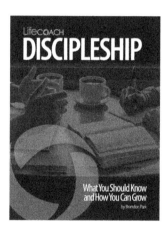

LifeCoach: Discipleship
LifeCoach: Discipleship is a tool for personal and spiritual growth and development that converges captivating media, practical content, and thought-provoking study questions all on the platform of interactive coaching relationships. This book comes with a free app for iPhone, iPad, and Android users. Studies have shown that we grow best when we have someone to invest in us and walk with us in life. That's why we want to help you learn how to be a *LifeCoach* and learn how to invest your life into others. This journey is designed for the participant to become a coach. The goal is for the mentee, the one being discipled, to become a mentor to multiply other disciples. You were made to be a disciple and to make disciples. As you spend time with God and His Word each day, read with a "learn and return" mindset. You're not only learning and growing just for yourself; you're also learning for the person you will someday disciple in following Jesus.

Available at

ABOUT THE AUTHOR

Dr. Brandon Park is a communicator, author, coach, and the Lead Pastor of Connection Point, a multisite church in the Kansas City suburbs.

Brandon has been in a senior leadership role as Lead Pastor for more than 18 years. With a focus on outreach, systems for church health, one-on-one discipleship, and small groups - each church he has led has been blessed with substantial growth. Connection Point Church near Kansas City, Missouri, has been listed twice in *Outreach Magazine* as one of the fastest growing churches in America.

He has earned four degrees including a Bachelor of Science degree, two master's degrees, and a doctorate. He is also the author of five books including *LifeCoach: Discipleship*, *Weathering the Storms of Life*, and *The Five Essentials of Life*.

Brandon is not only a pastor but is also a personal growth expert and certified Executive Coach to CEOs and business owners. He is also a sought-after speaker for corporations and non-profits. His life mission is to engage audiences through his communication abilities, to equip them with practical resources to succeed in life and leadership, and to empower individuals to multiply their influence.

He is married to his college sweetheart, Carrie, and together they have three children: Austin, Ava Marie, and Ainsley (plus a Yorkie named Biscuit). They currently reside in Kansas City, Missouri.

Visit Brandon Park at www.BrandonPark.org
Follow Brandon on Twitter @Brandon_Park
Connect on Facebook at facebook.com/drbrandonpark

To schedule Brandon to speak at your next corporate or non-profit event, visit his website at BrandonPark.org.

To order a case of 25 books (or more) at a discounted price plus free shipping, contact Connection Point Resources at 816-353-1994.

THE 5 ESSENTIALS OF LIFE

Developing a plan for personal growth in the areas that matter most

by Brandon Park

Copyright © 2018 by Connection Point Resources

All rights reserved. No part of this publication may be reproduced, stored, in a retrieval system, or transmitted, in any form or by any means, electronic, mechanical, photocopying, recording or otherwise, without the prior written permission of the publisher. Printed in the United States of America. For information, address Connection Point Resources, 10500 E 350 Highway, Raytown, MO 64138.

Cataloging-in-Publication date for this book is available from the Library of Congress.

First Connection Point Resources paperback edition 2018
First Connection Point Resources Kindle eBook edition 2018

Published by Connection Point Resources
www.connectionpoint.tv

Connection Point Resources books are available at special discounts for bulk purchases in the U.S. by corporations, non-profits, churches, and other organizations. For more information, please contact the Executive Assistant to Dr. Brandon Park by phone at 816-353-1994, by email at contact@connectionpoint.tv, or by mail at 10500 E 350 Highway, Raytown, MO 64138.

ACKNOWLEDGMENTS

This book is dedicated to...

My wife **Carrie Park**.
Thank you for how you encourage and support me to
reach my dreams and become all that God has created me to be.
You're the greatest wife any man could ever hope for.

My three kids: **Austin**, **Ava Marie**, and **Ainsley**.
Thank you for being patient with "boring Daddy" while he was
finishing this book. I love you with all my heart and I'm praying
and believing God for your success in each of these Five Essentials.

My church family, **Connection Point Church**.
It's an honor and a privilege for me to lead some of the
greatest people in the world. There's nowhere on earth I'd
rather speak than to you each and every Sunday.

My incredible staff team at Connection Point,
this project would not be possible without your partnership.
I would like to specifically thank the following people
who were most involved in this project...

Julie Herron, *my Executive Assistant*
Alyson Browning, *Communications Director*
Elise Cox, *Graphic Design and Layout*
Franklin Lugenbeel, *Graphic Design*
Mark Browning, *Editor*
Jeff Humphrey, *Executive Pastor*

CONTENTS

BEFORE YOU GET STARTED — 11
Understanding the Five Essentials — 13
Achieving a Laser Focus — 23
The Power of Habit — 29
Postponing Your Procrastination — 35
The Wheel of Life — 41

THE FINANCIAL ESSENTIAL — 47
The Greatest Financial Principle — 49
A Bulletproof Budget Strategy — 55
Accelerate Your Debt Reduction — 61
Pay Off Your Mortgage in 5 to 7 Years — 67
Invest for Tomorrow — 73
What the Wealthy Do Different — 79
The Rewards of a Generous Life — 85

THE PHYSICAL ESSENTIAL — 93
Nutrition: Eat This, Not That — 95
Your Guide to Health Supplements — 101
Exercise: Your Fitness Challenge — 109
The Five Rules of Fat Loss — 117
The Benefits of Intermittent Fasting — 125
High-Performance Sleeping — 131
Become an Early Riser — 137

THE INTELLECTUAL ESSENTIAL — 143
Invest in Yourself — 145
Develop a Clear Vision — 152
Determine Your Priorities — 160
Set Goals That Work For You — 167
Time Management Principles — 173
How to Rewire Your Brain — 181
Make Stress Your Friend, Not Your Enemy — 189

THE RELATIONAL ESSENTIAL — 195

The Foundation of All Relationships — 197
The Needs of Men and Women — 205
The Art of Listening — 213
How to Resolve Conflict — 219
Making and Keeping Friends — 227
The Science of Likability — 237
Working Your Networking — 245

THE SPIRITUAL ESSENTIAL — 251

Becoming God's Friend — 253
Seek Him First — 259
How to Pray with Power — 267
Discover Your Calling — 275
Increasing Your Faith — 287
An Attitude of Gratitude — 293
Five Things God Does Not Know — 299

CRAFTING YOUR GROWTH PLAN — 305

How to Get Motivated — 307
A Blueprint for Life — 311

NOTES — 322

Before You
GET STARTED

Understanding the Five Essentials

Are you living the life that you were meant to live?

Almost every philosopher in the world has dealt primarily with two questions: 1.) How can I be a good person? 2.) How can I live the "good life"? These are ways of asking what it means to flourish as a human being. It's hard-wired into us to seek the answers to these questions. But why do the answers to these apparently simple questions seem so elusive? Why is it that most people feel like they're not living the good life? What are they missing?

Life truly is a balancing act. Have you ever seen those guys spinning plates at the circus? By the time they get the ninth or tenth plate spinning, the first one they started with is starting to wobble and is about to fall. That's how a lot of us feel trying to make it through life, isnt it? We may feel like we're excelling in one area, but two or three other essential areas of our lives are mediocre at best — or falling apart at worst.

We've seen classic examples of this in our own experience. We've seen the guy at the gym that looks like he just stepped off the cover of a fitness magazine, but he has to get a ride home because his car had been repossessed by the bank. He may have 6% body fat, but is he really succeeding?

A well-lived life is also so much more than just well-handled finances. If you become a millionaire but lose your friends, family, and marriage in the process, is it really worth it? Furthermore, are you really "wealthy?" If you're the richest individual in the world and yet you live in chronic pain to the point that you can't even get out of bed, is that real wealth? So many people give their lives to their career to such an extent that they don't have anything left to give in terms of their relationships or any other aspect of their lives. Our problem is that our measurement of wealth today is too small. The word *wealth* comes from an old Middle English word that simply means "well-being." And that's the aim of this book. To help you live life with an overwhelming sense of well-being.

MindValley once did a survey among many of their subscribers as to in what areas of life they excelled. Their audience rated themselves strong in five key dimensions: 1.) Character, 2.) Spiritual Life, 3.) Intellectual Life, 4.) Romantic Life, 5.) Parenting.

> The idea is not to just be good in one area, but to thrive by finding growth and balance in the areas of life that matter most.

But here's the interesting part. A lot of people who are strong in these five areas have parallel weaknesses. The same people who are strong in character and spiritual life were weak in finances. The same people who were strong in their intellectual life were having difficulty in their romantic relationships. The same people who were strong in their romantic life and parenting wished that their careers and finances were better.

So the idea behind this book is not to just be good in one area and weak in another, but to thrive by finding growth and balance in the areas of life that matter most.

The Five Essentials of Life is perfect for you if you are…
- In search of a clear vision and strategy to turn your average, mediocre life into an *extraordinary* one.
- Curious to discover *what you're really capable of* in every vital area of your life.
- Feeling *stuck, uninspired, lost, or frustrated* with the rules and ideas of success that today's culture has imposed on you.
- If you're prepared to let go of the stubborn, limiting ideas you currently *believe about yourself* and discover what truly makes you happy and fulfilled.

What are the Five Essentials?

So what are the Five Essentials? Listed in order of priority, from the least important to the most important, here they are:

1. Financial
I've found in my own personal experience that income does not exceed personal development. Unless you develop yourself beyond your income, that income will usually stay back to where you are. So in the Financial section, we're going to deal with how we go about managing our spending, maintaining our level of contentment, retiring debt that's keeping us in bondage, investing for the future, growing in our generosity, and creating wealth for tomorrow.

2. Physical
Your soul and spirit lives inside a temple known as your body. If we don't take care of the temple we'll never be able to fulfill all that God has designed for us. So our nutrition, exercise, fat loss, musle gain, supplements, and rest are vitally important to our longevity and overall well-being.

3. Intellectual
The big challenge of life is that you can have more than you've got because you can become more than you are. Unless you change how you are, you'll always have what you've got. This section will focus on how we invest and manage ourselves. It will examine how we set goals, establish new habits, become more productive, have stronger emotional health, and rewire our thinking patterns.

4. Relational
This essential refers to the quality and quantity of our relationships with others. Your marriage, family, and friends ought to be the one of the most important things to you in this life. So we'll examine the foundation of all relationships, how to make and keep friends, how to strengthen your marriage, and how to improve your communication and conflct resolution skills.

5. Spiritual
The most essential of the Five Essentials is by far the most neglected. But when the Spiritual is prioritized, it adds life, vitality, and meaning to the other four. How you grow in your connection with God and the purpose for why He has put you here on this earth is critical if you ever hope to realize your potential.

This book will focus on the five areas of need in every life and provide you some practical steps you can take today in order to live a balanced life.

In life and in our education system, we learn a pre-set model of success. Often that has to deal with the size of your bank account, what kind of promotion you receive, and whether you live in a 3,000 square foot home with a three-car garage. Those are just cultural standards of how society measures success. I know this because I've been there. I'm an expert at comparing myself to others.

We live in a world where success is narrowly defined between two variables:
1. The amount of money in your bank account
2. Your career progression or job title and status

As a result, we've ignored the other vital areas that contribute towards our happiness and fulfillment. And this is the reason we live in a world where:
- Over 30% of Americans are obese (according to Center for Disease Control)
- 54% of Americans hate their jobs (according to Gallup)
- Most marriages will end in divorce (according to the American Psychological Association)
- Most of us experience life as a crippling roller coaster of ups and downs.

But it doesn't have to be this way. What if you could create a vision for your life that is pre-set to you? Where your only source of comparison is with the person that you used to be?

The Five Laws of the Five Essentials

There are several things you need to understand about how these Five Essentials work. There are certain "laws" if you will that govern their efficacy in how they structure our lives.

1. You must develop all Five Essentials simultaneously.
You cannot, in life, focus on only one aspect of yourself. You need to be growing and expanding in all of these areas simultaneously. Your life will look and feel distorted if it is overdeveloped in one ara and underdeveloped in another. The key is to be able to identify in what areas you are lagging behind so you can focus on those that demand more attention, bringing your life back into balance and harmony.

Darren Hardy said, "Have you ever seen a guy who has giant arms but skinny legs? Looks a bit ridiculous, right? That's how many people's lives look. Too much focus in one area and not enough in another. We all pity the man who has a big house on the hill filled with expensive cars and trinkets, yet no one to share them with." Their focus on the one area of life created a great imbalance with the other areas.

2. The Five Essentials are listed in the order of value and priority.
The lowest in the hierarchy of the Five Essentials is *Financial*. This may seem counter-intuitive at first glance because we spend our working lives striving for more of it. Yet studies have found that after a certain threshold of income is reached, obtaining more money has almost no effect on the overall happiness or quality of our life.

> After a certain threshold of income is reached, obtaining more money has almost no effect on the overall happiness or quality of our life.

The next priority is *Physical*. This refers to our ability to devote time and energy to people and projects. If we don't have our health, we will not live long enough to fulfill our God-given purpose.

The *Intellectual* Essential is prioritized over Physical because unless you know how to take care of your health, how to exercise, and the principles of nutrition and weight loss, your health will always struggle. Hosea 4:6 says, *"My people are destroyed for a lack of knowledge."* If knowledge is power, then learning is your superpower. Our capacity to learn dictates our capacity to grow in every other area.

The *Relational* Essential is next on the list. Should you lose your Intellectual, Physical, and Financial Essentials — hopefully you will retain relationships with someone to fall back on. The Relational Essential is next to the highest on the list because you can't really do anyting in life without relationships. It's what ultimately brings happiness and fulfillment.

The *Spiritual* element tops the list of the Five Essentials. When I refer to something as "spiritual," I'm referring to the depth of our relationship with God as a disciple of Jesus Christ. When we grow in the Spiritual Essential, it results in wisdom and power in our lives in a way that cannot be derived anywhere else. It's also what fuels success in the other four essentials.

Knowing the pecking order of the Five Essentials is vitally important. If the Five Essentials were publicly traded companies, you would want to invest more of your time, talent, and treasure in the fifth essential (Spiritual) and a descending amount in the other four.

3. The way we grow in one essential is by investing what we have in the other four.

A win in one essential is a win in the other four essentials. This journey will help you define and set up a win in every category. By the time you finish this book, you will have moved the needle in every single one of these essentials.

Let's say you are weak in the **Physical** Essential and wanted to devote more time and effort to growth in that area. To grow in that area might involve investing in a gym membership (Financial), asking a friend to work out with you or keep you accountable (Relational), reading a book or hiring a personal trainer to develop a workout plan (Intellectual), and looking at what Scripture says about the healthy rhythm of rest and work (Spiritual). You infuse the other four to grow in the one.

Maybe you want to grow in the **Relational** Essential. Maybe you have a lack of genuine friendships both in quantity and quality. You might need to set aside some funds to take individuals out for coffee or lunch (Financial) or to add value to friends by helping them with things you know how to do and sharing your expertise with them (Intellectual). Of course, just being present and spending time with friends is the quickest way to strengthen those relationships (Physical). But you'd also want to pray and ask God to direct you towards those He wants you to invest in or give a word of encouragement to (Spiritual). Again, you use the other four essentials to grow in the one you're focusing on.

4. All growth is spiritual growth.

In our society today, we have tried to compartmentalize that which is spiritual and that which is secular. But for someone who is a Christian, you simply cannot make those distinctions. There is no area of my life my faith does not touch. I bring my faith into every aspect of who I am. So how I grow physically is a spiritual decision. How I invest my money is spiritual. How I cultivate strong relationships is spiritual. Everything. Is. Spiritual.

Jesus models this for us as well. In Luke 2:52, it says that Jesus *"grew in wisdom* (Intellectual), *in stature* (Physical), *in favor with God* (Spiritual) *and man* (Relational). Jesus also devoted more time towards teaching about money and possessions (Financial) than he did on the topics of faith or prayer combined. The life of Jesus embodies the Five Essentials.

Think about all of the best-selling self-help books in the last century: *Think and Grow Rich, The Power of Positive Thinking, How to Win Friends and Influence People.* I've read them all and they are great books. But all of that information is in Proverbs. The Bible is the best book for success equations on how to live a better life. The Bible is just as practical as it is spiritual.

When Jesus was preaching the Sermon on the Mount, He said, *"Do not worry about your life, what you will eat or drink, or your body, what you will wear."* Jesus was basically saying that if you follow Him you can safely stop worrying about all of these things. People who don't know God are the ones who run after these things and worry about them. But your Father in Heaven knows that you need them. He promises to take care of you.

But this statement has always fascinated me. Jesus goes on to say, *"But seek first His kingdom and His righteousness, and all these things will be given to you as well."*

> The Bible is the best book for success equations on how to live a better life. The Bible is just as practical as it is spiritual.

In other words: "If you make it your top priority to be involved in what God is doing and have his goodness increasingly fill your life, everything else will be taken care of." The way to have it all is to make sure you're aiming past the target, pursuing the most valuable thing.

In essence, it's the Spiritual Essential that turns the gears on the other four. When your relationship with God is right and centered; everything else seems to fall in to place. Your relationships with others flourish; your mind grows with new ideas; your health improves; and your finances are brought under proper alignment. That's why Scripture says, *"Delight yourself in the Lord and He will give you the desires of your heart."* Everything fits and flows together when God is brought into the picture.

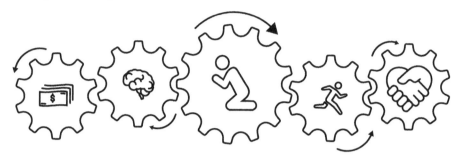

5. You don't grow in the Five Essentials by default. You must design a plan.
You don't just drift towards balance and maturity in these areas; you must enact a plan. In fact, without a plan, chances are you will drift further and further away from health in each of these areas. This book is all about giving you the tools you need to make more progress. The person you have become and what you have accomplished to date is only but a fraction of what's truly possible for you.

When you set a vision for what you want your life to look like in each of these five categories, you will watch your life's trajectory shift in a dramatic way and something beautiful emerges: a masterpiece of life being lived by design and not by default.

The F-5 Spiral

Let me give you an example of how these Five Essentials, when managed poorly, have a devastating effect on your life. But when managed efficiently, they lead you to towards new levels of growth and maturity and fulfillment. One way you can creatively remember the Five Essentials is by alliterating them into five F's. I look at each one of the fingers on my hand to remember them.

Finance - Look at your thumb. "Thumbs up" means that all is good, right? I want you to imagine someone looking over your financial statements and then giving you a thumbs up because they're impressed with how financially savvy you are.

Fitness - Look at your pointer or index finger. I want you to imagine that a coach or a personal trainer is pointing at you and the ground and telling you to give twenty pushups. When you look at your index finger, think fitness.

Focus - Your middle finger is the longest finger on your hand. Imagine that this finger is an arrow that's designed to hit a target. When you see your long middle finger, think about the long and arduous process of having a laser-like focus.

Family + Friends - This one is easy because it's your ring finger. When you make a commitment to give your life and love to your spouse, you put a wedding band on this finger to symbolize that commitment. The ring finger represents the relational aspect of life.

Faith - Your pinky finger is the smallest finger on your hand. It reminds me of that Scripture where Jesus said, *"If you have faith as small as a mustard seed…"* It doesn't take great faith; just faith in a great God.

I live in Kansas City, Missouri where we are known for severe thunderstorms that occassionally result in tornados. Back in the 1970s meteorologist Ted Fujita came up with this thing called the "Fujita Scale" and it's been adopted world-wide as a way to categorize tornadoes. Many people think that tornadoes are classified by their wind speed, but in reality they're classified by the type of damage that can be done, an F-5 being the worst case scenario. During a tornado-event of this magnitude, well built houses are entirely uprooted from their foundations, carried at incredible distances, and literally disentigrated in mid-air. Cars are sent hurling through the air like missiles. The tornado that struck Joplin, Missouri in 2011 was an F-5, and it killed 160 people.

When you are failing in the F-5's of life (Finance, Fitness, Focus, Family + Friends, Faith) it is catastrophically devastating to your life. The damage it can do you personally and to your future is far reaching. However, when you are focused and growing within these F-5's, they collectively spiral your life upward and result in balance, growth, happiness, and fulfillment in a way you would never expect.

My Story: How I Failed and Succeeded in the Five Essentials

So many books are written with the author's success in mind. This book is written with my weaknesses and brokenness as the foundation and how, by the grace of God, the Lord has brought me to where I am today.

I was blessed to have grown up with a great family. My parents are still my heroes. But my childhood wasn't free from any problems as I had some inherent challenges that plagued me in elementary school. I grew up with a speech impediment and a stuttering problem coupled with a really thick East Tennessee accent. Growing up in South Florida, I never really felt like I fit in. I was lonely much of the time. Shy and insecure. I was a skinny kid with no muscle, so sports and athleticism seemed completely out of the ballpark for me. To make matters worse, as soon as I became a teenager I developed a horrible case of cystic acne that made it pretty embarrassing to go out in public. It was unresponsive to a variety of treatments.

So I grew up with an overwhelming sense that I'm just not good enough. Interestingly, I responded by becoming this little achiever. I poured myself into my schoolwork. I graduated valedictorian of my senior class, not because I was the smartest kid in the room, but because I wanted to become the hardest working. I got my first job as soon as I got my drivers license and began working six days a week all throughout high school. I felt like the only way that I could prove my worth in the world was to outperform and outwork everyone else.

I became a pastor of a small country church at the age of nineteen and continued pastoring churches throughout my college and graduate degrees. My end goal was to earn a doctoral degree and pursue my dream of becoming a pastor of a large mega church.

> I grew up with an overwhelming sense that I'm just not good enough.

I did reach those goals ultimately. The problem was that I always determined my worth based on my achievement and success. In some ways, I had it. I led a thriving and growing church in Miami, Florida before becoming the Lead Pastor of one of the largest churches in the midwest: Connection Point near Kansas City, Missouri.

But even though I had achieved some modicum of "success" and reached my goals, I still felt empty.

We lost our home during the economic housing disaster of 2008. Because our mortgage was underwater by nearly $150,000, we had to start all over again so our *finances* were a mess. I had lost my retirement and all of my savings due to that situation.

Physically speaking, I was overweight. My body fat percentage got to 33% at my worst. I had no energy. And I was starting to develop some health issues such as high cholesterol and blood pressure even though I was only 30 years of age.

Intellectually, I always thought that if I just got that "Doctor" in front of my name, then I would feel like I was good enough. But I'll never forget the feeling of finishing my last course in my doctoral degree program. I went to Red Lobster afterwards to celebrate by myself as I was away from home. As I was sitting there, I remember thinking, "I pursued a terminal degree in hoping that it would give me the feeling of adequacy and finally being 'good enough'… but I've never felt more dumb and inadequate than I do right now." It reminded me of the quote: "Education is the progressive realization of your own ignorance." I never felt more ignorant than I did that day.

Relationally, I honestly had no close friend I could confide in, so I felt like I had to internalize all of the struggles I was going through on my own. Not only that but my marriage was on the rocks. Our three small children (all of which were in diapers at one point) became Carrie's focus and success became mine – to the exclusion of each other. During two difficult seasons in our marriage, Carrie and I were really worried that our relationship wasn't going to make it. Outside of our marriage counselor, no one knew about the problems we were experiencing because "pastor's are supposed to have it all together and never tell people their problems." So we struggled through it mostly on our own.

Spiritually speaking, all through this time I thought that I could earn God's favor by what I did *for* Him, not for who I was *before* Him. I was a human *doing*, not a human *being*. Even my time alone with God was done out of duty and not delight. I felt the pressure to even "perform" when it came to my daily time with God so that I could earn His love and approval of me.

My ministry was the one thing that made me feel like I was succeeding because, for the most part, I had the approval of people. But my self-worth was dependent upon just how many of those people showed up in the auditorium each weekend. If a lot of people showed up that Sunday, I felt like life was winning. But if a lot of people didn't show up — I felt like I was losing.

Eventually, I hit a wall and went through a time of deep depression and real soul-searching. I realized that I couldn't keep doing what I had been doing and expect different results.

My breakthrough came when I was on a plane coming back from doing a conference in Las Vegas. God showed me that there are really only five categories of life that we need to find balance and expansion in if we are going to live out our fullest calling. It was as if a lightbulb went off inside my heart and mind. I could clearly see where I had been lacking in each of these essential areas as well as where I was making progress.

That day led me towards a path of defining my purpose. Why had God placed me on this planet for such a time as this? What was I really crafted for and created to do? It was then that I began to design a plan for personal growth in the areas of life that mattered most - what I termed: "The Five Essentials of Life."

The result of going on this journey is that God has uniquely blessed me in each of these areas. **God always blesses whatever He is placed first in.**

In my *finances*, we went from losing our home and all of our equity to being able to purchase a 5,000 sq ft home that will be completely paid off in a few years. I went from barely surviving financially to learning new and creative ways, outside of my job, to make money while I sleep - more than I ever dreamed of making. As a result, we're able to live a truly generous life and I've been able to donate more this year than what was my entire annual income just 10 years ago.

In my *Physical* life, I'm now in the best shape I've ever enjoyed. Through the assistance of a personal trainer and understanding nutrition, I went from 33% to 14% bodyfat. I've gained twenty-five pounds of muscle in the last year and a half. I've literally gone from fat to fit. My blood pressure and cholesterol levels are now all within normal ranges.

Intellectually, I went from feeling stuck, lacking focus, trusting in my formal education, to developing a super memory, achieving a level of focus and productivity I never imagined possible, and being able to learn and master any subject or topic I invest my time in.

Relationally, my wife and I are now experiencing the marriage of our dreams. There's never been a time (even when we were dating) where we were closer than we are right now. The quality time that I'm able to enjoy with each of my three kids allows me to feel deeply connected to them. I'm also now enjoying some of the closest friendships I've ever had.

Spiritually, God has been teaching me throughout this process that He loves and accepts me just for who I am. Not some future version of me that could do better... but the person that I am today. I've always understood that truth with my head, but now I'm understanding it with my heart.

These discoveries are what led me to write this book *The Five Essentials of Life*. I want to help you to also live, lead, and succeed so you can find balance and expansion in the areas of life that matter most. I share my story with you because I want you to know that any diamond of "success" I have today is displayed on the black velvet of my past failures. I want this book to be a blessing and encouragement to you. As Carl Bard said, "Though no one can go back and make a brand new start; anyone can start from now and make a brand new ending." It doesn't matter where you are coming from. All that matters is where you are going. Let's get started on this journey together.

Achieving a Laser Focus

"The joy we feel has little to do with the circumstances of our lives and everything to do with the focus of our lives." — Russel M. Nelson

Sometimes life gets blurry and that's when we need to adjust our focus. By choosing to pick up this book and read it, you've separated yourself from the rest of the pack. 97% of the world's population don't give any thoughtful contemplation to designing their lives, much less charting a proper course that will help move them in that direction. People today are more disciplined about planning their next vacation than they are planning their life, their list of groceries over their list of goals.

Yet there is great power when we bring something into focus. Think about all of the light that is in the room you're sitting in at this moment. Diffused light has no power. But if you can take all of that light and focus it into a single beam, it could cut through steel. Nothing has power until it is brought into focus. Even Bruce Lee said, "The successful warrior is the average man, with laser-like focus."

> **People are more disciplined about planning their next vacation than they are planning their life.**

Paul lived his life with amazing clarity. He had a single mission in life: to pursue God by making disciples. Every Sunday, churches all across the world are still reading his writings. Towards the end of his life he wrote these words:

"Brothers and sisters, I do not consider myself yet to have taken hold of it. But one thing I do: Forgetting what is behind and straining toward what is ahead."[1]

If you want to achieve laser-like focus, that has to be your goal as well. Forget what's happened in the past; press on towards the goal that's in front of you.

Houston, We Have a Problem

When the Hubble Space telescope was being built, it took more than 6,000 men and women over the course of ten years to build it. It was a brilliant idea, really. What NASA wanted to do was place one of the most highly advanced telescopes ever built into outerspace orbit where it could collect data from high above the earth's atmosphere. And scientists figured that if they did this, they would be able to gather light from 20 billion light years away and it would tell us a lot about the universe. Specialists all over the country were brought in to supervise the development of thousands of these intricate parts. Solar panels were designed to help power this 2,500-pound telescope. The most precise system of gyroscopes ever built was put together so that the telescope could be aimed at objects hundreds of millions of miles away. And the cherry on the cake was the telescope's main mirror. This mirror was nine feet in diameter. It took six years to grind the concave contours to precise specifications. It had to be polished with microscopic instruments so that the mirror was absolutely flawless.

> You'll never hit the bullseye if you're aiming at multiple targets. If you try to chase two rabbits at the same time, both will escape.

So finally the date came – April 24, 1990 when the Space Shuttle Discovery was launched with a purpose of placing the Hubble Space Telescope into orbit some 300 miles above earth. After it was placed into orbit – thousands of people were gathered around a computer screen to see the first images that this Hubble Space Telescope would return to earth. Imagine their excitement after ten years of work and 6,000 individuals worth of manpower – they were going to see up close things that they had never been able to see before.

Yet to their horror, when the telescope was activated – all that they could see were blurry blobs – stars that were familiar to the naked eye were no more visible to the telescope. You couldn't tell the Milky Way from a Snickers bar! They couldn't figure it out – so they went to work. And you would never believe what the problem was. The lenses on the mirror wouldn't focus. They determined that the reason why they wouldn't focus was because the main mirror specifications were off by 1/50th of a sheet of paper. That's about the width of a human hair. Because the main mirror was off by that miniscule amount, the Hubble Space telescope was useless!

If you want to succeed at anything, you have to be focused. You'll never hit the bullseye if you're aiming at multiple targets. If you try to chase two rabbits at the same time, both will escape.

The two strategies used by almost all of the great achievers in the world are these:
1. an unyielding commitment to constant learning, and
2. clearly written goals that have specific laid out plans to achieve them.

At some level, your focus drives everything.

The F-O-C-U-S Formula

At some level, your focus drives everything. A lack of focus will lead to a lack of progress. There are three things that are always within my control: 1.) My level of discipline, 2.) My level of effort, and 3.) My level of focus. So here is a formula that provides five life hacks for achieving a greater level of F-O-C-U-S.

F - Feed your focus by starving your distractions.
We operate in a fragmented world. Distraction is becoming the norm. According to Udemy's survey, nearly 3 out of 4 workers (70%) admit they feel distracted when they're on the job, with 16% asserting that they're almost always distracted. The problem is biggest for Millennials and Gen Zers, with 74% reporting feeling distracted.[2] So ask yourself, what are the things that you're most distracted by? For me, it was getting email notifications in the upper right hand corner of my desktop screen that was really limiting my productivity. Maybe it's unnecessary notifications on your phone or an office environment that is limiting your ability to get things done. Starve your distractions, feed your focus.

One of the ways that you maintain focus is by making fewer decisions. Neuroscience teaches us that the more decisions you tend to make, the less effective you'll be over the long term. It results in what is called "decision fatigue." So you want to minimize the level of decisions you're making. Here's a tip: stop browsing. The more time we spend on Facebook, Twitter, or channel surfing, the more prone we are to being distracted when we are actually trying to get work done. It's easier to become distracted the more you allow distractions into your life.

O - Observe the outcome; not the obstacle.
If I were to put a 2 x 4 board on the grass and asked you to walk across it, you could easily do that, right? Anyone could do it because we'd be focused on the board.

But what if I took the same 2 x 4 and put it 10 stories up high, stretched between two buildings? Could you still walk across that board?

That changes things doesn't it. It's hard to focus on the board because you're focused on your fear of falling.

We need to learn to become laser-focused on our goals and not be distracted by all of our obstacles or fears of the unknown. Concentrate on the 2 x 4 and take one stey at a time. You'll get it all done. Focus on the outcome, not the obstacle.

C - Channel all your energy towards only two or three objectives.
It's easy to take your eye off the ball if you don't even know where the ball is. Most people have never defined their mission. What are they trying to accomplish? Are you just reactive to the demands of others or are you proactive in setting forth the objective that you feel God has called you to do? That's the process I hope to help guide you in through this book. If you stick with it, we'll develop a growth plan that is personalized to you and your needs.

Researchers have often debated the maximum number of items we can be working on at any given time. Our conscious mind has what is called a "working memory" and a new study puts the limit at three, possibly four items maximum. Working memory relates to the information we can pay attention to and manipulate.[3] So ultimately, trying to work simultaneously on more than three or four projects at a time, is going to drastically limit your ability to focus.

> If you focus on results, you will never change. If you focus on change, you will get results.

It's not just what you do, it's who you are becoming on the way towards reaching that goal. As Michael D'Aulerio puts it: "Don't focus on what you can see, focus on what you can be." If you focus on results, you will never change. If you focus on change, you will get results.

U - Uphold your ability to say "No."
Sometimes what you don't do is just as important as what you do. Steve Jobs, co-founder of Apple said, "People think focus means saying yes to the thing you've got to focus on. But that's not what it means at all. It means saying no to the hundred other good ideas that there are. You have to pick carefully. I'm actually as proud of the things we haven't done as the things we have done."

We have to learn to do less with more focus. Remember that if you don't prioritize your life, someone else will. Greg McKeown, author of *Essentialism: The Disciplined Pursuit of Less*, said, "We can either make our choices deliberately or allow other people's agendas to control our lives." So if something isn't a clear yes; then it should be an automatic no. Do less with more focus.

S - Stop managing your time and start managing your focus.
It's a lack of direction, not a lack of time that's our problem. We all have the same 24-hour days. But if we don't know how to calibrate that time effectively, we'll never achieve anything worthwhile. One of the things that I've learned to do that has accelerated my level of focus and productivity is to use a technique called batching. I take my to-do list and put it on my calendar. So if my goal is to write a book, I'll block out a solid hour for writing. I don't necessarily set goals for how much writing I want to do. I just want to devote a solid hour where I am fully present and free of distractions to write.

Where focus goes; energy flows. Whatever we focus on grows and expands in our lives.

What White-Water Rafting Can Teach About Focus

This summer I had the opportunity to take my wife and kids to Colorado where we went white water rafting for the first time! If you've never done it, it's definitely something you need to add to your bucket list! Our trip was a category 3+ (on a scale of 1-5). So it was fast enough to give us a thrill but safe enough to at least give me some peace of mind knowing that the chances of us losing a kid were greatly reduced.

But how white water rapids work is a great lesson in success. Think of it this way. The wider the banks of the river, the slower the water. It has kind of a lazy, drifting effect. The narrower the river, however means that the gorge has to be even more focused. The same volume of water has to flow through the narrower banks. That means that the water must push through deeper, harder, and faster. It also means that the momentum builds and those sitting in the raft can't just coast along casually anymore. Within moments, we would go from taking in the beautiful Colorado scenery on a lazy river, to digging our feet into the bottom of the raft and paddling as if our very lives depended on it - because they literally did!

Succeeding in life is the task of taking the wide banks of the river and narrowing them to result in greater power, focus, and momentum. Using this analogy, the river always starts as a spring or waterfall. That's passion. The passion continues as long as the river gushes. In time though, the force of the water will cause the banks to widen, and the river to flatten. Eventually, the river becomes a slow, lazy drifter. For the river to regain power-- call it momentum or passion--the banks have to become narrow once again. Sometimes engineers will even do this and cause the river to move more forcefully once again.

You might have a lot of passion regarding what it is that you feel God has called you do. But passion alone isn't enough. You've got to narrow your river banks. Focus in on your ideas so that it becomes a singular focus. As Tai Lopez says, "Double down on what's working. Cut the rest." Perfection is achieved not when there is nothing more to add, but when there is nothing left to take away. It's the idea behind one of the most challenging books for life and business: *Essentialism: The Disciplined Pursuit of Less* by Greg McKeown.

Over the last few years, I've been able to focus in on why I believe God put Brandon Park here on earth, what my purpose is based on the passions and callings He's placed on my life. That three-fold purpose centers around three keywords: Engage, Equip, Empower.
- I'm here to *engage* people to see their hearts and minds transformed through my passion for public speaking and communication.
- I'm here to *equip* people to reach their full potential by writing and developing resources.
- I'm here to *empower* people to multiply their influence and truly make a difference in the lives of others.

Living life with a narrow focus isn't easy. Like a raging river, it can actually be scary at times. But that's where you gain the greatest momentum and trajectory in discovering your calling. It's also where the greatest adventure awaits!

> Perfection is achieved not when there is nothing more to add, but when there is nothing left to take away.

NEXT STEPS

Do you have a "mission statement" for your life? If so what is it?

How would having a laser-like purpose empower your ability to focus?

What's your one takeaway from this lesson?

The Power of Habit

"We are what we repeatedly do. Excellence, then, is not an act, but a habit." — Aristotle

So often, we're faced with the challenge that comes when we see people who are more successful than we are or have achieved more and accomplished more and we feel helpless and inadequate. We wonder to ourselves, "What are the big things that they're doing that I must not be capable of doing to acheive that kind of success?"

Yet here is the key truth that we need to get permanantly downloaded into our hearts and minds: **It's so often the small things that no one sees that result in the big things that everyone wants.**

William James wrote in 1892, "All our life, so far as it has definite form, is but a mass of habits."

Duke researchers in 2006 came to the same conclusion. They discovered that 40% of the actions that people perform each day aren't actual decisions but *habits*. This has become one of the most important discoveries in the fields of psychology and success - that so much of what you *think*, *feel*, *do*, and *achieve* is the result of habit.

> **It's so often the small things that no one sees that result in the big things that everyone wants.**

There is immeasurable power within our habits--or we might say our disciplines--because we are what we repeatedly do.

So before we jump into this topic, let me ask you a question. Would you say you are a disciplined person or an undisciplined person?

> We are what we repeatedly do.

I would argue that even if you think you're not disciplined that you inherently are! You have some disciplines that you are consistently doing. And you have other disciplines that you do that just aren't as good or helpful disciplines. But every single one of us is disciplined in different ways.

You might be disciplined to hit the snooze button every day, to play video games in your free time, or to eat a lot of fried food. We're all disciplined; we just don't always have the right disciplines and the right habits.

Discipline is choosing between what we want now and what we want most.

Chances are you're successful in some specific area of your life. And if you take a magnifying glass to that one area and look at it closely, you will discover some consistent disciplines.

Maybe you've got a good marriage. If you do, I can promise you there are some consistent disciplines you and your spouse have built into your relationship.

Maybe you're successful financially. Chances are, it's because you've developed some money-savvy habits in this area of your life. You're likely living on less than what you make. You're investing wisely and being generous with your resources.

Yet the opposite is also true. If you have an area of your life where you feel like you're not succeeding, then you've got some disciplines but just not the right disciplines.

It was Aristotle who once said, "We are what we repeatedly do." Another way we could say it is, **we create our habits and then our habits create us.** When you study the most successful individuals, you find that they all create empowering habits.

Breaking Bad Habits

Chances are, there's not one person reading this chapter who does not want to change *something* in their life.

Once I was teaching on the power of habit, and I had a volunteer from the audience join me on stage to illustrate a point. I picked a big burly fellow out of the audience and I had him clasp his hands together while I took a spool of thread and wrapped it around his wrist. I just wrapped his wrist with that thread two or three times and then asked him if he could break the thread - which he could do easily. But then I continued to teach on the power of habit all the while wrapping nearly the entire spool of thread around his wrist. By the time I was done, he was unable to easily break free.

In Scripture, even the Apostle Paul dealt with the strongholds of bad habits. He said, *"For I have the desire to do what is good, but I cannot carry it out. For I do not do the good I want to do, but the evil I do not want to do—this I keep on doing"* (Romans 7:18-19).

I just love his vulnerable transparency. Can you relate to that? But in the same chapter, Paul acknowledges where his power to overcome bad habits comes from. It's derived from the power of God that resides in him. With God's help, I can change. By His power, I can be transformed. Paul's answer wasn't found in a principle, it was found in a Person. Christ in me is stronger than the appetites within me. I'm not looking to be self-disciplined; I'm looking to become spirit-disciplined because the Spirit inside of me is what empowers me to do what I myself am incapable of doing. God can help give you the power to become more disciplined in these five areas of life that matter most. We must choose what matters most over what we want right now.

But here's where a lot of us go wrong when it comes to breaking bad habits. Changing behavior without changing your deepest desires and beliefs is mere behavior modification, and it usually doesn't last. What you need is a changed heart. There will never be lasting or true change without a changed heart because the heart of the human problem is the problem of the human heart.

Here's what we need to understand: Bad habits cannot be erased; they have to be replaced. You can never truly extinguish a bad habit. Those old cravings and the things that led to the bad habit will always be there in a sense. You can't just erase them; you have to replace them with a *better habit*. It's why smokers have to replace their routine. Our society today doesn't teach this too well. Pastors are good at telling people what *not* to do; but we don't always tell them what they *should* do. So nothing ever really changes. Whatever you feed grows stronger; and whatever you starve grows weaker. This applies to both your good and bad habits. So we need the formation of new habits.

Building Good Habits

It's been said that people never decide their future. They decide their habits and their habits decide their future.

Here's a statement I want you to try to remember: Resolve won't change what routine created. In other words, a lot of us would *love* to change. Many of us will even *resolve* to change by setting resolutions for the New Year. And you might change for a week maybe even a month. But we all know what inevitably happens: we go right back to the same routine and the same pattern we held before.

There is great power in the pattern because we are what we repeatedly do. So ask youself, what patterns are evident in your life? When a habit gets set in your mind neurologically, your brain goes into autopilot. It becomes your default level of thinking and behavior.

Resolve won't change what routine created.

So what do you need to change a habit? Charles Duhigg wrote a book on this topic entitled *The Power of Habit*. In his book, he examines scientifically what constitutes a habit. Any habit requires three components:
- A Cue
- A Routine
- A Reward

The *cue* is the trigger that tells your brain to go into automatic mode and which habit to use.

Then there is the *routine* - the behavior itself - which can be physical, mental, or emotional.

Finally there is the *reward* - the resulting flood of chemical reactions within your neurotransmitters helps your brain figure out if this particular habit is worth remembering for the future.

Over time, this loop: *cue, routine, reward, cue, routine reward* becomes more and more automatic as the cue and the reward become neurologically intertwined.

Let's take working out for example. Studies have shown that people who identify simple cues and clear rewards are more likely to establish consistent running habits. When I wake up, the first thing I do is I put on my workout clothes and my sneakers before breakfast (that's the cue). Then I go to the gym and workout (the routine). Then I log my workout on a clipboard I have in my gym bag. Knowing that I showed up to the gym that day and recorded how much weight I just lifted gives me the sense of accomplishment and fulfillment that my brain has grown to crave. After a couple of months of doing this, my brain has grown to anticipate the *reward* (craving the feeling of accomplishment and seeing my log book get filled with a new personal record). Because of this, there's a measurable neurological impulse to exercise each day.

So remember, you can't eliminate a habit. You can only change it for a better alternative. For years, I used to have a bad habit. I'd crave and eat junk food about an hour before I went to bed. My wife and I would settle in to watch something on Netflix and as soon as my butt hit the couch, I would have cravings for candy, ice cream, potato chips--you name it. To change that habit, I had to identify the cue that was preceding my junk food binge. Research indicates that most cues fit into five categories: location, time, emotional state, other people, or the immediately preceding action.

So I learned that whenever my junk food craving habit hit, I noticed where I was, what time it was, how I felt, who else was around, and what I had just done. Pretty soon the cue was clear. I always felt the urge to binge on Hot Tamales at around 9 pm, right after we got the kids to bed, right as we were about to watch our evening show on Netflix. Once I figured out the cue and reward, it was fairly simple to shift the routine. If you can perceive the pattern, you can address the problem.

Life isn't as mystical as we sometimes make it out to be. Yes, sometimes things do just happen. But the majority of our problems are the result of patterns. If you'll change the pattern, you can change the product!

You don't always have to be stuck like you are now. You can get a new pattern. That's why Scripture says, *"do not be conformed to the pattern of this world."* You can choose your pattern.

> If you can perceive the problem, you can address the problem.

Those whom you admire for where they are in life aren't successful by accident. They've learned the value of establishing good habits over the years. Bruce Lee once said, "I don't fear the man who practiced a thousand kicks, I fear the man who practiced one kick for a thousand days." The key to success is not attempting a thousand new ideas, but to home in on your calling and skill and practice that a thousand times so you become the expert at it. The product of your results are tied to the patterns in your life.

So the question I want you to wrestle with today is this: What do you need to do now to have what you want most? What one discipline do you need to add to your life now that will help lead you toward what you ultimately want most?

NEXT STEPS

Name your biggest bad habit or an area where you lack discipline in the Five Essentials:

Financial:

Physical:

Intellectual:

Relational:

Spiritual:

Postponing Your Procrastination

"When there is a hill to climb, don't think that waiting will make it smaller."
– Anonymous

I'm a recovering procrastinator. Maybe you are as well. In the past, I've always thought procrastination worked to my advantage. In school, if I gave myself 10 hours to do a project, it would take precisely 10 hours. But I soon discovered that if I gave myself only five hours to do the same project the night before, I could get it all done in that amount of time and still manage to land a decent grade.

Procrastination works for us and against us. Interestingly enough, if you're a person who has a vision for your life - you also simultaneously are gifted with the unfortunate nature of being a procrastinator.

As a visionary, you see your future so clearly--the business you want to build, the book you want to write, the kind of life that you want to create for your family--is all fully-formed in your mind's eye. If anyone should be sprinting towards the finish line with their eye so clearly on the prize, it ought to be the man or woman of great imagination.

But it doesn't work that way. Because as you may have already discovered from life experience, visionaries are sometimes the very worst procrastinators.

The graphic on the left is how people with a low vision for their lives perceives their progress:

The inner circle is their "realized world" that they are currently experiencing. It's the sum total of what has been built up to this point. The outer circle is the "imagined world." It's the realm of possibility; what isn't but could be. It's the life they have imagined for themselves.

But if you are a person who has a big vision for your life, the graphic on the right is how you likely see your progress.

In this case, your "realized world" is the same size as the man with low vision or imagination. But your *imagined* world is enormous!

Here lies the problem: You would think that the grandeur of your "imagined world" would spring you to action. But it's not the size of the worlds that matters; **it's the size of the gap between them.** As a person who has a great vision for your life, the gap between where you are and where you desire to be is crushingly large and daunting.

Even if you were to expand your realized world at the same exact speed as the person of low vision; his progress will seem great but your progress will seem inconsequential and insignificant. You'd still see yourself far removed from where you want to be.

Our problem, many times, is not that we are lazy or burnt out. Our problem is that we get paralyzed by the gap. So what's the answer? Just having a castle-in-the-sky vision is not enough. You must redirect all your energy, all your passion, and all your obsession towards expanding your realized world.

Stop running in a multitude of directions looking for the next idea. Take one single idea--any idea--and make it real. Free-floating vision with no action can become most debilitating. We have to learn how to get off the pipedream of procrastination and put some work to our ideas.

Make Your Clock Count

One of the greatest enemies you and I will ever face is procrastination. How many people know in their heart what they should do (they have many good intentions) but they just keep putting it off. The interesting thing about procrastination is that it's so easy to justify:
- One day, I'll start that new business.
- One day, I'll get on a budget
- One day, I'll go back to church.
- One day, I'll hire a personal trainer and get fit.

So often we know what we should do, but we just don't do it. I want to challenge you today to be a "Now" person. Start doing what God has placed upon your heart today. It's been said that *wisdom* is the art of spending your time prudently. The Psalmist said *"Teach us to number our days that we may apply our hearts unto wisdom"* (Psalm 90:12). Let me give you three basic thoughts concerning our time:

1. **Time is a gift from God.** God is the creator of time. The Lord has given you enough time to work, time to play, time to laugh, and time to labor. We need to learn to perceive every day as a gift from God. Has it ever occurred to you that for you to cease living, God doesn't have to take your life. All that God would have to do is stop giving life to you. Every day is a gift from God.
2. **Time equals opportunity.** You need to see time not just as something that is passing; but rather as an incredible opportunity. Scripture tells us that we should be *"redeeming the time"* (Ephesians 5:15-16) which simply means we must live each day making the most of what we've been given - buying up the opportunity that is before us.
3. **Time is temporal.** I read somewhere that in a lifetime, the average American will spend five months tying his shoes; six months sitting at red lights; eight months opening junk mail; one year looking for misplaced objects; four years doing housework; five years waiting in line; six years eating; fifteen years working; and twenty years sleeping. Here's the greatest shocker of all! By the time a person reaches thirty-five years of age, they will only have 500 days left to *really live* (if you subtract all the time spent sleeping, working, tending to personal matters, and so forth.)

Our problem with procrastinating is that we tend to overestimate how much time we have left. Good stewardship of our time begins with the realization that God has given each of us a certain number of days to live.

A scholar once surveyed the Scriptures to discover the most significant words in all the Bible. He wanted to find the saddest word, the happiest word, the most emotional word, and so on. When he came around to the Bible's most *dangerous* word, he identified it as *tomorrow*. He said "That word is a thief that robs dreamers of their dreams and the talented of their greatest achievements."

There is no such thing as a successful person who is a procrastinator. If you describe yourself as such you're basically saying, "I'm planning on avoiding a successful life." When you find men and women who found great success, you

> **Our problem with procrastinating is that we tend to overestimate how much time we have left.**

will inevitably discover that they were people who took their time seriously. If you don't sacrifice for what you want, then what you want becomes the sacrifice.

Six Ways to Stop Procrastinating

James L. Clark shares six methods to stop procrastinating so you can put that time-thief in lock up and live a better life. These tips helped me and maybe they'll help you too.

1. Put it all down on paper.
If you write a comprehensive list with due dates and other details, you're much more likely to get things knocked out. Charles Schwab, a multi-millionaire businessman, once hired a man named Ivey Lee to help him become more productive. Lee gave Schwab a pan of underwhelming simplicity. He said, "Each evening, write down the six most important things you should do the following day. List them in order of their importance. The following morning, come into work and do whatever tops the list. When you're finished move on to the next."

Schwab said, "How much do I owe you for this advice?"

Lee said, "Use it for several months and then decide on the value of my plan and send me a check." Several months later, Charles Schwab sent Ivy Lee a check for $25,000! Put it all down on paper.

2. Eat little bites until your plate is empty.
You know that old question "How do you eat an elephant?" The answer is fairly straight forward: "One bite at a time." That's how you get anything done to be honest. Break big tasks into more manageable smaller tasks, and before you know it—you're done.

3. Go somewhere else to get it done.
Sometimes you need to get out of Dodge or change your workspace if you want to finish a task or project. When I write books for example, I really need to hide myself away so I can focus. It's much harder for me to complete a paragraph, let alone a chapter or more, when I can be easily interrupted. If you find yourself stuck, try doing the same thing.

4. Partner up with someone like-minded.
It's always easier to stay on point when you have someone else involved helping keep you from getting side tracked. By working with others, you can both keep each other accountable, focused, and marching forward.

> The longer you put things off, the harder they are to do.

5. Don't try to be perfect.
Perfectionists have serious difficulty getting anything finished; they may get close, maybe even 99%, but they struggle completing projects because they won't let things go. It's never good enough. The danger of course, is you never get anything done and you fall behind.

6. Quit making excuses and just get it done.
Be like Nike said, just do it. Don't leave it. Don't make excuses. Pony up. Step up to the plate and take a swing, and every other cliche statement. Really, that's the only way to stop

procrastinating: just don't procrastinate. It's like running a marathon—you can't learn to do it if you never go out and run.[1]

Get It Done

So I want you to think once again about the Five Essentials. What is the one thing you've been putting off when it comes to your finances, fitness, focus, friends and family, and your faith? Some day, every single one of us will have to stand before God, giving an account of ourselves for how we used our time. And it will be based on what we have actually done, not what we intended to do.

> Time is the ballot that records your vote on what really matters in life.

Have you noticed that the longer you put things off, the harder they are to do? I noticed the label on my carpet cleaner one time. In the directions on how to remove a stain it said, "The quicker you do it, the easier it is to remove." The same is true about life, isn't it? The quicker we take action on something, the easier it is to do. The longer you put things off, the more difficult it's going to be.

You can have as big of a bank account as you would like to have. I don't know of any bank that is going to limit what you put in. You can even brag to your friends that you have a million dollars in the bank when in reality you've only got $10. The bank won't have a problem with you bragging. The only problem is when you try to take out more than what you have put in. The banker will say, "Now wait a minute, unless you invest some more, you cannot receive any more." You can't take more out of the Five Essentials of Life than what you have put in.

Remember: Time is the ballot that records your vote on what really matters in life. You will always have time to do what you decide in your heart to do. When something is truly a priority for you; you find the time. When it's not, you find an excuse.

NEXT STEPS

What was your biggest takeaway from this lesson that you would want to remember?

The Wheel of Life

"An unexamined life will eventually become an under-developed life."

The goal of *The Five Essentials* is that you acheive whole-life success, in not just one but every major area of your life. As you look over your goals and personal growth plan, it's imperative that you set goals that represent every area of your life in a balanced way.

Your Five Essentials life plan will be the road map by which you navigate the direction of your life. So before you begin this journey, let's take a moment to reflect where you currently are. Let's suppose you were coming over to my home one night for dinner. You're driving around in your car and you're lost. You can't find my house. So you call me up on the phone and ask for directions. What would be the first question I ask you? *"Where are you?"* You can't know where you need to go until you first know where you are and where you've been. So I'm going to lead you through an exercise to help you take a step back and do a 30,000-foot-view evaluation of your life.

For this exercise, we're going to use the F-5 alliteration when referring to the Five Essentials. Knowing that we might assess our friendships and family relationships very differently, you will assess those two relational aspects separately using the same assessment statements.

Rate the following on a scale of 1 to 5, 1 being Least True and 5 being Most True [1]:

Financial

I have a completely detailed budget and unfailingly stick to it.	1 2 3 4 5
I have the financial means to be very generous with my money.	1 2 3 4 5
I have a professionally designed and diversified financial portfolio	1 2 3 4 5
I have no credit card debt that cannot be paid off within one month.	1 2 3 4 5
I have a dedicated six-month reserve account completely funded and set aside.	1 2 3 4 5
I feel that I am compensated adequately according to my worth.	1 2 3 4 5
I live well below my means and never spend money imprudently.	1 2 3 4 5
I have a detailed retirement plan that will accomodate exactly what I need to live after retirement.	1 2 3 4 5
I'm always learning new ways to manage money effectively and build new wealth.	1 2 3 4 5
I'm giving 10% of my income to my local church and growing in my generosity.	1 2 3 4 5

TOTAL SCORE: _____

Fitness (Physical)

I am cognizant of the nutritional value of everything I put in my mouth.	1 2 3 4 5
I am currently doing strength training at least three times a week.	1 2 3 4 5
I am currently doing some type of cardiovascular exercise at least three times a week.	1 2 3 4 5
During a typical day, I watch no more than one hour of television.	1 2 3 4 5
I don't eat fast food… ever.	1 2 3 4 5

I am aware of the health dangers of sitting too long, I utilize a stand-up desk or walk often.	1 2 3 4 5
I have undisturbed, quality sleep for at least 7-8 hours every night.	1 2 3 4 5
I drink at least 8 glasses of water per day.	1 2 3 4 5
I know where my body is deficient and take health supplements daily.	1 2 3 4 5
I am satisfied with my current body fat percentage and overall health.	1 2 3 4 5

TOTAL SCORE: _____

Focus (Intellectual)

I read something instructional or inspirational for at least 30 minutes a day.	1 2 3 4 5
I listen to something instructional or inspirational for at least 30 minutes a day.	1 2 3 4 5
I seek out ways to grow in my personal life and in my field every day.	1 2 3 4 5
I have determined and set forth priorities for my life.	1 2 3 4 5
I always say no to requests or obligations that don't fit my core values or objectives.	1 2 3 4 5
I have clearly written goals for my life placed in prominent areas to be reviewed each day.	1 2 3 4 5
I review what I am grateful for each day.	1 2 3 4 5
I manage my time effectively and plan my day before I live my day.	1 2 3 4 5
I rarely get over-stressed.	1 2 3 4 5
I take time out to daydream and visualize my future every day.	1 2 3 4 5

TOTAL SCORE: _____

Family + Friends (Relational)

All of my friends are a positive influence in my life.	1 2 3 4 5
I spend as much time as I want with my friends + family.	1 2 3 4 5
There is no one in my life whom I haven't completely forgiven.	1 2 3 4 5
I am actively engaged in learning how to be a better spouse/parent/friend.	1 2 3 4 5
I find it easy to make friends and keep friends. People tell me I'm a likable person.	1 2 3 4 5
I know how to manage conflict well. I am able to peacefully resolve any conflict immediately.	1 2 3 4 5
My family and friends know that I prioritize my relationships with them over my work.	1 2 3 4 5
The relationship I have with my spouse is stronger than ever and continually growing.	1 2 3 4 5
I get together with my closest friend(s) at least once a week.	1 2 3 4 5
I have great interpersonal relationships when it comes to networking and meeting new people.	1 2 3 4 5

TOTAL SCORE: _____

Faith (Spiritual)

I have peace with God and I know what it means to have a personal relationship with Him.	1 2 3 4 5
Others who know me would consider me a spiritual person.	1 2 3 4 5
I consider myself a person of great faith who walks daily with God.	1 2 3 4 5
I study my spiritual beliefs daily.	1 2 3 4 5
I practice my spiritual beliefs daily.	1 2 3 4 5
I teach my spiritual beliefs daily.	1 2 3 4 5
I live completely in accordance with my spiritual beliefs.	1 2 3 4 5

I consistently use my faith to help me resolve my personal problems.	1 2 3 4 5
I consistently use my faith to help others in their lives or in their walk with God.	1 2 3 4 5
My prayer life is getting stronger and stronger each year.	1 2 3 4 5

TOTAL SCORE: _____

To determine your level of balance in each of the Five Essentials, take your scores from the previous pages and plot them on the wheel. Start from the center of the wheel and use the key to make your current status. Then connect all the dots and see how balanced your wheel is or isn't.

KEY: Score of 5 = 1 notch. Score of 6-10 = 2 notches. Score of 11-15 = 3 notches. Score of 16-20 = 4 notches. Score of 21-25 = 5 notches. Score of 26-30 = 6 notches. Score of 31-35 = 7 notches. Score of 36-40 = 8 notches. Score of 41-45 = 9 notches. Score of 46-50 = 10 notches. Use the same score for both the Family and Friends line.

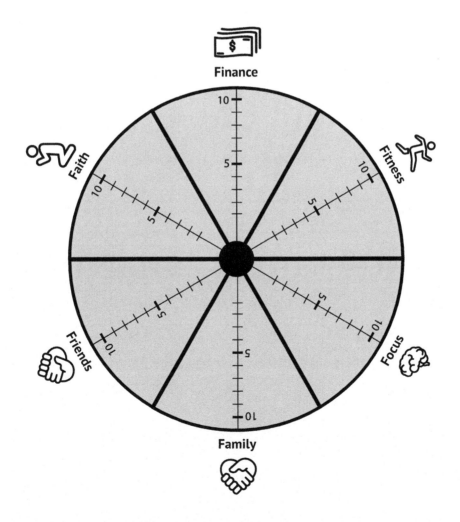

NEXT STEPS

Which essential was your highest score?

What were your two lowest essentials?

Do you agree with your own assessment of your life? Why or why not?

Which essential are you most committed to work the hardest on improving?

The FINANCIAL Essential

The Greatest Financial Principle

"To be content doesn't mean you don't desire more, it means you're thankful for what you have and patient for what's to come." — Tony Gaskins

Let's face it, money is important to me — and chances are money is also important to you. **You need it to function in life.** You need it to pay bills, buy food, and take care of your family. Frankly, you need money to survive. In a nutshell, the greatest financial principle is not a tip or technique--it's a state of mind. It's not how you manage your money; it's how you manage your heart.

In 1 Timothy 6:6-7 we read, *"But godliness with contentment is great gain. For we brought nothing into this world, and it is certain we can carry nothing out. And having food and clothing, with these we shall be content."* It says that godliness with contentment is great gain. Some translations use "great profit." Are you content? Contentment is probably the most powerful financial principle there is. If you are ok with where you are in life, where you are with your wardrobe, where you are with your house, and where you are with the vehicle you drive, then you can start attacking your debt, building your savings, and learning to live a generous life. All of a sudden, your life starts to flow the way that it's supposed to.

> It's not how you manage your money; it's how you manage your heart.

Here's a key thought to consider: **Contentment occurs when your earning power is greater than your yearning power.** That sounds great, but instead, we often live in a "feverish acquisition" mode where we get all we can, can all we get, sit on the can, and poison the rest. Epicurus said, "Do not spoil what you have by desiring what you have not; but remember that what you now have was once among the things you only hoped for." How quickly we forget just how far we've come. We get a pay raise and then we wonder how we ever made it before we had that extra money.

As Dave Ramsey says, you need to learn to "act your wage." We need to learn to live on less than what we make. We are Congress. We don't get to raise the national debt ceiling every time we want to spend more money. Many Americans seem to feel that living within their income is a fate worse than debt. Proverbs 21:20 says, *"The wise man saves for the future, but the foolish man spends whatever he gets."* If you spend everything that you make, that truly is a foolish way to live. Not only that but you will never have a chance to make it towards financial security if you spend everything that you make. We must learn to live on less than what we earn. Plato said the greatest wealth is to live content with little.

Did you know that the average American is exposed to 560 advertisements every single day (on TV, newspapers, radio, and even the billboards we drive past on our way to work). The marketers on Madison Avenue spend around $450 billion dollars every year trying to make you unhappy with who you are, with what you have, with how you look, and with what you do.

"If only I had this new ab machine; I'd be ripped like that guy in the commercial."

"If only I had these new golf clubs, I'd hit a ball like Tiger Woods."
Slowly but surely, we're being eaten alive by the Monster of More. At its core, advertising is designed to make us ungrateful and to feed our greed by showing us what we don't have and eliciting a desire to buy it.

If you find yourself saying (or thinking) these words: "If only I had…" then you have a problem with contentment. One sociologist discovered that in 1900, the average American wanted seventy-two things and considered eighteen of them absolutely essential. In the year 2000, the average person wanted 500 things and considered 100 of them essential. How can you tell if you have some heart issues with money? There are several tell-tale signs:
- You are far more excited about getting money than you are about giving money.
- You are placing normal daily expenditures on credit cards because you don't have the cash to pay.
- You continue to borrow money to buy luxury and depreciating items.
- You are consistently late on paying your bills.
- Your thoughts are dominated by what it would be like to be rich.
- You are dishonest in your financial dealings.
- You find it difficult to give and be generous with your resources to God and others.

Some people go through life thinking that contentment is just "one more something" away. If they could just relocate they would be content. If they could just get another job they would be content. If they could just get a raise they would be content. If they could just get more square footage they would be content. But Paul stated these words that I aspire to live by as well, *"I have learned in whatever situation I am to be content"* (Philippians 4:11).

The key to contentment is not having everything you want but actually wanting everything you have. Having is not wrong; it's when the having *has you* that it becomes wrong. The Greek word for "content" actually means *contained*. It was a word that was actually used in ancient Greek literature to denote a little country that supplied itself with no need of outside imports to sustain it. Does that describe the state of your heart? That you just don't need anything from the outside of you to be happy? The secret to having it all is believing that you already have it.

It's been said that the key to happiness is spending your money on experiences rather than possessions. Trying to just "keep up with the Joneses" is never going to bring you satisfaction. The Jones' family is living a lie and up to their ears in debt. So remember, *contentment is destroyed by comparison.* You need to appreciate what God has given you. Many people try so hard to get ahead, while, if they would just stop and take stock of what they have, they would realize that they're already ahead. Socrates sums it up well: "The secret to happiness, you see, is not found in seeking more, but in developing the capacity to enjoy less."

I'm not saying that you shouldn't make progress in your finances - to earn more, invest more, save more, and give more. That's what this whole section is about. But what I am saying is that if you can't be content with where you are now and curb your spending, adding more zeroes to your net worth isn't going to make any difference.

The 70% Principle

The 70% Principle of lasting wealth is another great technique that always ensures that you're living on less than you make. This is a real concise formula that's easy to remember, but not always easy to do. We have to learn to tell our money where to go instead of wondering where it went. So this framework gives you a basis upon which to do that.

Let's suppose $100 comes into your life. The first thing you do is you do't close your fist around that $100. You open your hand and say, "God, thank you for giving me these resources. How do you want me to use it?"

The first 10% of all that I earn goes to what's called my *tithe*. This is a generosity principle taught in Scripture. The word tithe simply means "tenth." I offer to God the firstfruits of my income to him as an act of worship and generosity. He's the one who gave me the strength, the energy, and the brain to make that money, so I'm acknowledging Him with it and giving it back to Him. This is where a blessed budget starts.

> We have to learn to tell our money where to go instead of wondering where it went.

The second 10% goes to *debt*. We will cover this more in detail in a later chapter. But if you are debt free, then you use this second 10% to go towards personal investments. When you don't have debt, your money can do anything you want it to. But since you've hopefully developed the discipline of saving this 10% by now, you'll continue building your wealth through investments. Wealthy people invest first and spend what's left and broke people spend first and invest what's left.

The third 10% goes to *savings*. Saving is the way that you fulfill some of the wants you have in life. God promises to give you all you need, but if you want something, you can actually save for it. Scripture tells us to save first and then buy it. American culture does just the opposite. It says buy it now, and don't worry about saving anything. As Warren Buffet would suggest, "Do not save what is left after spending, but spend what is left after saving."

One of the principles that Dave Ramsey advocates for is to make sure that you have three to six months of reserves set aside in savings. Imagine how much that would free you up! Let's say your car broke down--you're prepared. Let's say your washing machine just went out — you could take that out of savings and you could replace it.

The last 70% is what you live on. Unfortunately, many people are living on 110% of their income. They are spending more than they make and digging themselves deeper into the hole of debt. Now, I know what you're thinking: "Sure, Brandon. If I made a lot more money, I could do this. I could live off of just 70%." But that's not true. If you don't build this discipline into your life now, then when your earnings go up; your yearnings just go up even higher. With enough planning, you can live on 70%.

Proverbs 21:5 says, *"Careful planning puts you ahead in the long run. Hurry and scurry will put you further behind."*

Think of your net worth as an airplane. You are trying to take off and get it into the sky. But we have a big problem. Here on earth, we are all subject to the same gravitational force. The larger you are, the more that force exerts on your body. If you weighed nothing, you'd just float up to the sky like a balloon.

When it comes to finances, our net-worth airplanes are subject to the same financial pull. What neighborhood you choose to live in, how you choose to live, the products that you buy, and so forth all determine how large and heavy your plane must be to hold all that stuff. The greater the need (monthly expenses), the more thrust (income) you'll need to take off.

Money Is a Mirror

Did you know that your money is not only important to you — it's also important to God. The Bible has five times more to say about money than it does the subject of prayer. There are 500 verses on faith, yet there are 2,000 verses in the Bible about money. The reason why God has a lot to say about money is because your attitude towards it says so much about you. Money is a mirror that reflects our personal strengths and weaknesses with amazing clarity. Your attitude and approach towards money represents your heart. And God wants your heart.

Jesus made a thought provoking statement in Matthew 19. He said, *"It is easier for a camel to go through the eye of a needle, than for a rich person to enter the kingdom of God."* This quotation has been misinterpreted and taught incorrectly by many over the years. What did Jesus mean when He said it was easier for a camel to get through the eye of a needle than for a rich person to enter God's kingdom?

Well, back in those days, this was a proverbial phrase that was commonly used for something that was very difficult. So everyone back then who was hearing Jesus speak, understood this idiom. They knew it referred to something that was difficult and it was rooted in an occasion that almost everyone had encountered at some point in their life.

> Money is a mirror that reflects our personal strengths and weaknesses with amazing clarity.

In ancient times, the road system wasn't as advanced as it is now, but they still had roads upon which peopled traveled. Most of the time, you would travel with a group of others in a caravan since there was safety in numbers. Yet in the natural landscape, those roads would often weave into what would appear to be a narrow opening or a small passageway between the walls of a cliff or a natural land bridge. And this small narrowing passageway was referred to as "the eye of a needle." In order for the caravan to work through the eye of a needle, they had to condense themselves to almost a single file line. In many cases, the only way a camel can go through is to kneel.

I don't know if you've ever ridden a camel before, but I have in Israel — and camels do kneel. It's an arduous process as the camel starts to lower one leg, then slowly lowers the other leg, and then eventually gets down on the ground where they have some possessions of everyone who owns the camel on their back.

What Jesus was teaching us was this — it's easier for that camel to physically kneel than for you and I to spiritually kneel when it comes to our finances, because kneeling carries with it the symbolism of humility. Jesus says it's difficult for a rich man to enter the kingdom of heaven, but it's not impossible.

Jesus was once approached by a rich young man who asked, "What must I do to inherit eternal life?" Scripture notes the response of Jesus that has always perplexed me: *"Then Jesus, looking at him, loved him, and said to him, 'One thing you lack: Go your way, sell whatever you have and give to the poor, and you will have treasure in heaven; and come, take up the cross, and follow Me.' But he was sad at this word, and went away sorrowful, for he had great possessions."*

Christ knew this man's heart. And without beating around the bush, he touched the root of this young man's heart. But this passage always bothered me. It seems presumptuous. I know people who are dirt poor and go from church to charity asking others to support their lack of self-discipline.

But Julian Archer made an interesting observation that instead of "sell all that you have," a better translation would be "Sell all that has you." Are your possessions controlling you?[1]

No matter what income you make, there will likely come a time in your life where you are financially broken. It is within that moment that you shouldn't try to pull yourself up by your own bootstraps and try to hack it out on your own. You need to reach the point where in your heart your bend your will to God's will. You acknowledge that you can't do this on your own, that everything that you are and everythign that you think you own really belongs to Him anyway. And there's the great truth: God will always bless whatever we put Him first in. You put God first in your heart and even within your finances and watch what He can do. When you trust God with your money, He will replace your stress with His peace.

Now follow this line of thinking: If you trust God with your resources, then you're acknowledging that your money is God's money. And if all your money is God's money — *then every spending decision you make is a spiritual decision.*

NEXT STEPS

How well do you "act your wage"?

What do you believe is the most valuable information you've gained from this chapter? What do you struggle with the most?

What aspect of being content do you struggle with the most?

A Bulletproof Budget Strategy

"Too many people spend money they haven't earned, to buy things they don't want, to impress people they don't like." — Will Rogers

The Space Shuttle Challenger was made from over a million intricate parts, all beautifully crafted and fitting together with great precision. Every part was necessary in order for the Challenger to lift off from the launching pad on earth to outer space orbit. However, a single O-ring was found to be the cause of the tragic explosion of the shuttle resulting in the deaths of its crew. Although 99.99999% of the Challenger was working flawlessly, that one simple, tiny defective part resulted in those fatalities. It's the small things in life that make a difference.[1]

There are many things that could be causing you to miss out on building a strong financial platform of wealth building. But chances are, not having a budget that you adhere to could become the fatal O-Ring in your dreams of becoming financially secure.

A budget is telling your money where to go instead of wondering where it went. Proverbs 21:20 says, *"There is desirable treasure, and oil in the dwelling of the wise, but a foolish man squanders it."* When you don't have a budget, you end up squandering everything that you have—and then some. This proverb teaches that the wise person invests in things that

> When you don't have a budget, you end up squandering everything that you have.

have lasting value and they focus on more than just temporary wants and desires.

One of the keys to keeping your contentment in check is being disciplined enough to live on a budget. It's not your salary that makes you rich, it's your spending habits. Unless you control your money, making more won't help. You'll just have bigger payments. That's why Psalm 62:10 says, *"If riches increase do not set your heart upon them."* I like how the New Living Translation puts it: *"If your wealth increases, don't make it the center of your life."* Since money is a necessity in our world today, God wants you to manage it rather than be controlled by it. Money makes a good servant, but a poor master. You need to master your money instead of having your money master you.

I believe we all need some luxuries in life — it helps keep our morale up. But let me remind you that 3 billion people in the world live on less than $2 a day while another 1.3 billion people get by on less than a dollar a day. All of us living in America are wealthy by the rest of the world's standards. My point is, no matter your cash flow situation, you can probably get by with less so that your income exceeds your outgo. Benjamin Franklin said one time: "Contentment makes a poor man rich and discontent makes a rich man poor."

Planning + Prioritization = A Budget

There are two components that go into any budget: planning and prioritizing. Dave Ramsey teaches that when making a purchase, you should consider opportunity cost. What else could you do with that money? What future enjoyment are you sacrificing for tomorrow due to your greed of what you want today? There's a Swedish Proverb that states: "He who buys what he does not need steals from himself."

A wise man once said, "Let's say your shirt is $24 and you get paid $8 an hour. You are wearing three hours of your life." Wow. Let that sink in for a second and change your outlook on money. Rich people stay rich by living like they're broke. Broke people stay broke by living like they're rich.

"Don't tell me where your priorities are," James W. Frick says. "Show me where you spend your money and I'll tell you what they are." So how do we go about using a budget to control our priorities?

Step 1 - Know your monthly income.
This seems like common sense, but let me ask you: do you know what your monthly income is down to the exact dollar? You'd be surprised... most people don't. Your budget is based on your net income, after your taxes. So get out those pay stubs and calculate exactly what your monthly take-home pay is.

Step 2 - List all of your fixed monthly expenses.
Your expenses come in two categories: "Need to have" and "Like to have." Unless you want to be homeless, your mortgage or rent payment is a "need to have" expense. So are your utilities. "Like-to-have" expenses are your cable bill. We'll look at the "like-to-have" category later, but for now, just focus on listing the fixed expenses that you know you need in order to survive.

Step 3 - List all of your variable expenses.
These are things that can change depending on usage and vary each month: your groceries, clothing, restaurants, entertainment. These are the costs that you do have control over. And they can be adjusted or removed entirely depending on your goals.

Step 4 - Prioritize where your money is going to go before it's spent.
To create a budget that works, you have to take a really hard look at what is truly necessary. Whenever I get paid, the first thing I do is take the top 10% of my income and immediately give it back to God. Without His grace and goodness in my life, I wouldn't have an income to begin with, so this is my first priority expenditure. It's an act of worship and gratitude to God. The second 10% goes towards my debt retirement, the next 10% goes towards savings, just like we discussed in the last chapter (the 70% Principle). My remaining 70% is what I actually budget. If you don't take care of that top 30% of items first, you will automatically spend it on lesser things. As much as you think you need the latest iPhone upgrade, it's in the "Like-to-have" category and can only be purchased as long as the other things are prioritized first.

Step 5 - Eliminate what's not necessary.
If you want to find out where your money is going, start digging into your variable expenditures and cut whatever's unnecessary. Look through your bank statements and analyze where your money is going. You might be surprised to discover how many monthly fees and subscriptions you are losing money to. Here are some suggestions:

> "Let's say your shirt is $24 and you get paid $8 an hour. You are wearing three hours of your life."

Cell phone usage. Do you really need unlimited texting on your phone? Is there another carrier that would offer you the same level of service for a cheaper price? You might be surprised how your own cell phone carrier will be willing to negotiate a new price to keep your business.

Your subscriptions. Do you really need those magazine subscriptions? What about the monthly charges that keep coming out of your account every month. How many of those can you eradicate?

Cable TV. Do you really watch all 437 channels on your cable TV? If not, then downgrade to basic. The average cable bill is $86 a month. Imagine what you could do with an additional $1,032 a year. I recently cut my cable entirely and replaced it with Hulu and Netflix and saved nearly $50 a month.

Entertainment. In 2015, the U.S. Bureau of Labor Statistics reported that the average American spent nearly $3,000 on entertainment in one year! So there's a huge potential to find money by looking more closely at your entertainment expenses.

Coffee. If the average "designer coffee" costs $3.28, then you're spending $23 per week on fancy coffee. That's $1,200 per year! Is the coffee really that good? I'm not saying you need to give up the coffee habit, but simply cutting your coffee trips in half could save you a lot. Ditch the landline. This is a newer trend, and it makes sense. If you're still paying for a landline but you also have a cell phone, you might want to cut the cord for good. A landline might only cost $25 a month, but it adds up to $300 per year!

Mow your own lawn. If you're paying a landscaping company to cut the grass, this is an easy way to quickly save money. By cutting your own grass, you'll save money and get some good exercise!

Insurance rates. When was the last time you shopped rates on auto, life, and homeowner's insurance? If you're like most people, it's probably been awhile. But if you shop around using an independent agent, you could save a huge amount of money each year. You could save $500 a year just by getting better insurance rates.

Cook more meals at home. The average family spends half of their food budget on meals outside the home. You could potentially save hundreds of dollars over the course of a year just by cooking and eating more meals at home.

Now here's what I want you to do: take all of the money that you have found in your monthly expenditures that you can cut and multiply that by 12. That's the total amount of money that you could be saving just by taking an in-depth analysis of your budget. So many people think of a "budget" as restricting. But a budget actually gives you more freedom because you have permission to spend money on things that are important to you!

Step 6 - Track your spending.
Here's the exciting part. When you start tracking your spending, you'll find even more money you never even knew you had! You can track your spending in many different ways. Of course, you can do this the old-school way with a check register or a computer spreadsheet, but I want to encourage you to utilize some of the latest technology that makes tracking your spending pretty cool and convenient. Here are several resources I would recommend:

EveryDollar website and app. This tool was developed by Dave Ramsey so it's an excellent budget tool. It offers both a free as well as premium paid plan. It's easy to use and intuitive and you can get your budget up and running in under 10 minutes.

Mint website and app. I've been using Mint for years and in my opinion, it's the best app for managing your money. It's developed by the same company behind QuickBooks and TurboTax. *Mint* is an all-in-one resource that enables you to create a budget, track spending, and reach your goals. You can tie in all of your bank and credit card accounts, and even get reminders about your monthly bills.

Wally. This is perhaps the best app out there for tracking expenses. Instead of manually entering your expenses at the end of the day (or week/month), Wally lets you simply take a photo of your receipts.

You Need a Budget. This is a great app for getting out of debt or reaching your financial goals. This app forces you to live within your actual income. If you happen to get off track, the app will show you what you will need to do differently in order to balance your budget.

When you finally start tracking your spending accurately, you're going to identify patterns and see ways that you can streamline and cut your expenditures even more. This enables you to make adjustments along the way and empowers you to be the master over your money.

Step 7 - Evaluate monthly.
Once a month, take a look over your financial landscape. How are you doing on your savings goals? How much debt were you able to retire over this month? Is this in keeping with the annual goals you have set? Are you growing in your generosity? I always look over my finances on the last day of the month so that I can plan for any adjustments that might need to be made before the 1st of the next month.

To wrap it up, a B.U.D.G.E.T. allows you to:
B - Be Powerful
U - Understand where the money is going
D - Design your desired lifestyle.
G - Go after your dreams and goals.
E - Experience peace and less worry.
T - To have fun!

Unless you find an effective means to budget your money and track your spending, you'll never be financially free. Anna Lappe says, "Every time you spend money, you're casting a vote for the kind of world you want." So let's make sure you're voting for a future that leaves you financially secure!

> "Every time you spend money, you're casting a vote for the kind of world you want."

NEXT STEPS

What's your current monthly income?

What's your current fixed expenses?

What financial tool or app do you want to investigate more?

What is your goal in creating a monthly budget?

Accelerate Your Debt Reduction

"You might get 85 years on this planet—don't spend 65 paying off a lifestyle you can't afford." — Cait Flanders

Tmost important thing to do if you find yourself in a hole is to stop digging. **Debt has a way of bringing you to the edge of ruin.** Many lives and even marriages have severely damaged by it. In fact, debt is the second leading cause of divorce in America today.

Nothing causes us more stress than dealing with debt. That's why they put bumper stickers on cars that say, "I owe, I owe, so off to work I go." I wonder how many of you feel like the former pro golfer from Georgia, Doug Sanders, who said, "I am working as hard as I can to get my life and my cash to run out at the same time. If I can die right after lunch on Tuesday, everything will be fine!"

Solomon said, *"The rich rules over the poor, and the borrower is servant to the lender."*[1] The New International Version renders that verse by saying the borrower is a slave to the lender.

Kristen Kuchar wrote about the emotional effects of debt.[2] She said that while we can argue the virtues of good debt and bad debt, the truth is that any debt has serious emotional and psychological consequences. Countless studies have shown that debt can lead to depression, anxiety, resentment, and denial.

So what kind of debt have you accumulated to date? Maybe it's student debt, car loans, mortgage, credit cards. Every manner of debt is zero fun. It might start off small, but before long you feel like you're drowning in it. So what's the way out? Here are some helpful tips to assist you in accelerating your debt reduction.

What You Should Never Go into Debt For

If you buy things that you don't need, pretty soon you will have to start selling things that you do need. When I was in my 20s, one of the best words of advice I ever received was this: *never go into debt for depreciating liabilities.* A classic example of this is buying a new vehicle. Did you know that a new car loses 70% of its value in the first four years of ownership? Good debt is when you leverage your equity to buy additional assets (things that will make you more money). Cars can be the biggest liability of them all. They depreciate 10-20% in value just by driving it off the lot! Your used car may not be as sexy as a new one, but being wealthy is! The car I'm currently driving is 11 years old. I keep waiting for it to die as I've got enough money saved up to buy a new one, but that hasn't happened yet, so I keep driving it! Meanwhile that money that would normally be invested in a vehicle, is able to be invested in other ways, which is earning me more money. Instead of making a car payment to a bank charging you interest, make that same car payment to your savings account.

> **Never go into debt for depreciating liabilities.**

Also, never lease a car. According to Edmunds.com, *Smart Money magazine*, and my calculator, leasing is the most expensive way to operate a car.

Boats can be another depreciating asset. It's been said that the best two days of owning a boat is the day you buy it and the day you sell it. Not only do they depreciate like a car, but they are expensive to maintain. I suggest renting a boat for the few times during the year that you want to go out on the water.

If you have to do into debt for anything, make sure that it's debt to buy an asset (real estate, a business deal, etc.). People get into trouble when they use debt to buy toys and liabilities. A lot of people go into debt just to keep up with those who already are. Don't be like them. Be different. Be financially viable, sustainable, stress-free, and secure. Don't confuse a person's debt-worth with their net-worth. They may appear wealthy, but their debt may very well have brought them to the brink of bankruptcy. As Dave Ramsey says, "Live like no one else, so you can live like no one else."

Schedule a Plastic Surgery

Dave Ramsey famously quipped that if you want to get out of debt, you might need to do some "plastic surgery"—cut up your credit cards. The average American in 2018 had a credit card balance of $6,375 which was up nearly 3% from the previous year, according to Experian's annual study on the state of credit and debt in America. Total credit card debt has also reached its highest point ever, surpassing $1 trillion in 2017, according to a separate report by the Federal Reserve.[3] Consumer debt has tripled since 1980, and

43% of American families spend more than they earn each year. That means that a good percentage of people have more month than they do money, more bills to pay than dollar bills to pay them.

The first step to debt acceleration is to cease debt accumulation. Being willing to delay pleasure for a greater result is a sign of maturity. Just because you can afford the payments for something doesn't mean that you can afford the item that you're trying to purchase.

Thomas Jefferson said, "Never spend your money before you have it." The first step to taking control over your money is to stop borrowing. It's far better to *want* than it is to *owe*. Will Rogers used to say, "The quickest way to double your money is to fold it over and put it back in your pocket."

> Just because you can afford the payments doesn't mean you can affort the item.

Somewhere along the line, you're going to have to make some budget cuts to get yourself out of the debt hole. You can't expect to get out of debt by keeping the exact same lifestyle that got you into debt to begin with. Cut out everything except the basics. Then take whatever funds you've freed up and begin throwing them towards that debt! If you get a bonus, a tax refund, or even a birthday gift — any sum of unexpected cash--send it straight toward your debt. Resist the temptation to spend it on something frivolous. The pay off will be worth it when you're finally debt free!

List Al That I Owe and All That I Own

To seriously attack your debt, you have to get started and figure it out. You have to get the facts and put them down on paper. Most people don't really have a clue how much debt they have accumulated totally. You can't live in that state of unknown. When I first did this, I realized I had a negative net-worth. I owed a whole lot more than I owned. Once you get it all down on paper, you can work the plan. Proverbs 21:5 says, *"Good planning and hard work lead to prosperity."* The flip side of that principle is also true. Poor planning and laziness will lead to poverty. We have to own the fact that if we have a surplus of debt, it's likely poor planning that brought us to this point. A problem defined is a problem half-solved.

Avalanche vs. Snowball

There are two primary debt repayment strategies: the debt avalanche method and the debt snowball method. Let's look at each strategy more in depth:

The **Debt Avalanche Method** pays debts in order of their interest rate (starting with the debt that has the highest interest rate first). The focus is on paying off one balance at a time in order of interest rate while still paying the minimum balance on all the other debts. The benefit of this method is that you will pay debts off faster and pay less interest.

The **Debt Snowball Method** pays off debts in order of balance amount. You start with the smallest balance first, pay that debt off completely, then take all the money that you were putting towards that debt and add it to the payoff of your next smallest debt. Of course, if two debts have the same balance then you put the debt with the higher interest rate first. The focus is on paying off one balance at a time, in order of smallest to largest, while still making minimum payments on other debts. The greatest benefit of this method is that it results in *quick satisfaction*. You get an immediate dopamine rush when you see one of your debts completely wiped out and it motivates you to keep implementing the strategy. This is the strategy that I used and I'm proud to say that, with the exception of my home (which is on track to be paid off in a few years), I am completely debt free!

Creditor	Total Debt	Regular Payment	Regular + Extra Payment	New Payment
Target account	$450	$25	25 + 200	$225
Shell account	$600	$40	40 + 225	$265
Master Card account	$850	$75	75 + 265	$340
Parent Loan	$1,200	$150	150 + 340	$490
Car Loan	$8,000	$350	350 + 490	$840

If you just make the minimum payments on your credit card (as most people do), you will be in debt for a minimum of 120 months! That's ten years--and possibly many more--to pay off your debt!

After you've determined how much you can pay each month, automate your payments. Almost all banks offer this service. This will ensure you never forget and also make saying goodbye to your cash a little easier.

Remember that slow progress is still progress. Don't get discouraged. If you keep following this process and plodding along—without adding any new addition debt—you will succeed!

One resource you may want to utilize is a web tool called digit.co. Digit analyzes your spending and automatically saves the perfect amount every day, so you don't have to think about it. Once you share what you're saving for (paying off a credit card, saving for next vacation, or putting money away for a rainy day), Digit does the rest. So if you don't feel like you're disciplined enough to achieve these payments, a tool like this should really help.[4]

Remember that slow progress is still progress.

Most money problems are not because people don't make enough money, but rather because they don't manage the money that they make. Let me encourage you: money management is easy if your priorities are right and if you have discipline. You're not going to become debt free overnight, but you can make a decision to move in that direction. Every decision that you have ever made starts with a commitment.

Here's one last challenge. However long you think it will take you to do get out of debt, make a commitment that you will do it in *half the time*. Just commit it to God and say, "Lord, maybe with Your power, I will be able to do this in half the time." With God's power, miracles can happen. Jesus said, *"What is impossible from a human perspective is possible with God."*⁵

You know what you can do when you no longer have to make payments on debt? Anything. You. Want. When you're debt free, your money can do anything you want it to. Being totally in control of your finances is perhaps the greatest stress reliever there is. Romans 13:8 says *"We should owe nothing to anyone except love."* That's a vision for your financial future that's worth pursuing! Do something today that a future version of yourself will thank you for.

NEXT STEPS

Assess exactly how much debt you owe. Do this by calling your bank, sorting through mail slips, going online, and parsing through the numbers. Once you know the damage, you can set your plan in motion.

List your current debts, amounts, and interest being paid here:

What's your accelerated debt strategy: Debt Avalanche or Debt Snowball?

How are you going to keep yourself accountable? What's your target date for being debt free?

Pay Off Your Mortgage in 5 to 7 Years

"Compound interest is the eighth wonder of the world. He who understands interest, earns it. He who doesn't understand interest, pays it." — Albert Einstein

The word *mortgage* literally means "death contract." That's how I used to feel about it too. Did you know that having a mortgage is actually the most expensive and least efficient way to finance your home? I know what you're probably thinking, "I know, Brandon, but what other option do I have?" I want to let you in on what I believe is the greatest wealth management secret I've ever discovered — a systematic plan to pay off your mortgage that most people can accomplish within five to seven years.

Imagine what you could do if you got rid of your thirty-year mortgage and paid off your home in such a short amount of time. A couple of years ago, I was driving home from work and began thinking about my own thirty-year mortgage and how old I would be (past retirement) if I paid off that home by maintaining the same payments. I began to pray and said, "Lord, there has to be a better way. Show me how to pay off this home quicker." That very night while I was at the gym listening to YouTube videos, I stumbled across a video by Michael Lush, who has served as my financial advisor through ReplaceYourMortgage.com. What he has taught me has been a game changer. I've been implementing this strategy for a year now, and already I have paid down my principle more this year than what it would have taken me seven years paying on my traditional thirty-year mortgage. I am well on my way to having my house paid for.

I know what you're probably thinking: "If it sounds too good to be true, it probably is." But I want to encourage you to realize that this isn't magic; it's just math. So stick with me and try to understand this wealth-building principle. It could drastically alter your future net worth.

The Problem with Traditional Mortgages

If you've ever really studied an amortization schedule of your mortgage statement, it almost makes you nauseous. The truth of the matter is, we don't really own our homes, we just rent them from the bank at exorbitant costs.

Let's just take a simple side-by-side comparison of a mortgage vs. A HELOC. If you have a thirty-year mortgage for a $300,000 home at 4.25% interest, the payment is going to be $1,475 per month. Now let's take that same debt and transform it into a Home Equity Line of Credit. You still have the $300,000 loan on the home, but now we're going to take that same payment of $1,475 and apply it to it the same way. Guess what? You will actually pay off your home in 24.5 years as opposed to 30. If you are unclear on this, stick with me as I attempt to explain.

The power of this strategy is that you are now treating the HELOC as your checking account, thus accelerating this debt reduction even further. On average, most people can pay it off in five to seven years, without changing anything with their budget. So if you're accustomed to getting paid and depositing your money into your checking account and paying your bills out of your checking account, that's all that's involved in utilizing this strategy with a HELOC. It replaces your checking account.

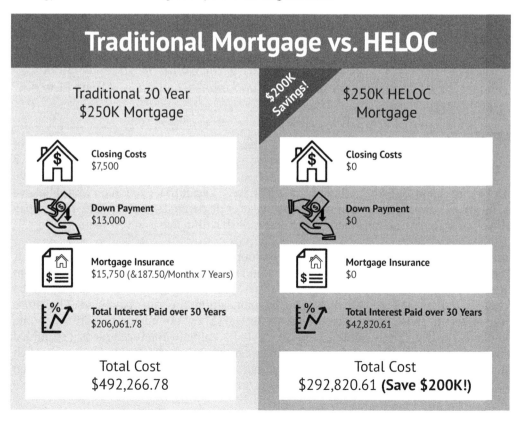

How Does the Strategy Work?

Basically, what I have done is I have replaced my mortgage with a Home Equity Line of Credit (HELOC for short). The line of credit calculates interest daily on the outstanding principal balance and requires an interest only payment.

HELOC's are bank-owned products. They are not regulated by the mortgage industry. Their terms differ from bank to bank but the basic principle is the same. Most banks will issue you a HELOC if you have a loan to value ratio of 80%. Let's say your home is valued at $200,000. If your current loan balance is $160,000 or less, you should be able to qualify for a HELOC.

> We don't really own our homes, we just rent them from the bank at exorbitant costs.

A mortgage is a closed-ended account - meaning that you can put money in, but you cannot take money out. A HELOC is different. It's an open-ended, simple interest account much like a credit card. You pay interest on the daily balance. If tomorrow's balance is less, then you pay less interest. You can deposit and withdraw money from it as much as you would like over the course of a ten-year period. What if you can't pay off your home in ten-years you might ask? Well, just go get another HELOC from another bank. It's that simple.

So how do I leverage this strategy to work in my favor?

First of all, 100% of all of my income go directly into this account. I've been working for years to have multiple income streams: my salary, my wife's income, my book royalties, executive coaching fees, speaking fees, and so forth. All of those funds go directly into this account. I don't have a separate savings account, or a money market account, or an additional checking account. Again, I want to emphasize that 100% of my money goes into the HELOC. So every time I get paid or get some additional income, I immediately transfer that amount from my checking account into my HELOC account, thus driving down the daily principle balance which results in less interest being paid.

Secondly, none of my money is being escrowed by the bank. When you have your taxes and insurance escrowed and held for annual payment by the bank, who's making interest off of that money? Definitely not you. The bank is. By not escrowing your money and keeping it within the HELOC, driving down the daily principal balance until it has to be paid, you are paying less interest and therefore paying off the loan faster.

Third, all of my expenses are placed on a 0% interest credit card. You can qualify for a credit card that offers 0% interest for twelve months or even eighteen or twenty-four months. I ask for the highest loan balance on that credit card. Currently, my maximum loan balance for my 0% interest credit card is $25,000. So guess what balance of expenditures I keep on that credit card? You guessed it: $25,000. Because that money is being held interest free, it enables more of my income to go towards my HELOC, further driving down the daily principal balance and further accelerating the debt payoff. Once the twelve-month 0% interest offer expires, I pay the full amount of the credit card out of my HELOC account and go and get another 0% interest credit card for the next year.

Fourth, all major purchases are made out of the HELOC. I can't emphasize this enough. You have to make a commitment to yourself that you are never going in debt for any other purchase ever again. You are now your own bank. So now when I need to replace my car with a used vehicle, I go to the dealership and pay for it out of my HELOC. If you don't consolidate your debt in this way, it will take you even longer to pay it off and build wealth.

And finally, I set annual targets to reach my payoff goals. I use the calculator on ReplaceYourMortgage.com to set milestones along the way. If my goal is to have my home paid off in seven years, then I can use that calculator to help me determine how much my loan balance should be by year one, by year two, and so on. If I'm tracking on target, then we may have some extra money to go on vacation. If I'm falling behind, then that helps me to also tighten the belt on expenditures.

Why Don't Most People Do This?

About six months ago, I was talking to a friend at my local gym. He owned his own mortgage company and recently sold it. I told him about my strategy and I expected him to be critical or at least skeptical as his background is within the mortgage industry. Once I told him my strategy, his response surprised me, "Ah!" he said, "That's what a lot of my doctor and lawyer friends do to pay off their homes quickly. Most people will never take the time to learn that strategy though so they will always come to people like us to get their traditional mortgages." Here was a mortgage expert acknowledging to me that this was the most effective and efficient way of financing a home.

But perhaps you're wondering, "Why don't more people do this?" That's a legit question. There are several reasons:

1. Bankers and those in the loan industry don't even know about this strategy. When I applied for my HELOC at my local credit union, no one there had ever heard of using a HELOC as a first-lien position loan to pay off a house. It was a completely foreign concept to them even though it's a common concept in foreign countries.
2. Because banks don't make as much money from them. Banks are in the business of making money, so if there is a more profitable product to sell, they will sell it. Not only do they lose a significant amount of interest that is front-loaded to your mortgage amortization schedule, they also lose the closing fees which amount to thousands of dollars. Mortgages are big business.
3. Most people aren't willing to take the time to learn new and better ways to build wealth--so they stay stuck where they are financially. Ironically, this is the system for home financing that is commonly practiced in Australia and parts of the UK. They think we are crazy for getting the types of mortgages like we do.

Who Can Qualify?

1. You have to make more money than you spend. This is important. If you don't have cash flow positivity where you are making more money than what you spend, this strategy will not work for you. You have to be disciplined and have a budget.

2. You have to have a good credit score to qualify for a HELOC. Your credit score should be at least 640. Depending on the bank, they may have a different credit score requirement.

3. Some banks have seasoning requirements before you can qualify for a HELOC. That means you may need to have lived in your home for at least a year or longer in order to qualify.

4. You have to be uber disciplined with your money. When you start seeing your equity increase drastically (and you will) the temptation will come to use some of those funds to buy a new car or to take a more elaborate vacation than you normally would. You have to fight that temptation to spend that money.

Imagine what your life would be like if you didn't have to worry about a mortgage anymore. This is by far the greatest wealth building secret I've ever discovered. I can personally vouch for the success of this system. My financial advisor is now encouraging me to look into purchasing rental homes and investment properties using this strategy. Every six months, he buys a new rental property and purchases it by using his HELOC. You would think that spending $50,000 or even $100,000 would put you far backwards from being able to pay off your own primary home; but the reality is, the additional rental income coming back into your HELOC actually helps pay off the total loan balance faster! You could literally become a real estate mogul and secure for yourself your own retirement pension plan just by using this strategy.

> Eliminating a mortgage is by far the greatest wealth building secret I've ever discovered.

There's so much more that I would like to cover on this topic but it would be impossible to do so in such a short chapter. I would encourage you to do what I did and contact the experts at ReplaceYourMortgage.com. You can schedule a free session where you can discuss your finances and determine if this strategy is right for you. And please do me a favor and let them know that Brandon Park recommended you to them.

NEXT STEPS

What excites or concerns you about the HELOC strategy?

What other valuable insight did you gather from this chapter?

Invest for Tomorrow

"When you invest, you are buying a day that you don't have to work." — Aya Laraya

Sometimes **I get frustrated with our educational system today.** I wish I was taught in high school what is perhaps the number one skill that has earned me the most money to date—the power of investing. Two decades have gone by since I've graduated high school and not once have I used what I learned in algebra or calculus, but investing is something that I do every day. I had to be self-taught and my only regret about investing is that I didn't learn these skills sooner. Of course, there isn't enough time in one chapter in this book to cover this or any of these topics, but I hope to just whet your appetite a bit and point you in the right direction to get you started in building your own investment portfolio.

It Doesn't Take Much to Earn Your First Million...

...it just takes a lot of time to earn it. People think that becoming a millionaire is this elusive pie-in-the-sky dream. It doesn't have to be. You just need some *Investing 101* basic knowledge, and you need to get started *early*, preferably while you're still in your 20s. The earlier you can begin, the greater your financial payout will be in the end as you approach retirement. Investing and the ability to win with money is about 80% behavior and only 20% head knowledge. Most of us know what to do; we're just not doing it. We

> $100 a month invested in a decent growth-stock mutual fund from age 30 to age 70 will be worth $1,176,000!

know we should be investing; but we're piddling our money away on frivolous things.

Did you know that $100 a month invested in a decent growth-stock mutual fund from age 30 to age 70 will be worth $1,176,000? That's a serious amount of money just by investing $100 a month! If you were to just cut out your coffee expenses and your cable bill, you could retire with dignity! Invest for your future.

Did you know the average car payment in America is now $523 and requires five years and nine months to pay off?[1] But if you were to follow my advice in an earlier chapter and buy a used car with saved up cash, then you could free up money that could be invested. If you were to take that same payment of $523 and invest it in a decent growth-stock mutual fund from age 30 to age 70, you would have $5.3 million dollars! I hope you enjoy your car. Perhaps this is why Solomon said, *"The wise man saves for the future, but the foolish man spends whatever he gets."*[2]

When it comes to investing, remember that time is always on your side. Warren Buffett says, "The rich invest in time, the poor invest in money." So get started as early as possible. Like the ancient proverb states: The best time to plant an oak tree is 25 years ago; the next best time to plant a tree is today. The best time to get started with investing is yesterday; but the second best time to get started is today! Don't lose out on potential earnings by waiting till tomorrow. As the old saying goes: The early bird catches the worm…or, in this case, gets to retire in style. The sooner you put your money to work, the more it has time to grow.

Think about this: If you invested $10,000 and left it to grow for 40 years (assuming an average return per year of 8%), you would end up with $217,000. But if you waited 10 years and invested $20,000 — that's *twice* as much — you would only end up with just over $200,000.

Remember the Rule of 72

The rule of 72 is an investor's way of easily determining a return on investment. To find the number of years required to double your money at a given interest rate, you just divide that interest rate into the number 72.

For example: 72 divided by 8% = 9 years. So if you take $10,000 and put it in an interest bearing account that yields an average of 8%, it will take 9 years for that $10,000 to become $20,000.

Let's say you have a current balance of $350,000 in your 401k. If you invest it at 8% interest, you will have $700,000 within 9 years. That's the power of compound interest. Your money multiplies in an exponential way. Interest is bad when it's on a credit card; but it's extremely lucrative when it's tied to your investments.

In 2017, Bitcoin was all the rage. Interestingly enough, if you had just invested $100 in bitcoin in 2011, it would be worth $2,053,278 in 2018.[3] I think all of us have investor's remorse when it comes to missing out on that opportunity. However, we can fall into a lot of trouble though when we treat the stock market as another "get-rich-quick" scheme. "An important key to investing," Peter Lynch says, "is to remember that stocks are not lottery tickets." I did this when I first started investing. I bought pretty much only penny stocks (stocks valued at less than $5 a share, although most of my first investments were less than $2 a share). I made a lot of money in a relatively short time; but I also lost most of the money I made in those early years. The key to the stock market is making wise choices, investing conservatively, and backing away from it.

Ric Edel in his book *The Truth About Money* noted that the stock market is like a little boy with a yo-yo. If you watch the yo-yo of the stock market too much, you will become fearful and bail out completely. But if you take a step back, you'll notice that while the yo-yo is going up and down, the boy is walking up a hill. We can see the stock market going up and down (even with major market corrections every ten years or so) but the overall trend is upward.

Tools for Getting Started

If you were like me, you probably want to invest, but you don't have the foggiest idea where to get started. So let me offer to you a few tools that are a great launching pad.

Robinhood is my favorite app to learn investing. The best part about it is that it's free! Whereas other stock brokerage accounts charge you money to buy and sell stocks, with Robinhood, it's all completely free. They've "cut the fat" that makes other brokerages costly, like manual account management and hundreds of storefront locations, so they are able to offer zero commission trading. There's an app for both Google and Android as well as their website. If you don't have an account, you can also click my free link and receive a free stock to get you started! You could receive a stock in Apple, Ford, or Sprint just to name a few. Just type this link in your browser: share.robinhood.com/brandop101 and you and I both will receive a free stock. That's a win for both of us!

Acorns is a great tool if you're having trouble finding the money to get started with investing. What acorns does is it invests your spare change. You can set up what's called "Round-Ups" where the app will set aside the spare change that you make from the purchases you make as you go about your day and automatically transfer that into your stock accounts. For example, if you purchase a cup of coffee for $2.60, then Acorns will round up and take $.40 cents and invest it for you. You can also set up recurring investments.

Betterment.com is another tool that falls into the category of robo-advisor to build your wealth. If you're not familiar with how robo-advisor's work, here's a brief rundown. Basically, when you sign up for their services, you provide information about your goals, your income, and your risk tolerance. A computer software program then uses that information to choose investments for you and automatically rebalances your assets over time. This is a great tool if you're new to investing as the minimum investment to get started is much lower than with traditional financial advisors. The management fees are also considerably lower as well since many robo-adisors push cheaper funds—like ETFs—that carry fewer fees than other investments.[4] On average, Betterment claims that their investing principles can increase returns by 2.66% when compared to the typical investor.[5]

> You have to put off what feels good now in order to enjoy your long-term goals.

Automate Your Investments

If you have to think about whether or not you're going to invest in a particular month, chances are you won't do it. One of the best books I read in my twenties is a book called *The Automatic Millionaire* by David Boch. In it, he talks about the importance of setting up in your online banking these automated bill payments. On the same day that your direct deposit hits your checking account, use the online billpay to set up an automatic transfer of money to fund your retirement account, emergency savings account, and even your regular bills. Most people who are saving for retirement are only putting away 3-4%. That's just not enough. Aim for at least 10% of your income going towards retirement. That might be hard to get to immediately, but if you make it your goal to increase it by 1% each year, most people can get there without even feeling the effects on their budget. Think of this as paying your future self first.

When it comes to investing, people tend to focus more on the actual investment than on the amount that's being invested. Yet a 2011 study found that a person's savings rate is more important for wealth building than what that person actually invests in. So keep that in mind. Invest as much as you can. In Hebrews 11, it says that Moses forsook pleasures for a time because he saw a greater reward. It's that same principle of diligence and tenacity of self-sacrifice that will ensure long-term success. You have to put off what feels good now in order to enjoy your long-term goals.

Dividend Stocks

A big investment strategy that many investors go for (and many even use this strategy to live off of their passive income) is dividend stocks. A dividend is a distribution of a portion of a company's earnings to holders of its stock. When a company makes money, it has the option to share that profit with you as a stockholder or retain that money as earnings, which it is then free to reinvest. Let's say you own 1,000 shares of a company's stock and that company's board of directors make the decision to pay a cash dividend in the amount of $10 a share. Your payment would therefore be $10,000! Smart investors look for stocks with high yields and a track record of increasing their divident payouts every year for several years. Here are a few examples:
- Coca-Cola: 3.2% dividend yield (52 years of dividend growth)
- Target: 2.8% dividend yield (47 years of dividend growth)
- McDonald's: 3.43% dividend yield (38 years of dividend growth)
- Pepsi: 2.83% divident yield (32 years of dividend growth)[6]

Diversify

Don't put all your eggs in one basket. Never test the depth of a river with both feet. We've got a lot of pithy sayings that encourages us to diversify. Scripture even tells us *"But divide your investments among many places, for you do not know what risks might lie ahead."*[7] Successful investors also know not to put all of their money eggs in one basket— or two baskets, for that matter. They spread their wealth across a variety of investments, from stocks, mutual funds, ETFs and bonds, to real estate, collectibles and startups. A diversified portfolio means that you can potentially take advantage of multiple sources of growth and protect yourself from financial ruin if one of your investments bombs.

NEXT STEPS

How "savvy" do you consider yourself in matters of finance and investment?

Think of several people you know who could serve as resources on the topics from this chapter.

What the Wealthy Do Different

*"Tell me how you use your spare time,
and how you spend your money,
and I will tell you where and what you will be in ten years."*
– Napoleon Hill

Every year, Forbes magazine releases their list of the richest people in the world. The top five richest (in estimated worth) in 2018 were:

#5 - Mark Zuckerberg (founder of Facebook) - worth $71,000,000,000.
#4 - Bernard Arnault (French business magnate) - $72,000,000,000.
#3 - Warren Buffett (business investor) - $84,000,000,000.
#2 - Bill Gates (founder of Microsoft) - $90,000,000,000
#1 - Jeff Bezos (CEO of Amazon) - $112,000,000,000

It's hard to imagine that amount of wealth isn't it? I've always been fascinated with super rich people. I remember as a kid watching the TV show *Lifestyles of the Rich and Famous*. Some of these people live in a completely different world. However, the book

The Millionnaire Next Door presents a different perspective. As it turns out, a lot of millionaires--maybe the majority--don't live the super-lavish lifestyle like we might imagine. In fact, they live such modest, humble, and generous lives that you would never cause you to suspect they were sitting on a large nest egg.

As difficult as it is to imagine, there are some major lessons that we can learn from the very wealthy. Chances are, there are certain things that they do differently than you and me. They have a different attitude and approach towards money and building wealth that we can learn from.

I remember what it was like to be poor and not to have enough money for groceries. I can identify with the comedian who said, "I used to be so poor that I'd find myself rubbing cologne from magazines on my shirt. When people said to me, 'Oh you smell good, what is that?' I'd say "Page 12." Maybe you've been there. Bill Gates used to say, "If you are born poor, it's not your mistake. But if you die poor, it is your mistake." His point is that we are all given the chance in America to improve the financial situation and circumstances that you were born into — but we have to make the right choices and commit to growth and learning.

You may not ever become a millionaire, but if you develop their same mindset you will most assuredly improve your financial situation. So how do you do it?

Commit to Learning about Building Wealth

First you learn and then you remove the "L" (you earn). Paul Martinelli of the John Maxwell Company once asked a group of participants at a conference I attended this thought provoking question. He said, "How many of you have ever give more than 10 minutes of thought a week as to how you will make your first million." I had to be honest. Although, like all of us, I had fantasized about what it would be like to never have to worry about money, I had never given any thought to an actual strategy for building lasting wealth. That's the problem for a lot of us. We want to be rich; but we're not willing to put in the diligence to follow the process.

Anyone who will tell you that accumulating wealth is easy is lying to you. If you hear a "get-rich-quick" scheme; it's precisely that… a scheme. It takes time to research and to learn about money, including interviewing and talking to others who have accomplished more than you and learning from their success. T. Harv Eker said it best: "It's simple arithmetic: Your income can grow only to the extent that you do."

That's why most CEOs read an average of one book a week. Compare that to the rest of the general population who just read two books *a year*. Warren Buffett recommends reading 500 pages a day and he states that knowledge "builds up, like compound interest."

First you learn and then you remove the "L" (you earn).

Throughout the Bible, Scripture tells us that the diligent shall be made rich. Research does in fact back this up: 80% of self-made millionaires become wealthy *after* the age of 50. That's nearly half a century of personal growth, learning through trial and error, and due diligence. In the book, *The Millionaire Next Door*, it says that most millionaires take eighteen years to reach their first million. Are you willing to be patient and save and invest diligently?

Somebody once said that if you took all the money in the world and divided it up equally among everybody, it would soon all be back in the same pockets. Success is something that you attract by who you are, it's not something that you pursue. Instead of going after it, work on yourself. Jim Rohn says, "The major question to ask on the job is not what are you *getting*. The major question to ask on the job is, what are you *becoming*." True happiness and fulfillment is never within what you get; it's who you become.

Do What Others Won't

You must be willing to do the things today that others won't do in order to have the things tomorrow that others won't have. What are the things that others won't do? You can start by making discipline a major force in your life. Don't you think that if you had been more disciplined, you would have been further along in reaching your goals than you are now? Socrates said, "The undisciplined life is an insane life." The man who does more than he is paid for will soon be paid for more then he does. But the flip side of that same coin is that those who don't manage their money will always work for those who do.

> Rich people stay rich by living like they're broke. Broke people stay broke by living like they're rich.

It's been said that rich people stay rich by living like they're broke.
Broke people stay broke by living like they're rich. Have you ever met someone who is unassuming and modest and found out later that they're actually rolling in the dough? Millionaires are all around us, and many of them are probably not who you would think. This is because they wisely live below their means and save their money rather than showcasing it. The trick is adopting a "less is more" mentality and sticking with it, even when your income and net worth increase in the future.

Not only do the wealthy spend their money wisely but they also spend their time wisely. They outsource tasks that aren't a productive use of their time because they understand that time is more important than money. They have no problem outsourcing chores like cleaning or household maintenance because they know they could make more money in that time than they'll spend paying someone else to do it. Not only that, but it also decreases stress and frees up mental energy for more important things.

Develop a Side Hustle

I once read somewhere that everyone needs three hobbies: a hobby to help them relax, a hobby to keep them in shape, and a hobby to help them make money. Not everyone is cut out to be an entrepreneur, but it's always good to have a plan B if your current employer decides there are cutbacks for unknown reasons. Check out Chris Guillebeau's books *The $100 Start Up or Side Hustle* to get your creative juices flowing on what you could potentially do as a side business.

If you have a marketable hobby or talent (think photography, fitness, crafting, baking or music) then brainstorm some ways that you might be able to profit from doing what you love. Spread the word to your family and friends and look for the best outlet to market your services.

Les Brown said, "My definition of success is doing what you love to do and finding somebody to pay you to do it." Working hard for something you don't care about is called *stress*. Working hard for something we love is called *passion*. You want to master your talent. Do what you love to do. Then explore ways to earn a living doing that.

> Those who have become wealthy have also mastered the art of having more than one income stream.

Those who have become wealthy have also mastered the art of having more than one income stream. Apparently, 65% of self-made millionnaires have three streams of income. 29% of millionaires have five or more. The most common include dividend income, real estate rental income, royalties, capital gains, income from businesses they own, and interest on savings and bonds.[1] Millionnaires rarely rely on just one income stream, because they know it's a risk.

Passive Income Ideas

Warren Buffett famously quipped: "If you don't find a way to make money while you sleep, you will work until you die."

Here are a few of my favorite passive income ideas that might help spark your imagination of what could be possible.

Invest in Real Estate with a REIT. Did you know that 90% of all millionaires become so through owning real estate. Real estate is almost always part of the wealth building arsenal of those who are wealthy. But it can be hard to get started if you don't have enough capital. That's where a REIT can come in handy. REIT stands for Real Estate Investment Trust. The REIT owns the property so you don't have to worry about any logistics like a landlord would. They also pay higher dividends than stocks, bonds, or bank investments. You can also sell your interest in an REIT whenever you want making it more liquid than owning actual real estate. Check out a site like Realty Mogul if this interests you.

Rent your own space. Due to the rise in popularity of Airbnb, you can now use your own space as an alternative for people who are looking for something other than a hotel. So if you have an unused home, a spare room, or even a furnished basement—your own property can become a way to generate extra income.

Buy a blog. Notice I didn't say start a blog. Everyone's doing that already. But there are actually thousands of income producing blogs that are in the process of being abandoned by their owners every year. Most blogs make money through Google AdSense, which provides a monthly income based on ads that Google places on the site. You can go to Flippa.com and see what blogs or websites are for sale. As a general rule, a blog usually sells for twenty-four times their monthly income. So if the site generates. $250 a month in average income, then the blog will sell for $6,000. Not a bad investment for $3,000 a year in additional cash flow.

Teach online courses. I personally know of people who make over $30,000 a *month* selling their online courses. Some even make seven figures. Do you have a niche that you love to learn about and teach others about? Then consider launching an online course. Platforms like Teachable.com or Kajabi.com make this easier than ever before. You'll need to master a funnel to get leads and it's some work getting the online course up and running; but once it's done you'll be able to make money in your sleep.

Become an affiliate partner. By selling other people's products on my website and in my seminars, I actually make a little bit of effortless money. Many companies allow you to join them as an affiliate partner by rewarding you with a one-time "finder's fee" or a commission based on you recommending their products or services to others. If you find a product that you absolutely love and rave about, contact the company and ask if they offer an affiliate program.

Sell products online. When people think of selling products online, they might think of eBay but Amazon's FBA (Fulfillment by Amazon) program enables you to do that as well. You can have products shipped directly from the wholesaler to Amazon's warehouse where they can be sold. Many have found this to be so lucrative, that they've made it their full-time job.

Do the Most with What You've Been Given

In Matthew 15, Jesus shared the parable of the talents. It's a story of how a man called his own servants and gave them a differing sum of money called a *talent*. A talent was the equivalent of twenty years of wages for the common worker. We're talking an insane amount of money here. By today's standards, one talent would be equal to roughly half a million dollars! To one of his servants, he gave five talents ($2.5M), to the second two ($1M), and to the third one he gave one ($500k). Notice that although everyone was given gifts equally, not everyone had equal gifts. Matthew 15:15 tells us that each man was given his talents *"according to his own ability."* That's an important distinction to note. Your income cannot grow until you do.

The master went away on a journey and left his money with his servants to steward. The man who had received five talents went and invested and traded with them and earned five more! (He went from $2.5 million to $5 million dollars!) And he who had received two gained two more also (he went from $1 million to $2 million). But what about the last guy who received the least? Scripture says that this guy went and hid it in the ground. He didn't want to take any risk.

In the parable, Jesus says the master chastised the servant who hadn't done anything with the resources he had been given; but the servants that did steward their resources well were given even greater responsibility. It's interesting that God values those who have ambition and who are looking to maximize the resources that they are given rather than just holding on to what little they have and burying it in the ground.

Les Brown said, "If you're not willing to risk, you cannot grow. If you cannot grow, you cannot be your best. If you cannot be your best, you cannot be happy. If you cannot be happy, what else is there?"

Can God trust you to be wise and diligent with the resources you've been given? In their working lifetime, most people are going to handle $2 to $6 million dollars. We have to act and be responsible—both on paper and on purpose. Sit down and give every dollar a name and agree on it with your spouse. And always remember that money is a servant; you are the master. We get into trouble when it's the other way around.

> "As we made all that money, it didn't fix our lives — it just made us more of who we already were."

A wise man who had millions of net worth invested in real estate and earned a yearly disposable income of $250,000 once said, "As we made all that money, it didn't fix our lives — it just made us more of who we already were." Even if you're one of the lucky ones who achieves his or her materialistic dreams, money only amplifies that which is already present. It's been said that a person's character is put to the test when he suddenly acquires or quickly loses a considerable amount of money. Why? Because wealth doesn't make you a better or happier person. Money only amplifies what is already there.

NEXT STEPS

What one idea was sparked in your mind after reading this chapter?

What is one passive income idea that you can begin investigating this week?

The Rewards of a Generous Life

*"The law of prosperity is generosity.
If you want more, give more."* – Bob Proctor

One of my favorite topics to teach on is the subject of generosity. This is probably because, quite honestly, I was not a generous person for a long time. In fact, I was the opposite of generous--I had the spiritual gift of being a tight wad. But God has truly done a work in my heart and helped me to learn the power of living a generous life.

Interestingly enough, when you read the Bible, half of all the parables Jesus shared were about money and possessions. Jesus talked more about money than He did about the subjects of Heaven or Hell combined. One out of every six verses in the Gospels (Matthew, Mark, Luke, and John) deals with the topic of money and possessions. Why does the Bible devote so much time to this one topic? It's because God knows that our attitude towards money and possessions is a barometer of our heart's condition and it shows what we really value in life. And God wants us to live lives that are blessed. Proverbs 11:25 says, *"A generous man will prosper; that he who refreshes others will himself be refreshed."*

There are five rewards or blessings, if you will, when we learn to be generous with our resources:

#1 – I Always Receive More When I Give

Luke 6:38 reveals one of the greatest generosity principles in all of the Bible. It states: *"Give, and it will be given to you. Good measure, pressed down, shaken together, running over, will be put into your lap. For with the measure you use it will be measured back to you."*

One of the most common mistakes people make about this verse is assuming that Jesus is speaking only of money. In reality, He's revealing a principle that applies to every single area of our lives.

What do the terms a "good measure, pressed down, shaken together, and running over" mean? Sounds almost like a dance doesn't it? In reality, these were farming terms, agricultural terms used to describe a bushel basket. People would make their living back then farming wheat and other crops. At the end of the week, the employer would then pay his laborers a measure of wheat–it was what was going to sustain their families.

Good employers would customarily take these baskets and make sure that you first had a *"good measure"* (not just a partial measure or a half measure). Your pay was going to fill the basket.

Then they would *"press it down"* to compress the grains together to make more room for additional wheat. After topping off the basket again, they would then shake it to eliminate any space between the grains.

Having done all that, you would then pour in as much grain as you possibly could--heaping it up over the rim until it spilled over and was *"running over"* the sides.

It was one thing to receive a basket of grain – it was quite another thing to receive a basket that was a *"good measure, pressed down, shaken together, and running over."*

That's a pretty amazing promise when you think about it! But it has only one condition: you must give. The point Jesus was trying to make was, "Whatever you give, you're going to get a lot more of the same in return. Now remember, God's not some kind of cosmic vending machine where you put your money in, press the button and *poof*, He gives you exactly what you want. I don't want you to hear that, but I do want you to realize that God does bless those who give. God gives us this promise not to create our motivation for giving, but rather to free us from fear and show us the reward of giving.

> **You need to sow based on how much you want to harvest.**

Here's the principle: You need to sow based on how much you want to harvest. Jesus said in Luke 6:38, *"With the same measure that you use, it will be measured back to you."* Did you get that? This is a powerful principle to grasp: God doesn't decide how blessed you are. You get to decide how blessed you are. You have a measure. If you're a really generous person, then you have a large measure. If you're a chintzy, selfish, greedy person-- then you have a very small or non-existent measure.

Imagine a farmer going out to his farm and saying, "What! I

only have ten stalks of corn in my field! I can't live on this!" His friend says,

"Well, how many seeds did you plant?"

"Well... I only planted ten."

According to your standard of measure, it's going to be measured back to you in return.

#2 – I Lessen the Effects of Greed and Materialism

Another benefit of giving is freedom. Nothing breaks the bonds of greed and materialism faster than generosity. A lesson from high school physics can teach us a great truth about our mindset on money. The greater the mass, the greater the hold that mass exerts. That's why a 100-pound man on earth would weigh just 33 pounds on the moon but would weigh an astounding 351 pounds on Jupiter!

> Money leads; hearts follow.

In a similar way, the more things we own - the greater their total mass - the more they have a tendency to grip us, setting us in orbit around them. Finally, like a black hole, they suck us in.

When we give, it changes that tendency. It breaks us out of orbit around our "stuff." We escape our possessions' strong gravitational pull and orient ourselves to enter a new orbit around our treasures in Heaven.

Jesus said this about money: *"For where your treasure is, there your heart will be also."* One day, when I was teaching on this principle, I brought a heart-shaped helium balloon with me on stage. On the bottom of the string attached to the balloon, I tied a $100 bill. The heart-shaped balloon represented our heart, our desire, and our will, while the money on the other end of the string represented how we manage our resources. I held on to the balloon and dragged the $100 bill behind me and explained that this is how most people see their relationship to money. They think that whatever things they cared about, wherever their heart went, their money would follow. Makes sense right? We think that it's our hearts and our desires that lead to where our finances are spent.

However, Jesus teaches just the opposite. He says that *"where your treasure is, there your heart will be also."* In other words, Jesus says that it's not your heart that leads around your finances, it's where you spend your money that determines where your heart is going to go.

Money is sometimes stronger than our mind and our will--and our will bends to where our money goes. So we invest our money in giving extravagantly and generously--and soon our heart and desires will follow that. That's a big distinction!

Before I bought stock in Apple, I could care less what value it was trading in per share. But after I bought stock in Apple, I found myself keeping up with Apple news. What happened? I put some of my treasure there and my heart followed.

Money leads; hearts follow. So if you want to develop more of a heart for missions or to help the poor; invest your money in those initiatives and watch what happens to your heart. Remember, it's not your heart that determines where you money goes; it's where you invest your money that determines where your heart goes. The only way to be freed from greed is to give. Nothing snaps the chains of greed and selfishness more quickly than generosity.

#3 – I Am Infused with Joy When I Give

The happiest people in life are the givers, not the getters. When I speak on the topic of giving at conferences, donor gatherings, and churches, I repeatedly see people with joy in their eyes telling how God has touched their lives through helping the needy, in hands-on ways, as well as through their giving.

When Jesus spoke of the man who found the treasure in the field, he emphasized how "in his joy" the man went and sold all that he had to gain the treasure (Matthew 13:44). We're not supposed to feel sorry for the guy because it cost him everything. Rather, we're supposed to imitate him. Sure, it cost him, but it also gained him everything he wanted! Scripture says he was "filled with joy." The benefits vastly outweighed the costs.

The more we give, the more we delight in our giving—and the more God delights in us. Our giving pleases us and brings us joy. But more importantly, it pleases God: *"God loves a cheerful giver"* (2 Corinthians 9:7).

God delights in our cheerfulness in giving. He wants us to find joy. But if we don't give, we're robbed of the source of joy God instructs us to seek!

The bottom line is that people who give generously feel great about it and find themselves blessed in ways they never expected. Great things happen in them, and great things happen to those around them. It's the ultimate win-win situation.

We get a lift when we give don't we? Whenever we go out of our way to help or encourage someone, we feel encouraged and positive. It causes others to want to be around us as well. Something happens on the inside. It's good for us and good for others.

I've had the opportunity to travel to Israel on two occasions leading tours of the Holy Land. One of the most memorable stops on that tour is the Dead Sea. The salt content of the Dead Sea makes this body of water a truly eerie experience. You literally can't sink. It's impossible. Not only that, your body sort of bobs on the surface of the water. But the reason it's called the Dead Sea is because it's just exactly that - dead. Nothing can live in its waters. But why? Turns out that there are numerous channels and tributaries that all run into the Dead Sea--including the Jordan River. As they travel to the Dead Sea, each one of these rivers and channels brings additional deposits of not just water, but also salt and other minerals. Experts say that if the Dead Sea had an outlet--if it had a way to give--it wouldn't be dead. But because it has no outlet, because it has no means by which to give out of its own supply--it's dead.

Isn't that a perfect picture of life? When we have no outlet to give, we die a little bit on the inside. Generosity is what helps bring life to our body, soul, and spirit.

#4 – I Reap What I Sow

Galatians 6:7 says, *"Do not be deceived, God is not mocked; for whatever a man sows, this he will also reap."* Now if you've ever raised a garden or planted flowers - you can understand the laws of the harvest. They're very simple:

You reap WHAT you sow. If you put good seed into the ground - you're going to reap a good harvest. If you put bad seed into the ground - you're going to reap a bad harvest. The harvest is always the product of the seed. If you sow corn, you're not reaping strawberries. You reap what you sow. So therefore you need to plant what you want to harvest. You have to give what you want to receive. You reap what you are willing to sow.

> The harvest is always the product of the seed.

You reap MORE than you sow. If a farmer sows a kernel of corn, does he reap just one additional kernel of corn? Of course not. He reaps an entire stalk that will bear two ears of corn and hundreds of kernels. When you sow an acorn, you don't just reap another acorn. You reap an entire oak tree. You not only reap what you sow, you always reap *more* than what you sow. Jesus taught that when you give, you will be given back more than what you gave. Proverbs 11:24 says, *"There is one who scatters, and yet increases all the more, and there is one who withholds what is justly due, and yet it results only in want."* God blesses what He possesses.

You reap LATER than what you sow. Any farmer knows you don't sow on Monday and reap on Tuesday. There's a process of cultivation and irrigation and incubation--and then the harvest comes.

The Chinese bamboo tree is an peculiar plant. Once you plant it in seed form, you water that tree for the first year and *nothing* happens. You water and feed it for the second year and *nothing* happens. You water it and feed it the third year, *nothing* happens. Fourth year... still *nothing*. But in the fifth year - within just six weeks - that bamboo tree will grow ninety feet. But if that bamboo tree had not been watered, nurtured, and cultivated during the five years leading up to it sprouting out of the ground, nothing would have ever happened.

Sometimes we don't see the immediate effects of our generosity. That's okay. Just know that you are planting seeds in the ground and the harvest will eventually come.

#5 – I Can't Outgive God

God will not allow you to outgive Him. Proverbs 19:17 says, *"Whoever is kind to the poor lends to the LORD, and he will reward them for what they have done."* When you give generously to others in need – God says you've just made a loan to God. And guess what? He pays back with interest!

I truly believe that God prospers me not to necessarily raise my standing of living, but to raise my standard of giving. And when you know what God's word teaches about generosity and the promises that He makes back towards you, it empowers you with the boldness to be generous.

A husband and his wife owned a cat. The husband absolutely despised the cat. But his wife loved the cat so much he really couldn't do anything about it. One day, this cat did something that was the last straw for that husband and he couldn't take it anymore. So while his wife was away, he took this cat down to the post office and had it shipped to Africa — never to be seen again.

> I truly believe that God prospers me not to necessarily raise my standing of living, but to raise my standard of giving.

The wife came home and, since the cat would wander from the house, she didn't suspect anything. After a day passed, his wife said, "Honey, I can't find the cat."

The husband said, "Oh I wouldn't worry about the cat, I'm sure it will come back."

Well, several days went by and the cat didn't return. So just to make sure that he wasn't suspected of wrong-doing and to make himself look like a hero, he said to his wife, "Honey, I know how much you loved that cat. I'll do everything I can do help find it."

He went around the neighborhood and put up signs saying that he was offering a reward of $5,000 to anyone who found his wife's cat. His buddy said, "Why in the world would you offer $5,000 for a cat that you absolutely hated?"

The man smiled and said, "When you know what I know — you can afford to be very generous."

When you understand what God says about money, you can afford to be generous. When you really know in your heart and experience in your life that you cannot outgive God, it enables and empowers you to live a life of generosity.

Recently, I was leading a seminar for a group of bi-vocational pastors. These are pastors who lead small churches that are too small to afford to pay their pastor a full-time salary, so they also have to find another job to be able to make ends meet.

At the end of the seminar, one of these pastors had told the group that he was struggling in a few areas in his life. So before we dismissed, we all gathered around him and prayed over him. While praying this voice said to me: "Give him what's in your pocket." I knew exactly what God was trying to do, but still I hesitated.

God continued to speak to my spirit: "Give him what's in your pocket." It was a roll of cash, five $20 bills totalling $100. While we were there praying, every head bowed and every eye closed, I rolled up that cash and very carefully began tucking it inside this pastor's pocket pants pocket (which admittedly was rather awkward). I didn't want him to know that it was me giving it to him (and he still doesn't know to this day). I thought to myself, "What is this guy going to think if he catches another man sticking his hand down his pocket?" Still I slid it in there as we continued to pray over him.

We finished the seminar and I headed home. I remember thinking, "Well, Carrie and I don't have our 'Date Night' money anymore, but I'm glad that the Lord used those resources to really bless this struggling pastor."

I remember thinking, "Lord, I know it's been said you can't outgive God, but I think that I just did. I gave away our date night money simply because You wanted me to. But I'm not complaining Lord, you are so worth it."

I pulled into my driveway and went to get the mail. Opening up the mailbox, I spied a check written out to me for $1,000. It was for the speaking engagement that I just did where this bi-vocational pastor was in attendance. And I wasn't even expecting to get paid for it! God rewarded me ten-fold, literally instantly. Friend, you truly can't outgive God.

NEXT STEPS

What is the biggest obstacle to you living a life of generosity?

Can you think of a time when God has demonstrated His faithfulness in response to your generosity?

The PHYSICAL Essential

Nutrition: Eat This, Not That

"The foods we eat impact our well being, not just on a cellular level, but on a whole life level—how we feel, how much energy we have, how strong we are, how capable we can be." — Dr. Josh Axe

Health is really the first form of wealth. No one on planet earth has ever uttered the words: "I wish I wasn't so healthy." We take it for granted until it's gone. Yet what you eat today will impact how you live tomorrow. For most people, health is not valued until sickness comes.

We need to remind ourselves that medicine is not health care. Food is health care. Medicine is sick care. That's why Paul Coletta, CEO of Urban Remedy, said, "Let's pay the farmer, not the pharmacist." There's an Ayurvedic proverb that states: "When diet is wrong, medicine is of no use. When diet is correct, medicine is of no need."

Today, Americans lead the world in heart disease. We have more cancer here in our country per person — than anywhere else in the world. We are also the heaviest country with the most people

> We need to remind ourselves that medicine is not health care. Food is health care. Medicine is sick care.

overweight. This is mainly caused by the eating habits we've developed as a culture and the wrong foods that we've been eating.

A lot of times, we're praying that God will give us a miracle saying "Lord, take away this pain. Take away this sickness." But what we need more than anything is a lifestyle change. Scripture teaches us in 1 Corinthians 3:16, *"Don't you know that you yourselves are God's temple and that God's Spirit dwells in your midst?"* Your body is the vehicle—the temple—that God wants to use to do good in the world. When we recognize that our body is not our own, that it belongs to God and we're to be stewards of it, it helps to keep us accountable. We need to develop better habits to take care of our temple. Eating well is a form of self-respect.

There are a lot of things we cannot control in life (the weather, the air we breathe, the people around us) but we can control what we put in our mouths. Many people don't realize that the reason why they don't feel well, the reason why they have no energy, and the reason why they have chronic illnesses is simply because of what they are putting into their system every day.

I grew up eating shortening. We put it in everything. But they say that you can take that stuff and put in in your garage with the lid off of it and check back 20 years later and it will still look the same! Nothing causes it to break down. Can you imagine what that's doing to our bodies, our arteries, and our digestive systems? Our bodies weren't created to handle things like that.

Another example of processed food would be lunch meats: cold cuts, bologna, hot dogs, and others. Packaged lunch meats are full of nitrates which are a major risk in causing cancer.

In Hosea 4:6, God says, *"My people are destroyed for lack of knowledge."* In other words, what you don't know will hurt you.

Avoid Processed Food at All Costs

> The food in America was designed to sustain life, but it was not designed to sustain health.

The food in America was designed to sustain life, but it was not designed to sustain health. A hundred years ago, we didn't have the levels of heart disease and cancer that we have today. What changed? Our diets. We live off of much more processed and refined foods that have chemicals and preservatives in them to make them last longer; but they're not necessarily good for us. Tim Ryan says, "Our bodies are not meant to deal with fake food." In other words, if it came from a plant, eat it. If it was made in a plant, don't. We've got to eat less from a box and more from the earth. Amanda Kraft says, "When you start eating food without labels, you no longer need to count calories." Did you know that about 80% of the food on shelves of supermarkets today didn't even exist 100 years ago!

A lot of times people like to use the excuse that it costs too much to eat healthy. "Buying organic is expensive," they say. If you think the pursuit of health is expensive and time consuming, try illness! According to Linus Pauling, "Good nutrition will prevent 95% of all disease. You can trace every sickness, every disease, and every ailment to a nutritional deficiency." Your own body keeps an accurate journal of the quality of food and nutrients you've been feeding it. So the food you eat can be either the safest and most powerful form of medicine or the slowest form of poison.

You don't necessarily have to eat less, but you do have to eat right. A healthy outside starts from the inside. We need to remember that when our body is hungry, our brain is signaling, telling us it wants nutrients, not calories. Most people have no idea how good their body is designed to feel. We just never experience it because we're filled with so much processed junk.

> If it came from a plant, eat it. If it was made in a plant, don't.

Another example of processed food would be white flour and "enriched" foods. Beware whenever you see the word "enriched" on your food. All that means is that it is so enriched they have taken all the nutrition out of it. White bread and white flour slows down your digestive system because it has no fiber. When you eat whole grains, because of that fibrous outer shell of the grain, it takes your body longer to strip the shell off and get to the "goodies" inside which means the rate at which carbohydrates are delivered into your blood is slowed down considerably. Your blood sugar levels will stay nice and steady and you'll stay full longer. When you let machines do this work for you by taking the wheat germ and ripping, grinding, and softening (literally pre-digesting it for you) your body doesn't get to do the job it was designed for and disease is the result. Another benefit to dietary fiber is that it also absorbs LDL (bad cholesterol) and helps rid them out of your body.

So whenever possible, buy twelve-grain bread (not just whole wheat or whole grain bread).

Eat Food as Close to How God Made It, and You Can't Go Wrong

After God created Adam and Eve, He gave them some very simple dining instructions. In Genesis 2:16, He said, *"You may freely eat of every tree in the garden."* Not every Krispy Kreme donut on the street or every potato chip in the bag. God told them to eat from the garden and we'd do well to stick to His advice.

It's been said that the people living in America today are overfed, yet they are simultaneously starving to death. How is that possible? Because they're not eating the right foods enough to receive the right nourishment.

Did you know that seventy to 80% of our food intake should be raw material? Enzymes are full of life, and cooking kills those enzymes. Those that put "live food" in their bodies have more energy than those who are putting "dead food" into theirs.

When you go to the grocery store, buy fresh vegetables instead of canned vegetables (even frozen vegetables are better than canned ones). A lot of times, we pick up a can of peas and feel proud of ourselves for eating healthy. But the fact of the matter is, by the time that can of peas gets on our plate at home, it's already lost 90% of its nutritional value. It may take more time to prepare fresh vegetables, but the results are worth it.

In our home, we eat a lot of chicken. But we have to be cognizant of the hormones and chemicals that are being used to raise chicken. Today, they are given hormones to make them grow faster. In addition, they are kept in small cages and force fed. Many times their feed is tainted with pesticides. So what's the answer? In most grocery stores, there is an organic section where you can purchase fruits and vegetables. These don't have the hormones and chemicals like the rest do. Sure it costs a little bit more money—but what price are you willing to put on your health? Whenever you can, buy organic.

When we eat our food in as close a state as possible to how God made them, we can't go wrong. As we've already stated; it's when foods are made by men in laboratories and factories that we get in trouble. Our bodies were not designed to get their nutrition in these forms. Our bodies don't know what to do with processed foods.

Think about it this way: Every thirty-five days, your skin replaces itself. Your liver, about every month. Your body makes these new cells from the food that you eat. So what you eat literally becomes you. You literally have a choice in what you're made of. Eat wisely.

Food Has the Power to Heal Us

You can restore your health one meal at a time. Food has the power to heal us. It's the most potent tool we have to prevent and treat many of our chronic diseases.

It's interesting to me how creation seems to bear certain signatures of our Divine Designer. There are certain natural foods that not only help parts of our bodies stay healthy, but they look just like those organs they're designed to help. Here are some examples:

Carrot - Eye. When you slice into a carrot, it looks just like a human eye. Growing up, my parents always told me to eat my carrots; they're good for my vision. Turns out they're right. Carrots are packed full of beta-carotene, a vitamin that decreases the chance of developing macular degeneration (or vision loss).

Tomato - Heart. When you slice open a tomato, it has chambers within it, just like the human heart, and both are red in color. Tomatoes contain lycopene, a heart and blood "food" that scientists believe reduces the risk for heart disease.

Walnut - Brain. Walnuts have a left and right hemisphere just like the human brain and they even have wrinkly folds that look like the neo-cortex. As it turns out, walnuts are "brain food" as they have tons of omega-3 fatty acids, which support healthy brain functioning.

Banana - Smile. If you're feeling a little down, eat a banana. They contain a protein called tryptophan, which converts to the feel-good, mood-boosting chemical serotonin when digested. Bananas work as a natural antidepressant.

Mushroom - Ear. A mushroom sliced in half resembles a human ear. Mushrooms not only have been found to improve hearing, but they contain plenty of vitamin D, which is vital for healthy bone functioning.

> ... you get three votes per day. Every meal you have is a vote for the kind of health you will experience tomorrow.

Grapes - Lungs. Grapes look quite a bit like the alveoli of the lungs, small branches of tissue that permit oxygen to pass through. Grape seeds contain proanthocyanidin, a chemical which appears to reduce the severity of allergy-triggered asthma.

Celery - Bones. Celery, bok choy, and rhubarb all look like bones. The sodium in them helps keep bones strong and replenishes our body's skeletal needs.

Ginger Root - Stomach. A ginger root resembles the stomach, and has been used for thousands of years as a digestive aid and cure for stomach issues. Ginger contains gingerol, which is listed in the USDA database of phytochemicals that can prevent nausea and vomiting.

Kidney Beans - Kidney. Kidney beans look like human kidneys, and no surprise, they help maintain kidney function as they're packed with vitamins and minerals.

Sweet potato - Pancreas. Seet potatoes resemble the oblong human pancreas. They help balance the glycemic index and promote healthy organ functioning.

Ginseng Root - Human Body. Ginseng has been used for thousands of years as a holistic treatment for a number of ailments including inflammation, heart disease, and cancer. People who regularly take ginseng report having more energy and sharper minds. Interestingly enough, many ginseng roots resemble a human body.[1]

Avocado - Uterus. Also known as the "Fruit of the Womb," avocado is a superfood with amazing benefits. It's high in fiber, contains twenty essential vitamins, and is generally recommended for women who are trying to conceive or already pregnant. It reduces the risk of cervical cancer and helps in the develpment the baby. As an added bonus, it also helps shed fat post-pregnancy.

Brazil nuts - Testes. The Brazil Nut is high in healthy fat, protein, and trace minerals but they can also increase a man's testosterone levels, increase sperm production and motility, and protect against prostate cancer.

Onions - Body Cells. Not only does a slice of onion look like a body cell (red blood cell) but they also help clear waste materials out of the body's cells.

Nutrition for Cancer Prevention

The National Academy of Sciences says that 60% of female cancers and 40% of male cancers are the result of poor nutrition. What does that mean? It means that if you and I would just take this message to heart and make some lifestyle changes, we would achieve a 50% lower chance of developing cancer. That should be enough to motivate you. If you don't want to eat healthy for yourself, do it for your family.

You can catch a cold but you can't catch cancer or heart disease. Did you know that every person has within their body abnormal, cancerous cells? Every single day we have cells that can harm us. But God made our immune system in such a way that it kicks in and destroys these abnormal cells when they are detected before they are able to take root and harm us.

But here's the problem. What if our immune system is not up to par? What if we're not receiving the right nutrition and our bodies are having to work twice as hard to produce the energy we need? What if our immune system is weakened because of all the sugars we're living off? What if our digestive tract is all clogged up and not eliminating the toxins like it should because we eat too much white flour and white bread or because we're not getting enough fiber and drinking enough water? It's under these kinds of conditions that abnormal, cancerous cells take root. Knowing about the cancerous cells in my body trying to gain a foothold, I find a whole new level of determination to stay healthy.

Don't Underestimate the Impact of Small Changes

What if you could make little changes in your diet today that would keep you from getting cancer twenty years from now? Many times, a small change will make a major difference. I'm not talking about being a fanatic and never eating another dessert or candy bar again. The point is to keep it all in balance and moderation. Those indulgent foods should be the exception, not the rule.

When you read the book of Daniel, you find a man who knew the importance of a healthy diet. When he was a young man, the king in that region told the officials to go and find the strongest and healthiest young men to serve in the royal court. Daniel was one of those men chosen. The officials were instructed to feed these young men from the king's rich, elaborate, and fancy foods. But Daniel was a breed apart. He knew that some of those foods had been offered up to idols, and on top of that, many of them were not good for him—they were outside of Jewish dietary law. So he told the officials, "I don't want to eat those foods, just give me some fresh vegetables and water." The official didn't know what to think, but he let Daniel try this food experiment for ten days. Ten days later, the Bible says that Daniel was stronger, healthier, and even smarter than the other men.

I wonder how much our quality of life would improve if we started eating the right foods. How much more energy would we have and how much more productive would we be? If it worked for Daniel, it can also work for you. Instead of grabbing for a cookie — grab a granola bar instead. Instead of all those sweets in the morning, how about a bowl of oatmeal? Instead of a candy bar, how about a piece of fruit? Remember this: you will develop an appetite for what you consistently feed yourself.

Don't dig your own early grave with a knife and fork. I can't control everything in my life, but I can control what I put in my body. The great thing about food is that you get three votes per day. Every meal you have is a vote for the kind of health you will experience tomorrow.

Your body is the only vehicle that you have to carry you through this experience called life. You want to be able to live life with energy and passion. So you have to develop a health plan. You cannot perform well if you don't feel well. It's not easy having a health plan and sticking to it--but you and your future make it worth doing it.

NEXT STEPS

What was the most surprising thing you gathered from this chapter?

What would keep you from putting some of these practices into action tomorrow?

Your Guide to Health Supplements

*"Take care of your physical body.
It is the only place you have to live."* – Jim Rohn

Modern healthcare may be good at treating ailments but it's horrible at preventive maintenance. But an old saying suggests, "It's easier to build a fence at the top of a mountain than a hospital at the bottom." It makes much more sense to prevent a potential problem before it arises. That's why holistic health doctors have risen in popularity. I recently started going to a doctor who assesses my health through a blood test and a series of other metric points as well as by analyzing my diet. The doctor then prescribes a number of health supplements that help address areas where I am deficient. Knowledge is power, and having this knowledge enables me to make sure that my health and nutrition are optimized to greatly reduce my chances of being diagnosed with a disease later in life. Of course, this type of doctor is *not* covered by most insurance plans and has to be paid out of pocket. But once again, you have to ask the question: "Is my health worth it?"

Dr. Mark Hyman says, "Food is the cause and food and is the cure of most disease." Hippocrates (the father of modern medicine) said in 376 BC, "Let food be thy medicine; let medicine be they food."

> "It's easier to build a fence at the top of a mountain than a hospital at the bottom."

Everything that you do ought to be for God's glory—including eating. That's why Paul said, *"So whether you eat or drink or whatever you do, do it all for the glory of God."* When God told Adam and Eve to enjoy and eat from every tree in the Garden of Eden (with the exception of eating from the tree of the knowledge of good and evil), God intended the fruit and nutrients of those foods to not only nourish them in the present but also to preserve them for the future. Every answer for every ailment that Adam and Eve would have, God had a solution for in His creation. This is why I'm such a big believer in health supplements.

Dr. Steven Gundry is a world renowned heart surgeon, whose influence, procedures, and contributions with technology over thirty years, have changed the way other doctors save lives. He did an interview once and recounted the story of a patient with severe obesity and heart issues. No other surgeon would do the much needed heart surgery on this patient, due to the high risk of death. When the patient finally came to Dr. Gundry, he had decided to become his own health advocate and had taken his own health in his hands. Six months prior, he had changed his diet and lifestyle, and had started taking a "shopping bag" full of supplements. The result was a major loss of weight, a reversal of blood markers that showed inflammation and disease, and a dramatic change in his health. Dr. Gundry was able to perform the surgery, and the patient came through it with flying colors. Up until that point, Dr. Gundry, as good of a surgeon as he was, was operating on two false beliefs. Number one, supplements only create expensive urine, and number two, diet and lifestyle do not make a huge difference when it comes to heart disease. How many times have you heard other doctors voice the same beliefs?

When he looked into his patient's shopping bag, he noticed that many of the supplements were ones that he himself used intravenously during transplants, but had never considered taking orally as a preventative measure. When he found out how his new patient was eating, he realized that it looked a lot like a paper he had written during medical school many years earlier. After turning the diet and supplement regime on himself, his own blood work improved significantly. Since then, he has used it on thousands of patients whose cholesterol improved, diabetes went away, and autoimmune issues such as fibromyalgia and rheumatoid arthritis decreased or disappeared.[1]

I have become a believer in health supplements and I take them morning, noon, and night. My own health has dramatically improved as a result of them. So here are a few of my favorite and most potent supplements in each category of health:

Top Supplements for Overall Health

Multi-Vitamin. This seems obvious, but your body may be deficient in a few key nutrients, vitamins and minerals. Your body will take what it needs from your multivitamin and excrete what it doesn't need.

Turmeric with curcumin is a supplement I can't live without. I take it religiously every day. It's not only one of the most popular spices in the world but its potentcy make it a superfood. It prevents inflammation in the body, improves brain function, reduces depression as effectively as Prozac, increases your immune system, reduces cholesterol as effectively as Lipitor, prevents cancer, improves digestion, relieves arthritis pain, delays aging, heals wounds, and even reverses the effects of diabetes. I can't say enough good things about this supplement.

Probiotics can serve as a great boost to your health. Did you know that there are billions, even trillions of living microorganisms in your body that play a significant role in your digestive process? This "good" bacteria lives in our small and large intestines, and if you are lacking in these beneficial microbes, it will cause you digestive and other health issues. Probiotics are "good" bacteria that line our digestive tracts and support our body's ability to absorb nutrients and fight infection. The greatest benefit I've experienced from probiotics has been to my immune system. The health of our gut directly affects our immune system. There have been numerous times when I have felt like I was coming down with an illness, but after popping a couple probiotics, I felt perfectly fine the next morning. One word of advice: don't skimp out on this purchase. Buy probiotics that are in the refrigerator of your local vitamin or supplement store and make sure that they contain at least 80 billion live cultures and at least thirty probiotic strains.

Vitamin D is important for strong bones, as well as muscular and overall health. Most of us probably get enough vitamin D from the sun during summer months (you only need 20 minutes of sun exposure). However, during the winter months, as many of us spend a lot of time indoors, we may benefit from a vitamin D supplement.

Magnesium is an important nutrient which plays a role in hundreds of enzymes including our body's ability to metabolize food, synthesize fatty acids and proteins, and transmit nerve impulses. This supplement is great to take in the evening as it enables you to have a better night's sleep and manage your stress levels.

Top Supplements for Heart Health

CoQ10 (Coenzyme Q10) primarily acts as an antioxidant in the heart and is involved in the synthesis of energy. It protects the "bad" LDL cholesterol from oxidizing and is useful in preventing damage to the heart during periods of stress.

Omega-3 Fish Oil has been shown to reduce the risk of having a heart attack or stroke and it helps decrease the risk of sudden cardiac death.

Niacin is accepted by even mainstream doctors because it lowers cholesterol. But it also lowers Lp(a), an independent risk factor for heart disease and heart attacks.

Red Yeast Rice is one that my doctor recommended to me due to my high cholesterol levels. The good news is that it worked, significantly lowering my cholesterol levels. Not only does it show reductions in total cholesterol but especially the "bad" LDL cholesterol and triglyceride levels.

Hawthorn Extract treats a variety of cardiovascular conditions. The most well-documented effect of hawthorn is to cause vasodilation and increased blood flow. A recent randomized study showed that 1,200 mg per day of hawthorn extract for sixteen weeks significantly reduced blood pressure in patients with diabetes compared to those who received a placebo.

Top Supplements for Fat Loss

CLA (Conjugated Linoleic Acid) is an essential fatty acid known for its fat-busting properties. For this reason, it's a top choice for smart dieters as one study showed its remarkable ability to break down difficult to shift, stored body fat. As an added bonus, CLA recently caught the attention of the scientific community as studies reveal its promise in warding off cancer.

Caffeine is America's #1 drug of choice and is a natural ingredient found in coffee, green tea, and dark chocolate. It can help you lose weight by boosting your metabolism by 3 to 11% and it also works as an appetite suppressant. If you use caffeine before exercise, it will boost your performance and endurance while also leading to a 30% increase in fat burning.

Green Tea Extract is loaded with powerful antioxidants known as polyphenol catechins. These substances fight the effects of free radicals in the body which can cause a number of health problems including heart disease and cancer. But when it comes to weight loss, Green Tea Extract contains ECGC which boosts the effects of a naturally occurring fat burning hormone in your body — norepinephrine. This hormone triggers the release of stored body fat by switching on fat cells and accelerating fat metabolism.

Yohimbine comes from the bark of a tree and it has the ability to release adrenaline, allowing it to work better, and being a rare example (supported by direct science) of improving fat loss in already lean athletes. The only downside is that its potency may not be good for some suffering from neurological conditions. This is a supplement that should not be taken by individuals predisposed to anxiety, panic attacks, or who have bipolar disorder.

Garcinia Cambogia is a small green fruit that resembles a pumpkin in shape. Its skin contains an ingredient known as hydroxycitric acid (HCA). The great thing about HCA is that it stops your body from producing enzymes that produce fats.

Top Supplements for Muscle Gain

Protein Powder. Your body needs protein in order to rebuild and gain muscle. I drink a protein shake every day after my workout. I'm pretty picky about the quality of my protein powders and how they taste but I've got one that I would recommend as my absolute favorite: Phormula-1 by the company 1st Phorm. It's a rapid assimilation protein which means it gets into the muscles quickly and begins repairing them fast.

Creatine is another great and inexpensive supplement for muscle gain. There are many variations of creatine but creatine monohydrate is the most researched with the most confirmation of its benefits. It enables your body's muscles to work harder and longer, which consequently can lead to an increased rate of strength and muscle gain. According to most research, this increase is between 5 to 15% for most people.

Branched-chained Amino Acids (BCAA's) are the amino acids that are the constituents of proteins and they're essential because the body can't produce them by itself. The advantage of taking them as a supplement is that they are absorbed directly since digestion is unnecessary and they help stimulate protein synthesis—which is what increases muscle growth.

Beta-alanine supplementation increases aerobic and anaerobic endurance and increases lean mass. It works synergistically with creatine and it also increases strength and allows you to train for longer periods of time.

L-Glutamine is an important building block of protein and is also critical to the immune system. Some research suggests that it can minimize the breakdown of muscle and has been shown to improve protein metabolism as well as help muscles recover faster and increase growth hormone levels.

Top Supplements for Brain Health

Have you ever wondered what your brain and body would be like if they got all the right things they needed to run? I recently started using brain supplements, also called nootropics. These supplements enable you to biohack your brain by improving your cognitive functions such as memory, creativity, and motivation. I am definitely sold on them because I can notice the difference. However, I do not use them every day as I don't want to build up a tolerance to them and no longer feel the effects when I need them the most! Here are a few of my favorites:

> Have you ever wondered what your brain and body would be like if they got all the right things they needed to run?

L-Tyrosine is a brain supplement that is known for supporting healthy brain function and mental alertness. As an added bonus, it also helps you to relieve stress.

GABA is a supplement that eases nervous tension and promotes relaxation.

Ginkgo Biloba works by increasing blood flow to the brain and improves brain functions like focus and memory. Some studies have also found that taking ginkgo bioloba supplements can help reduce age-related decline in brain function.

Lion's Mane is a mushroom that shows benefits not just for the brain but for the entire body. It could protect against dementia, relieve mild symptoms of depression and anxiety, speed recovery from nervous system injuries, protect against ulcers, reduce risks of heart disease, help manage diabetes symptoms, and may even help fight against cancer. I drink a special blend of coffee mixed with Lion's Mane and it tastes great. But you can also take it in supplement form as well.

Alpha Brain has become my favorite nootropic as it contains a proprietary blend of many of these brain enhancing nutrients. I have gotten to the point now that when I have a speaking engagement and don't have my Alpha Brain, I start to panic a little bit! It's helped me so much that I contacted them and became an affiliate partner. If you'd like to try a free sample of Alpha Brain, just go to my website, BrandonPark.org and click the resources tab.[2]

Top Supplements for Cancer Prevention

When a person has cancer it indicates the person has multiple nutritional deficiencies. These could be due to genetic, environmental, food, or lifestyle factors.

Once again, **turmeric** makes the list as a top supplement for cancer prevention. Research points out that this vital substance has a positive impact on DNA, cell survival, and reduction malignant tumors.

Resveratrol suppresses cancer-promoting inflammation, promotes cancer cell death, allows for DNA to repair itself, and puts the brakes on tumor growth. Will resveratrol become the next chemotherapy?

Glutathione is the most important antioxidant produced by your body and is a master detoxifier of every cell in your body. Studies have identified over sixty diseases that have low glutathione levels as one of their characteristics. So supplementing with glutathione will not only protect you against cancer, but also keep you away from fifty-nine other diseases. Another interesting fact: when researchers studied what makes centenarians (people who live to be over 100 years) different from the rest of us, they discovered that their bodies contained higher levels of glutathione.

Melatonin will not only help you sleep better at night but it's also a tumor suppressor and protector from many kinds of cancer, including breast cancer. Dr. David E. Blask found that night-time melatonin levels in the blood can slow breast cancer growth by 70%!

Selenium is a powerful mineral needed only in small amounts. It removes free radicals from the body, making it a potential defense against cancer especially when paired with Vitamin D and/or Vitamin E.

"We've seen the future of cancer research, and the future is food."

Acai Berries grow in Central and South America and are related to the blueberry and cranberry. They contain anthocyanins and flavonoids, both powerful antioxidants that protect the body from environmental factors and reduce the effects of free radicals. Freeze-dried acai berries have the highest antioxidant activity of any food reported to date. A separate study conducted at the University of Florida showed that extracts from acai berries generated a self-destruct response in up to 86% of leukemia cells tested.

Graviola (Soursop fruit) has shown to be highly effective at destroying cancer cells and warding off chronic disease. They help suppress cancer-causing genes. Other studies have similarly identified anti-cancer potential in soursop seeds, which contain various compounds that are selectively cytotoxic. This means they target cancerous and other malignant cells for destruction while leaving healthy cells unscathed. Research published in the *Journal of Natural Products* found that one of these compounds, known as "Compound 1," is selectively cytotoxic to colon adenocarcinoma cells (HT-29), with a potency up to 10,000 times greater than the chemotherapy drug adriamycin (doxorubicin).[3]

Dr. Mitchell Gaynor, director of New York's Strang Cancer Prevention Center, said, "We've seen the future of cancer research, and the future is food."[4]

Now I'm not saying that you can just pop a magic pill and make all your health issues go away. But health supplements can function precisely as to what they are called — they *supplement* a person who is trying to acheive a healthy, balanced life. If you are not taking care of the important things first, you might very well be wasting your money when using supplements. Supplements should be used to enhance your good efforts in maintaining a healthy lifestyle — not make up for slacking.

NEXT STEPS

What is one concept or idea that stood out to you the most?

What are some supplements you plan to purchase today (online) or this week (in store). Write down your list here:

Exercise: Your Fitness Challenge

*"The pain you feel today
will be the strength you feel tomorrow."*

Food is the most abused anxiety drug. Exercise is the most underutilized antidepressant. Exercise not only changes your body. It changes your mind, your attitude, and your mood.

We've all heard that exercise helps you live longer. But a new study goes one step further, finding that a sedentary lifestyle is worse for your health than smoking, diabetes, and heart disease. Dr. Wael Jaber, a cardiologist at the Cleveland Clinic and senior author of this study stated: "Being unfit on a treadmill or in an exercise stress test has a worse prognosis, as far as death, than being hypertensive, being diabetic, or being a current smoker...we've never seen something as pronounced as this and as objective as this. It [living a sedentary lifestyle] should be treated almost as a disease that has a prescription, which is called exercise."[1]

Mike Adams, said "Today, more than 95% of chronic disease is caused by food choice, toxic food ingredients, nutritional deficiencies, and *lack of physical exercise.*"

Your Body Is a Temple

> A sedentary lifestyle is worse for your health than smoking, diabetes, and heart disease.

Sometimes we feel like the comedian who said, "My body isn't a temple. It's a maximum security prison for my fat." But when we understand our body as the temple of God, that one truth has several implications and shows us that exercise is important for at least five reasons:

1. Your *physical* life is interconnected with your *spiritual* and *emotional* life. Every person is made up of three parts: spiritual, emotional, and physical. How we take care of ourselves physically will have a tremendous impact on our overall well-being. All three of these areas are interconnected. For example, what I eat affects my mood.

2. How I feel physically can affect my spiritual life. If I'm always tired and run down, I'm not going to feel like praying like I should. I won't be as sensitive to God's voice. My physical state will stifle my energy and my creativity. If I don't get enough rest at night, there's a good chance I'll be irritable the next day. If I'm not exercising regularly I won't have the energy I should. Some people are very good at taking care of themselves spiritually--they read the Bible, they pray, they go to church—but a lot of times these same people don't have the energy. They're moody, and they explain this by saying, "Oh, I'll just pray it away." But it's not a spiritual problem. It's a physical problem. And if you'll do your part to get the physical part right, then the other areas will come into balance as well.

3. God commands us to honor God with our bodies. In 1 Corinthians 6:20, Paul reminds us, *"for you were bought at a price; therefore glorify (honor) God in your body."* How do you honor God with your body? You take care of it. You respect it. You treat it as valuable. If you had a million dollar race horse, would you feed it candy bars? Would you feed it twinkies? Would you allow it to stay up all hours of the night and never get its proper rest? Of course not. You would only feed that horse the highest quality food. You would make sure that he trained properly, exercised regularly, and stayed in tip-top shape. You would go to great lengths to take care of your investment. Your body may not be an expensive race horse, but you are one of a kind--God has a purpose that He wants you to fulfill and if you die a premature death you won't be around to fulfill it.

4. Your body is the place where God's Spirit dwells. *"Do you not know that your body is the temple (the very sanctuary) of the Holy Spirit Who lives within you, Whom you have received [as a Gift] from God? You are not your own"* (I Corinthians 6:19).

What if you went to a church and it was run down: peeling paint, broken doors, smudged windows that didn't let the light in. You'd probably wonder about the pastor and the people that went to that church, wouldn't you? The church is God's instrument for celebrating the glory of God in this world. Some might wonder that if the people don't respect the church enough to keep it in good condition, what does that say about their relationship with God? The same principle applies to our body. Your body is your God-given instrument for experiencing life on Earth and for doing good works. To do the work that you were meant to do, you need to maintain the temple.

The Bible says that our body is the temple of the most high God. It's not only the house you live in--it's the house God lives in. In the Old Testament, God had a temple for His people; but in the New Testament, God has a people for His temple. If we are really going to honor and glorify God—we need to treat our body (the one He made in His image) as being extremely valuable.

5. Our body is not going to function up to par if we're not exercising and doing our part to stay in shape. But what are people's famous excuse for not exercising? *"I'm always too tired. I don't have any energy."* Let me remind you what happens when you exercise: When you get your heart rate up and you get your blood flowing, hormones known as endorphins are released throughout your system, naturally elevating your mood and giving you even more energy. God has designed our bodies to release all these chemicals to make us feel better when we exercise. God placed them in there—we have to do our part to get them activated.

Paul said in 1 Timothy 4:8, *"for, the training of the body has a limited benefit, but godliness is beneficial in every way, since it holds promise for the present life and also for the life to come."* I think if Paul could see our lifestyle today, he might see things a lot differently. Back in biblical times, they walked everywhere they went. Jesus routinely walked from His home in Galilee to Jericho – a 120 mile journey. If they wanted to carry something all those miles, they didn't put it in the car's trunk they put it on their shoulder. They were always on the go, but today we all live sedentary lifestyles. We take the escalator when we go to the mall and we get inside of our air conditioned cars. We mow the lawn on our riding lawn mowers. We complain because we have to put the dishes in the dishwasher. We are living in a different day. We inhabit a culture of comfort (and I wouldn't trade it for anything). But that means we have to be even more proactive in doing our part to compensate. The people who lived the longest and were the most healthy were those who still lived in the culture where they walked everywhere they went.

When I go for a while without getting any exercise, I can tell a big difference. Little things tend to irritate me more, I don't have as much energy, and I can't concentrate as hard and as long in my work. What's happening to me? I'm getting out of balance. I could just pray about that problem, but what I really need to do is get out and exercise. I believe that most of us have no idea how good we could feel if we would just get ourselves going physically.

You say, "Well, I'm older. This really isn't for me." No. You are never too old to stay in (or get in) shape. This is for everyone. Researchers once did a study of people in their 80s. They had them start lifting weights (not heavy ones of course) and they found that their bones stopped deteriorating and didn't get brittle or frail like other people their age. These seniors grew stronger and maintained their muscle mass. Today, we see a lot of osteoporosis, but historians say that there wasn't much of that at all a hundred years ago. It's because the people in the past stayed active. So what I am saying is that every one of us, regardless of our age, ought to be on some exercise regimen.

Staying Active

For this exercise routine, you need to find something that works for you. It could be walking, jogging, biking, swimming, lifting weights, gardening, tennis or racquetball, going for a stroll through your neighborhood, or any of a hundred other activities. Find something, and stay consistent.

Throughout the day, look for those little things that will help you stay in shape. Take the stairs instead of the elevator or escalator. Don't always look for the closest parking spot;

instead, park a long way out and walk the rest of the way. When you get home at night, turn off the T.V. and go for a walk with your spouse, go for a bike ride, or play ball with your kids. I used to think that if exercising was going to be profitable to me, I needed to get out and run at ninety miles an hour. No. Just get out and do something consistently. If you're having trouble keeping yourself motivated, find a partner to go with you.

They say that sitting is the new smoking. When you think of something that could threaten your life, you probably don't think about your office chair at work. But according to many researchers, it's the biggest potential threat to your health. Research shows that you can reduce your chances of cancer, type 2 diabetes, cardiovascular disease, and back pain, while also lengthening your lifespan, all with one simple lifestyle change: reduce the time you spend sitting.

I used to think that if I exercised every day, that that would offset the amount of time that I spend sitting. However, that's just not the case. As Katy Bowman, a scientist and author of the book: *Move Your DNA: Restore Your Health Through Natural Movement*, told Reuters: "You can't offset 10 hours of stillness with one hour of exercise."

Did you know that your metabolism slows down 90% after just 30 minutes of sitting? Gavin Bradley says, "The enzymes that move the bad fat from your arteries to your muscles, where it can get burned off, slow down. The muscles in your lower body are turned off. And after two hours, good cholesterol drops 20%. Just getting up for five minutes is going to get things going again."

One of the best ways that I've combatted this is by purchasing a stand up desk for both my office and my home. I've actually noticed several benefits by incorporating this new discipline. Not only does it keep my energy level up, but it also keeps me more focused for longer stretches of time. When I sit down, for some reason I'm more likely to engage in time-wasting activities. But when I stand, I'm more concerted and focused in my work.

Know Your Why

Why do you want to be physically fit? Maybe it's to look better. Maybe it's to honor God with your health. Maybe it's to be able to play with your grandkids. Maybe it's to reach a certain goal in weightlifting. Knowing your why will get you started, but discipline is what will keep you there.

Your goal for why you exercise really does matters. A study investigating reasons for exercise found that those focused on weight loss spent nearly a third less time exercising than those who said they wanted to feel better in day-to-day life.

> Knowing your why will get you started, but discipline is what will keep you there.

One of the greatest success principles you can master is action. If you wait until you feel ready, you'll be waiting the rest of your life. Likewise, if you wait until you "feel" like exercising or working out, you'll be waiting your entire life. The limit to your level of fitness is 100% mental. Your body won't go where your mind doesn't push it. Your desire to change must be greater than your desire to stay the same. I seldom ever feel motivated, but I've had to learn to be disciplined. Before the changes take place in the gym, they have to take place in your mind and in your heart.

The Benefits of Strength Training

There are plenty of good reasons to hit the weight room even if you're goal isn't to look like Arnold Schwarzenegger. Strength training can improve your physical performance, movement control, walking speed, functional independence, cognitive abilities, and self-esteem. In addition, it can also reduce your blood pressure, enhance your cardiovascular health, and decrease your chances of developing type 2 diabetes.

> The pain you feel today will be the strength you feel tomorrow.

Strength training is also beneficial for boosting your metabolism. Your muscle *is* your metabolism. The more muscle mass you have, the more calories you burn at rest. In addition, strength training creates a level of muscle damage that increases metabolism after you exercise during the recover and repair process. Everything being equal, the more muscle mass you have, the less body fat you'll have.

So how do you increase your muscle mass? There are really only three components involved: diet, progressive overload, and rest. Let's unpack each of those three:

1. Diet. Remember that fitness is 20% exercise and 80% nutrition. You can't outrun your own fork. If your goal is to build muscle, then you need to consume a lot of protein. About one gram of protein for every pound of body weight. That means since my weight is 170 pounds currently, I'm aiming to consume 170 grams of protein in a single day when on a bulking cycle. That's hard to do. But one good source of protein would be protein shakes.

Here's another important tip. Try doing your exercise or strength training in the morning before you eat breakfast. When you are working out in a fasted state, it enables your body to burn more fat since it won't have any carbs to work with as your "tank" will be empty. Did you know that for the first 15 minutes of your workout, your body is burning sugars and carbs. At 30 minutes, your body enters into the fat burning zone. So keep pushing yourself!

2. Progressive Overload. After three weeks of working out, your body reaches a point of homeostasis which means your body adjusts and adapts to the new stress you're putting on it. Your muscles get comfortable and they stop growing. So you want to always be pushing yourself to go just a little bit further either in intensity (weight) or frequency (try to eek out just one extra repetition).

I do this by keeping a detailed journal of my workouts. The one that I use is called *The One Year Challenge for Men* (they also make a version for women). It's based on the best-selling book by Michael Matthews, *Bigger, Leaner, Stronger*. The goal today is to go a little bit further than yesterday. It's that simple. One of the greatest moments in life is realizing that two weeks ago, your body couldn't do what it just did. Don't limit your challenges; challenge your limits. If you stick to it, I think you'll discover that the pain of a workout will eventually become the pleasure that you constantly crave. The pain you feel today will be the strength you feel tomorrow.

3. Rest. When you put your body through intensive resistance training your muscle fibers are damaged. This damage is known as microtrauma. Literally the muscle fibers tear individually and must be repaired. There are two things that your muscles need to recover bigger and stronger: protein and rest. You must always give your muscles plenty of time to recover and repair. This means getting eight hours of sleep at night and also rotating your routines so that your muscles have enough time to heal before those same fibers are torn again.

There are nine exercises that have proven to be the best for muscle growth:

1. **Deadlifts**. Considered by many to be the "king of mass building" for good reason. This movement activates about eight muscle groups simultaneously.
2. **Shoulder Press.** This movement hits all three heads of the deltoid shoulder muscle at the same time, thus achieving greater deltoid development and improved shoulder strength.
3. **Classic Pushup.** This exercise actives a chain of muscles - particularly in your chest, arms, shoulders, back, and abdominals. It's a great exercise for developing upper body strength.
4. **Pull-Ups.** This movement is great for developing the width of your back, but it also adds strength to your arms as well.
5. **Standing Barbell Curls.** Not only does this movement work the biceps and forearms, but it also increases your grip strength.
6. **Dips.** This is the best form of movement to develop your shoulders, chest, triceps, and even your back's thickness. It's also a great way to improve your pushing strength.
7. **Squats.** This will always be the best exercise for leg strength and growth. It also skyrockets your metabolic rate and improves testosterone production. With this one movement, you are training 40% of all the muscles in your body (quadriceps, hamstrings, and gluteous).
8. **Barbell Rows.** This exercise emphasizes your pulling strength which will help develop your back but also your traps.
9. **Bench Press.** This exercise is almost as synonymous as the gym itself as it has earned its place as one of the best measures of crude strength. The bench press is an amazing exercise for working on your pushing strength as it helps grow your chest but also your entire upper body in general.[2]

> It's not about "having" time; it's about making time.

Do you want to have a healthy body? Don't expect to see a change if you don't make one. You will never just find the time or even the motivation to workout. It's not about "having" time; it's about *making time*. Did you know that a 30-minute workout is just 2% of your day? Going to the gym when you don't want to to is going when you need to go the most. When you feel like quitting, talk about why you started. It's ok if you feel like you're not making much progress. Think about it this way: No matter how slow you go, you're still lapping everybody who is still sitting on their couch. Every step you take is a step further away from where you were and a step closer to who you're becoming. Just don't give up.

NEXT STEPS

It's been said that your body is a reflection of your priorities. Would you agree or disagree with that statement? Why?

What will be your new fitness routine?

What will be your action plan in staying active?

What's the most memorable tip that stands out to you from this chapter?

The Five Rules of Fat Loss

*"Losing weight is hard.
Being fat is hard.
Pick your hard."*

A lady was on a diet but she happened to drive past a Dunkin Donuts every single morning on her way to work. Finally she prayed and said, "Lord, if it would be your will for me to have a donut, would you allow there to be a parking spot right in front of the door?" Sure enough, on her fourteenth lap around the parking lot, she was able to find a parking spot right in front of the door.

It's so tempting to eat poorly, isn't it? I don't know too many people who don't struggle in either losing weight or maintaining their weight. In America, the average man is 5'9", weighs 196 pounds, and carries 41.2 pounds of fat (21% body fat). The average woman is 5'4", weighs 166 pounds and carries 46.5 pounds of fat (28%).

As you might expect, the dieting industry is a multi-billion dollar concern. There are all kinds of diets out there today—Atkins, Keto, South Beach, Paleo. Someone once said that the first three letters in the word "diet" spell "die" and that ought to tell us something. But the reality is, we don't need another diet; we need a lifestyle change. We need to identify the wrong eating patterns that are causing us to carry excessive weight.

> We don't need another diet; we need a lifestyle change.

Where most people go wrong is they starve themselves during the diet, lose the weight, then quickly lose their willpower and regain all that weight back again because their metabolism has slowed down to a creeping halt. For some people, they may have lost a total of 200 pounds over their lifetime. They lose twenty pounds and then gain twenty pounds (or more).

So what are the keys to losing fat and keeping it off? There are really only five rules of fat loss:

#1 – Burn More Calories than You Eat

Fat loss is really simple to understand. If you burn more calories than you consume, you'll drop the pounds. Metabolism is the process of your body taking the food you eat and converting it into energy. We literally "burn" the food to power ourselves, just like your car burns gasoline for power. The difference is that our bodies are designed to be more sophisticated than the nicest BMW. We can burn all kinds of things for fuel—chicken, potatoes, green beans, etc. And we can burn that fuel at different rates, from extremely fast to extremely slow.

When your metabolism feels sluggish--if you aren't burning that much energy--that means you don't have much energy to burn. You feel down. Uninspired. You can't quite wake up. Here's the problem: if you aren't using much energy but you are still "filling up the tank" with just as much food as usual, you're in trouble.

If you put more gas into your car than you need, the extra would just spill out of the tank. Our bodies don't do that however. There are millions of these flexible cells throughout our body that swell up with this extra "fuel" and save it for later. Want to guess what these cells are? *Fat cells*. If your body were a car, it would be like you had inflatable rubber tanks all over it that could fill up with unlimited gasoline.

We live in an unusual time in history where food is abundant and most of us have much more than what we need. Our ancestors were saved from famine by the fat they stored in their bodies during times of abundance. In fact just a couple hundred years ago, "fat people" were considered in art to be much more beautiful than skinny people. Obesity was a sign of wealth and affluence.

Too many people underestimate how much they eat and overestimate how many calories they burn. One of the best disciplines I ever did was to keep a food journal. I used the app MyFitnessPal and entered every single thing that I put in my mouth throughout the day. The first week, I was absolutely shocked! I would go to Cracker Barrel and sometimes eat two or three corn muffins before dinner. Imagine my shock when I realized that each corn muffin has nearly 300 calories! I may as well have been eating two or three donuts before dinner. Knowing your calorie intake is critical to losing body fat.

Remember: If you want to lose one pound of fat, that means you have to burn 3,500 calories. Make it your initial goal to start eating 500 fewer calories per day. You can do this by cutting back on your portion sizes and by limiting your carbs.

#2 – Focus on Getting Stronger and the Fat Will Take Care of Itself

Many people think that the key to fat loss is to do lots of cardio so they try to sweat the calories away on the treadmill, elliptical machine, or stair climber at the gym. Too much cardio along with a calorie deficit can cause you to lose muscle and make you weaker.

While cardio does help you burn some calories, there is a much more effective way. Lifting weights is the most efficient way to lose fat over the long haul. Even if your goal is to be smaller, you still need to lift heavy and build strength.

My personal trainer gave me this tip as I was trying to pursue a more healthy lifestyle. He said, "Focus on building muscle and the fat will take care of itself." That has proven to be true in my own experience. I never once tried to lose the 33% body fat that I had accumulated when I was at my worst. I just focused on making gains and increases in the gym. And as muscle increased, the body fat percentage naturally decreased. I was literally transforming my body composition.

Why does this work? Because one pound of muscle will burn seven to ten calories during the day, even while you rest. The more muscle you have, the more calories your body burns at its baseline as you rest. The rule also applies when you move: the more muscle you carry, the more calories get scorched when you're active.

"When you have more muscle, you burn more calories during everyday tasks such as housework, gardening, or even unpacking your groceries," confirms Lee Bell, who holds a masters degree in exercise physiology and is a lecturer at The Muscle Mechanic UK.

Not only that but when you lift weights, your body releases hormones that enhance insulin sensitivity, making your muscles more apt to take in sugar and carbohydrates.

Resistance training also improves something called "nutrient partitioning" which basically means that after lifting, your body is more likely to use the food you eat for good (building and repairing muscle) instead of evil (turning it into fat).

So the key is to focus on your health, not your weight. Remember that "I" is the only difference between FIT and FAT.

#3 – Stop Dieting – Change Your Lifestyle

What you eat in private is eventually what you wear in public. You have to eat clean to look clean. But you can't go on some starvation diet. You have to eat in order to lose weight. If you don't get much food, your body assumes that hard times are here and it does what it can to get you through. It slows down your metabolism until some good food comes around. It's kind of like when you know you don't have as much income coming in, you try to conserve as much as possible. You turn off the lights, turn down the heat, and try to travel as little as you can. Your body does the same thing and that's why diets backfire.

Someone has said, "There's one thing to be said for a diet — it certainly does improve your appetite." I think we can all relate to that. But the key is to not start a diet that has an expiration date; focus on a lifestyle that will last forever. The best diet is the one you don't even know you're on. It's become a part of who you are. It's your lifestyle. Don't focus on how much you eat, focus on what you eat. It's not about a short-term diet. It's about a long-term lifestyle change.

> What you eat in private is eventually what you wear in public.

Keep in mind during mealtime that it takes 20 minutes for your stomach to notify your brain that it's full. That tells me that we need to eat our meals more slowly. I have a tendency to woof down my food pretty quickly, and, as a result, I'm prone to overeating. You actually eat fewer calories when you eat at a slower pace. If we would just put our fork down, chew our food properly, and relax to enjoy our meals we would fill up a lot sooner.

Researchers gave a group of people a bowl of soup every night before dinner and over the course of three months they had each lost an average of eight pounds. Why? Because soup generally takes longer to eat (especially if it's hot). So by the time they got to their main meal, enough time had elapsed so their brain had already got the signal that they were full. When we eat in a hurry, we always eat too much. A half hour later we're feeling miserable and thinking to ourselves, "Why did I eat so much?" It's because our stomach is just getting around to sending the message to the brain.

#4 – Break Up with Your Sugar Addiction

Different foods affect the body in different ways and sugar is uniquely fattening. Sugar and high fructose corn syrup contain two molecules: glucose and fructose. Glucose is absolutely essential for our lives as every cell in our body burns glucose as food. If we don't get glucose from our food, our bodies can naturally produce it from proteins and fats. Fructose, however, is very different. Our bodies don't produce that. When we eat a lot of sugar, most of the fructose gets metabolized by the liver and there it gets turned into fat, which is then secreted into the blood. Fructose also causes insulin resistance and raises insulin levels in the body, which increases the deposition of fat into our fat cells. Fructose also causes resistance to a hormone called leptin, which makes the brain not "see" that the fat cells are indeed full of fat. This leads to increased food intake and decreased fat burning.

"Sugar is eight times as addictive as cocaine."

Dr. Mark Hyman, MD said, "Sugar is eight times as addictive as cocaine." It creates opiate and dopamine activity in the reward centers of the brain just like drugs of abuse like cocaine. In other words, sugar affects the same neural pathways as drugs of abuse. This activates powerful reward-seeking behavior that can drive overeating.

For me personally, overcoming my "sweet tooth" is by far the most difficult part of my own process of going from fat to fit. I knew my health journey was on the right path when my relationship with food changed from *compulsion* to *choice*. I knew I was going to have to break up with my sugar addiction and eliminate certain things out of my diet entirely.

Take soda for example. The average twelve-ounce soft drink has nine teaspoons of sugar in it and some people will drink four to five of those a day! Most of us take in over 400 calories a day from soft drinks and other beverages. If we would just switch over to water completely — we would not only be healthier, but we would lose an average of twenty-one pounds over the course of a year!

I know what some of you are thinking, "That's why I drink *diet* soda." However, according to *Prevention Magazine*, diet soft drinks are far more damaging to your body for five reasons: 1.) drinking diet soda is associated with a twofold increased risk of kidney decline according to a Harvard Medical School study. 2.) Diet soda is linked to a 34% higher risk of metabolic syndrome, the group of symptoms include increase in belly fat, high cholesterol, and higher risk of heart disease. 3.) Research has linked the acidity in diet soda to dental erosion. 4.) Drinking four or more cans of diet soda per day and you're 30% more likely to suffer from depression according to the American Academy of Neurology. 5.) Sipping more than one diet soda per day could increase your risk of stroke and heart attack by 43%.

I want to challenge you, over the next month or so to really pay attention to what you're eating. Many times, small changes will make a big difference. If you give up one soft drink a day, over the course of a year you can lose up to fifteen pounds. If you eat one glazed donut four times a week at the office, giving that up would let you drop twenty-one pounds. Three handfuls of potato chips five times a week will equal fifteen pounds in a year. So much of this is habit. We've got to pay attention to what we're eating and why we're eating it.

#5 – Eat the Top 10 Fat-Burning Foods

Fat in food doesn't necessarily correlate to fat around your waistline. Animal fats, real butter, coconut oil, nuts, and avocados are all fats that help reduce hunger and can actually help keep your body in ketosis, continually burning fat. There are many other foods that help assist you in this process though and here are a few of them you can add to your diet today:

Avocados – The fat that is in avocado is actually a triple-fat burner. Its monounsaturated fat plumps up cell membranes, enabling cells to better communicate with fat-burning hormones. It also switches off the body's fat storage hormones. Bring on the guacamole!

Almonds and Brazil Nuts – Almonds are rich in Omega-6 fatty acids, which aid in fat-burning, but don't overdo it—one handful of almonds per day is enough. Brazil nuts are actually little fat-burners. They help boost the metabolism by converting the thyroid hormone to its active form. They also bind up toxins that would otherwise store themselves in your fat cells and contribute to cellulite.

Wild Salmon – You can strip abdominal fat by consuming wild salmon on a regular basis. The omega-3s in wild salmon help improve insulin sensitivity, which shrinks fat from your waistline. Wild salmon also activates the thyroid hormone for a faster metabolism.

Coconut Oil – Coconut oil is rich in medium-chained-triglycerides (MCTs) which your body prefers to use for energy, leaving less opportunity for them to be stored as fat. A study published in the American Journal of Clinical Nutrition showed greater abdominal fat loss over a sixteen-week period when MCTs were consumed versus olive oil.

Coffee – Coffee stimulates adrenaline, which sends a message to your fat stores to burn fat. When you drink coffee 20 minutes before a workout, it also acts as an ergogenic aid enabling you to train more intensely. The key is to make it caffeinated and black, as milk reduces its fat-burning potential.

Whole Grains – Your body burns twice as many calories breaking down whole foods (especially those rich in fiber such as oatmeal and brown rice) than processed foods.

Green Tea – Drinking four cups of green tea a day helped people shed more than six pounds in eight weeks, the American Journal of Clinical Nutrition reports. Credit EGCG, a compound in the brew that temporarily speeds metabolism after sipping it. To up your intake, keep a jug of iced green tea in the fridge.

Hot Peppers – Capsaicin, the compound that gives chili peppers their kick, heats up your body, which makes you melt additional calories. You can get it by eating raw, cooked, dried, or powdered peppers. Add as much cayenne or hot sauce as possible to soups, eggs, and meats.

Asparagus – This is a great fat-burning food and is also a natural diuretic to rid unnecessary water deposits from your body. It contains the chemical asparagine, an alkaloid that directly affects the cells and breaks down fat. It also contains a chemical that helps remove waste from the body, which in turn helps reduce fat levels.

Lean Meats – Protein has a high thermogenic effect: You burn about 30% of the calories the food contains during digestion (so a 300 calorie lean chicken breast requires about 90 calories just for your digestive system to break it down. Protein also boosts your calorie burn throughout the day because protein takes more energy to digest than carbs or fat.

Six Simple Tips to Lose Weight Faster

1. Workout before breakfast to burn 20% more fat than after breakfast.

2. Take a 300 mg to 500 mg pill of green tea extract before your workout to burn an extra seventeen to 25% more fat.

3. Make it a HIIT workout (High Intensity Interval Training) to burn three times more fat than aerobic exercise alone.

4. Drink a green smoothie for breakfast to cut 250 breakfast calories and lose up to ten pounds in four weeks.

5. Drink two liters of water to cut more than 300 calories from your intake, increase weight loss by 44% and lose up to eight pounds the first week.

6. Replace processed food with whole food to cut up to 500 calories and lose up to twelve pounds in four weeks.[1]

When it comes to losing body fat, remember the golden rule: If you are persistent, you will get there. If you are consistent, you will stay there. The body achieves what the mind believes. When it comes to fat loss, remember that small progress is still progress. You can do this!

NEXT STEPS

How many of the "Five Fat Loss Rules" can you remember?

Which one of these five rules is the "weakest link" for you? Why?

Which "fat-burning foods" do you need to eat more of?

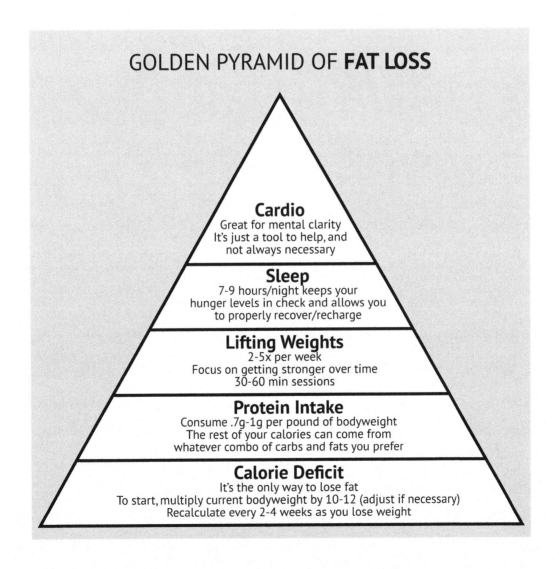

The Benefits of Intermittent Fasting

"Take away food from a sick man's stomach and you have begun, not to starve the sick man, but the disease." — E.H. Dewey, MD

I used to only think of fasting as a spiritual practice: the idea of going for a period of time without eating in order to focus your minds' attention and your heart's affection, praying through something with God. But it turns out that fasting serves not just a spiritual purpose but an important physical one as well.

In a nutshell, intermittent fasting is going without food for predetermined periods of time. So in this chapter, we're going to examine first the benefits to our brain and body when we fast intermittently as well as some practical steps that you can begin taking today to capitalize on this incredible biohacking tool.

The Health Benefits of Intermittent Fasting

The benefits of this type of fasting are almost too many to mention. It literally transforms every cell in your body, making you healthier and thinner. Here are a few of the incredible benefits:

Fat Loss – The greatest benefit perhaps is that you lose more weight than with mere dieting. After fasting for 12 to 14 hours, the body shifts from burning glucose for energy to burning fat, including stubborn, hard-to-lose belly fat. One study found that eating 500 calories every other day (and eating normally on the others) was as effective for weight loss as the best traditional diets out there. Generally speaking, intermittent fasting means you eat fewer meals and therefore consume fewer calories. But there are many other things going on in your body that facilitate fat burning. Lower insulin levels, high growth hormone levels, and increased amounts of norepinephrine all increase the breakdown of body fat and facilitate its use for energy. For this reason, intermittent fasting increases your metabolic rate anywhere from 3.6% to as much as 14%, enabling you to burn more calories. So intermittent fasting works on both sides of the fat loss equation — it boosts your metabolic rate (calories out) and reduces the amount of food you eat (calories in).

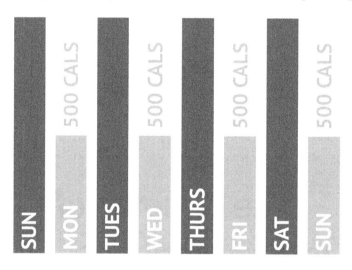

Heart - Fasting can lower levels of bad cholesterol by up to 32% and triglycerides by up to 42%. It also has a positive impact on blood pressure. Added together, those things could really reduce your chances of developing heart disease.

Muscles — You always lose muscle and fat tissue when you shed pounds. But fasting ramps up fat burning, so you may lose more fat and less muscle than on other diets. And the more lean muscle mass you keep, the more your metabolism stays revved up and continues to burn those calories.

Brain — What's good for the body is also good for the brain. Fasting increases your cognitive functions, promotes new brain cell growth, and can even boost your mood. How? Well, periodically restricting calories signals the brain to produce protective proteins that seem to also strengthen its neural connections. Interestingly enough, our body and brain are able to function at their peak while in a fasted state. In fact, studies show that reaction times and accuracy increase when an individual is hungry. Intermittent fasting also increases levels of a brain hormone called brain-derived neurotrophic factor (BDNF). When your brain is deficient in this hormone, it increases depression rates as well as other brain problems.

Liver — Early research suggests fasting might fight fatty liver. That's because it signals the production of proteins that control the liver's absorption of fatty acids and prevent excess fat from being stored there.

Skin — Exposure to free radicals can damage skin cells and cause wrinkles, spots, and fine lines. But fasting makes your cells more resilient, helping them withstand damage caused by oxidative stress, which could keep skin smoother and firmer.

Pancreas — After a meal, your pancreas secretes insulin to absorb glucose from food and use it for energy. But fasting makes the body more sensitive to insulin, so you need less of it to process the glucose. This promotes more stable blood sugar levels and protects against type 2 diabetes. After fasting, blood levels of insulin drop significantly, which facilitates fat burning.

Cellular Health — When we fast, our cells initiate a "waste removal" process called autophagy. This involves the cells breaking down and metabolizing broken and dysfunctional proteins that build up inside cells over time. This increased autophagy may provide protection against several diseases including cancer and Alzheimer's.

Decreased Risk of Cancer — Cancer is a terrible disease, characterized by the uncontrolled growth of cells. Fasting has been shown to have several beneficial effects on metabolism that may lead to reduced risk of cancer. A study published in *JAMA Oncology* collected data from 2,413 women with breast cancer over the course of four years. During that time, the women were asked to estimate the amount of time they "fasted" during the night. The study found that the longer the women fasted, the lower their risk for breast cancer recurrence was. One of the possible explanations for this is that after a long period of time without eating, the body starts to "eat" its own cells as a source of energy. And the cells that get targeted are the weakest and malfunctioning ones, which will then be replaced with new, healthier cells. This way the potential cancer cells can be used as an energy source so that healthier cells can be born instead of multiplying themselves as time goes by.[1] There are more and more studies coming out concerning this, but there's a lot to be optimistic about.

A study published in the *Journal of Translational Medicine* took thirty-four men and split them into two groups: an intermittent fasting group and a control group. Both groups had to complete an eight-week strength-training program.

The result were impressive. Whereas both groups of men built strength and muscle mass, it was the intermittent fasting group that had the additional bonus of a decrease in overall body fat.[2]

In my opinion, the greatest benefit of intermittent fasting is that it can help increase your HGH levels. In some cases, fasting has been proven to increase HGH by an astounding 500%. HGH, or Human Growth Hormone, is responsible not only for helping your body burn excess fat, but it actually builds lean muscle tissue. It strengthens your bone density, lifts your mood and overall sense of well being, and improves your performance during exercise.

Intermittent fasting may also extend your lifespan. Studies in rats have shown that intermittent fasting extends lifespan. Some of these studies produced dramatic results, including one in which rats that fasted every other day lived 83% longer than rats who didn't fast![3] Although more research is needed before we can definitively prove this to also be true in humans, the current research leads us to be optimistic.

The Ways You Can Fast Intermittently

Intermittent fasting basically means that you divide up your day with feast times and fast times. You know when you can eat and when you can't eat. Here are a few ways you can do it.

The 5:2 Method — This has actually been proven to be the most effective method for intermittent fasting, but it can also be the most difficult. The 5:2 method involves fasting for 24 hours twice a week. For five days out of the week, you eat like you normally would, and for two days a week, you fast for a full 24 hours. One of the more popular ways of implementing the 5:2 method is by eating your last meal at 5 p.m. and not eating again until 5 p.m. the next day.

The 16/8 Method — This may be the fasting method that's easiest to maintain. In a nutshell, this means that you fast for 16 hours and then you do all of your eating within an eight-hour window.

If you think that you just can't go 16 hours without eating, you can start out with 12, then gradually work your way up to 14, eventually reaching the 16-hour mark.

This is the type of intermittent fasting that I prefer to do and here's how I do it. I eat all of the food I'm going to eat that day between noon and 8 p.m. That means that my body is in a fasted state from 8 p.m. until the following day where I break my fast over lunch at noon. So in essence, I'm only missing one meal, breakfast. This seemed counter-intuitive at first as I've been taught my entire life that breakfast is the most important meal of the day. According to Dr. Joseph Mercola, that's absolutely wrong. In fact, skipping breakfast can be the most important thing you can do to maintain body weight and increase energy. Your body can only store energy from carbohydrates for a few hours.

The good news for coffee lovers is that you can still have your morning cup of coffee (as long as it's black with no cream and sugar). Black coffee doesn't add calories to your diet and actually helps boost your metabolism.

> **Fasting is taught in the Bible thousands of years before medical science really learned its benefits.**

I think it's interesting that fasting is something that is mentioned and taught in the Bible thousands of years before medical science really learned its benefits. Just as fasting helps rid your body of what's harmful and unnecessary, eliminating toxic waste and excess body fat, it enables you to live a more healthy and fit lifestyle. In a similar way, this is what fasting does for us spiritually.

Fasting for spiritual reasons is a time you set aside when you need God to perform a breakthrough in your life. It's intentionally denying the flesh in order to get a response from the spirit. It means renouncing the natural in order to invoke the supernatural. When you fast, you say "no" to yourself and "yes" to God. When we fast, we're saying that the cry of our souls is greater than the cry of our stomachs. It's more important that God feed us and meet our spiritual needs than to take that time to meet our physical needs for food.

What can you expect from God when you fast for spiritual reasons? Isaiah 58:6 says, *"Is this not the fast which I have choose, to loosen the bonds of wickedness, to undo the bands of the yoke, and to let the oppressed go free and break every yoke?"* You fast so that God can get deep into your heart and break the chains that bind you. Fasting also takes your eyes off of yourself and puts them onto the needs of others: *"Is it not to divide your bread with the hungry and bring the homeless poor into the house; when you see the naked to cover him; and not to hide yourself from your own flesh?"* (vs. 7). Verse 8 then tells us the end result of what God does in response to our fast: *"Then your light will break out like the dawn."*

As you examine the power and purpose of fasting for both the physical and spiritual dimensions of life - I want to encourage you to put this discipline into practice. You might be surprised at the changes that take place in you - body, soul, mind, and spirit.

NEXT STEPS

Which health benefit of intermittent fasting appeals to you the most?

Which method of intermittent fasting could you see yourself trying?

High Performance Sleeping

"Sleep is the golden chain that binds health and our bodies together."
— Thomas Dekker

You're going to spend a third of your life doing it; eight out of the 24 hours of your day will be spent in bed, yet most people don't think about the best ways to optimize their sleep. When you're focused on personal growth and top performance, you're typically only thinking about how to go farther faster. But we don't think much about rest, recovery, and restoration. We think it's in our best interests to minimize and trivialize our sleep, but nothing could be further from the truth. In fact, the only way to truly maximize our productivity and well-being is to optimize our sleep.

Dr. Michael Breus, dubbed the "Sleep Doctor," one of the foremost experts on this topic, has authored three best-selling books and has dedicated years of research towards helping others optimize their sleep. From his writings and research, here are seven science-based tips that will help you get the best night's sleep possible.

#1 – You May Not Need Eight Hours

As a matter of fact, Dr. Breus himself gets six hours of sleep every night - and he's "The Sleep Doctor." He writes, "Everybody's sleep need is different. Eight hours is a myth, let's just start right there. Not everybody needs eight hours."

> The world's top performers get an average of 8 hours and 36 minutes of sleep per night

Does that blow your mind? It did mine. I've always grown up hearing that if you don't get your full eight hours of rest per night, you were essentially digging your own grave. It turns out there's a reason why the "eight-hour myth" got started. Your body needs approximately five sleep cycles per night and we've been told that a sleep cycle is 90 minutes long. This is where we get our popular sleep metric--since five 90-minute cycles amounts to just under eight hours of sleep.

However, new research has shown that not everyone's sleep cycle is 90 minutes long. The length of a sleep cycle can range anywhere from 75 to 90 minutes. Which explains why some people can get away with only six hours.

So how can you figure out how many hours of sleep you need? Dr. Breus teaches us how in three easy steps.

Step 1 - Set a standard wake up time. Most of us have a socially determined time to wake up. I wake up at 5 a.m. on most days. Depending on family and work schedules, I sometimes have to push that back to 6 a.m. But for the most part, I've settled into a consistent wake up schedule--even on my days off. That's the key. Find a time that is a *consistent* time that you can wake up every single day.

Step 2 - Set a time when you'll go to bed. Let's say you need to get up by 6:30 am. Count seven and a half hours backwards from 6:30 a.m. and make 11 p.m. your new bedtime.

Step 3 - Note when you naturally wake up. Of course, don't forget to set your alarm in case this experiment goes horribly wrong, but note what time you naturally wake up. If you naturally wake up at 6 a.m. (not 6:30 a.m.) then perhaps your body only requires that you get seven hours of sleep. However, if you find that you're still groggy and can barely get yourself out of bed, you might need to set an earlier bedtime. (Note: Don't feel bad if you require more sleep. The world's top performers get an average of eight hours and 36 minutes of sleep per night.)

2 – Analyze Your Sleep Patterns

Just by missing out on one of your five sleep cycles, your cognition can go down by as much as a third. Interestingly enough, your level of risk taking increases and your ability to think rationally about the risks you're taking decreases.

Sleep is absolutely essential to have a healthy brain. When you sleep, your brain consolidates short-term memory to long-term memory. Not only that, but when you sleep, you also enable your body to remove the plaque inside your brain that can eventually lead to dementia and Alzheimer's disease.

#3 – Watch Your Caffeine

Did you know that caffeine has a half-life of six to eight hours? What that means is that seven hours after you've had a cup of coffee, half of that caffeine is *still* in your system. It's for this reason that Dr. Breus teaches that you should go "caffeine-free" after 2 p.m. each day.

#4 – Invest in the Right Sleep Gear

For optimal sleep, you need the optimal sleep environment. Those closest to me sometimes make fun of me for being a "sleep diva" with all the sleep paraphernalia that I have, but I'm all about investing in the tools that are necessary in helping me get a good night's sleep.

Body Pillow – I'm a side-sleeper so having a body pillow on both sides of me that I can put between my knees helps keep my spine in proper alignment.

ChiliPad Cube – I'm fairly hot natured and if I can't get cool enough I can't sleep. Doctors have even proven that the sixties are the best temperatures to achieve the deepest, hibernation-mode sleep. So this new invention is one of my favorites, especially during the summer months. The ChiliPad is a mattress pad with a cooling and heating temperature control system. It regulates the surface temperature of your mattress by circulating water through a network of micro tubes. You can cool your bed to as low as 55 degrees or heat your bed in the winter to as high as 110 degrees.

White Noise Sound Machine – Ever have trouble falling asleep because your To-Do list won't stop buzzing around in your head? White noise can help. A white noise sound machine also masks sounds in your home that might interrupt your sleep. And if you do wake up, it's often easier to fall back to sleep.

Gravity Blanket – Engineered to be 7-12% of your body weight, a weighted blanket helps relax the nervous system simulating the feeling of being hugged or held (without the body heat). This increases serotonin and melatonin levels and decreases cortisol levels which both improve your mood and promote a restful sleep at the same time.

#5 – Exercise Daily, but Not Too Late

We've already established the importance of exercise for your health and wellbeing in earlier chapters, but did you also know that exercise can actually improve your quality of sleep?

Even just half an hour of moderate exercise will do the trick. Walking, jogging, biking, swimming, weightlifting--pretty much anything that will get your heart rate up consistently for half an hour will help make falling asleep and staying asleep easier.

However, any type of exercise that is four hours before bedtime could be too exciting for your body and could actually *prevent* you from falling asleep.

#6 – Mind Your Exposure to Light

Your laptop computer, TV, tablet, and your phone emit blue light which shortens REM sleep and makes it harder to fall asleep. God designed light to give us energy and keep us awake. Did you know that if you get tired during the day, you can go outside and take a "sunshine break" instead of a coffee break. The spectrum of light known as "blue light" which is on the spectrum of 400-495 nm) is a high-energy spectrum that basically turns off melatonin (the chemical that makes us sleepy).

So if you're using electronic devices late at night before you go to sleep, they are literally prohibiting your natural ability to produce melatonin and make you "sleepy."

There are many ways to overcome this. You can purchase glasses that block blue light. I personally purchased some very stylish glasses from GammaRay Optics through Amazon for less than $10. You can also replace the light bulbs in your bedroom with GoodNight bulbs (also available on Amazon).

#7 – Master the Art of Napping

Napping has long been taboo. People used to think that you were being lazy if you took an afternoon nap. Yet the latest research shows that it could become one of the greatest things we can do to increase our performance.

Even large corporations like Google are discovering the benefits of what "power napping" can do. They even offer high-tech nap pods where employees can go and recharge so that they are more productive at work during the last half of their shift. Why would a huge company like Google not only encourage their workers to take a nap on the clock but also provide a sophisticated and expensive sleeping pod in which to do it? Simple. A 26-minute nap increases performance by 30%.

That's the key. The best nap is 26 minutes. A mid-morning nap will boost your memory and creativity. An afternoon nap (siesta) will boost your alertness. And an evening nap can also help revitalize your focus. Now I'm not saying you should be taking three naps a day! But you should encourage yourself to nap based on the needs of your circadian rhythm.

> A 26-minute nap increases performance by 30%.

Dr. Breus recommends a bio-hack that he has dubbed the Nap-A-Latte. It's a creative way to boost your focus, alertness, and memory for at least four hours. He encourages you to chug a six-ounce cup of cooled or iced black coffee. Once the six ounces are down the hatch, lie down and take a 20-minute nap. The coffee won't affect your ability to sleep as it takes 20 minutes for the caffeine to reach plasma concentration levels and really kick in. As you're napping, you'll rid your body of the biological molecule that is making you drowsy and sluggish (adenosine). After about 20 minutes, your adenosine reserves are depleted and then the caffeine from the coffee kicks in hard and you feel like a million bucks. According to Dr. Breus, this tactic should work for about four hours.

One of the best things you can do if you can't sleep is simply talk to the Lord. Make prayer the bookends of your day - your first response when you wake up and your last action before you fall asleep.

Psalm 3:5 says, *"I lie down and sleep; I wake again, because the LORD sustains me."*

Psalm 4:8 says, *"In peace I will lie down and sleep, for you alone, LORD, make me dwell in safety."*

And Proverbs 3:24 says, *"When you lie down, you will not be afraid; when you lie down, your sleep will be sweet."*

If something is weighing on your heart and mind and is keeping you awake, just give it to God and turn it over to Him. He's going to be up all night anyway.

NEXT STEPS

What is your biggest obstacle towards getting a good night's sleep?

Based on what you read, are there any new attempts you could try to get a better night's sleep?

Become an Early Riser

"Create the life you can't wait to wake up to." – Josie Spinardi

Benjamin Franklin famously quipped, **"Early to bed and early to rise makes a man healthy, wealthy, and wise."** Turns out, the research proves him right. Those who regularly get out of bed by 7 a.m. are more likely to be happier and even thinner.

I used to always be a night owl. I hated mornings. It's been said that there are two kinds of people in life: Those who wake up and say, "Good morning, Lord!" and those who wake up and say, "Good Lord, it's morning." I used to be like the second guy.

But over the last few years, I've actually trained myself to become an early riser where I get up at 5 a.m. most days. The rewards have been amazing. I now feel like I accomplish more before 8 a.m. than what I used to be able to accomplish in eight hours of a normal working day. Muhammad Ali said, "The best way to make your dreams come true is to wake up." Terri Guillemets said, "The time just before dawn contains the most energy of all hours of the day. This has helped me become an early rise and and early doer."

Five Benefits of Getting Up at 5 A.M.

Proverbs 13:4 says, *"Lazy people want much but get little, but those who work hard will prosper."* People who wake up early have an insane productivity advantage. Most of the great leaders and thinkers today get up early every morning. For example, Richard Branson

(CEO of Virgin) wakes up at 5:45 a.m., Tim Cook (CEO of Apple) wakes up at 4:30 a.m., and Howard Schultz (CEO of Starbucks) is up no later than 6 a.m. So why do most successful people get up so early? You've heard the maxim: "The early bird gets the worm." That may sound silly but it's true. Here are five benefits to waking up at 5 a.m.:

1. You enter the "Flow State." This means that you are completely involved in an activity for its own sake. Every action, movement, and thought flows from the previous one with no distraction. Your whole being is involved and you're using your skill to the utmost. Flow means that you're "in the zone" and it enables you to do deep work and make some progress.

2. You remove ego depletion. This is a term coined by scientists to refer to the tendency for our willpower to come in finite amounts. Think of your willpower like a battery. As you go through your day exerting your willpower, the "battery" goes down. Have you ever had a day at work where everything was going wrong, and then when you got home you noticed that you were easily triggered or irritated by the smallest things? That's because your willpower battery is low, and it's harder for you to resist the urge not to get upset or angry. So if you can do your most intensive and most important tasks in the early morning while your willpower is high, you are on your way to insane productivity.

3. It allows you time to have a morning ritual. A morning ritual is your own personal routine that you do every single day. Maybe it's having a quiet time for 20 minutes, exercising, writing, beginning work on your most important task, or something else. Morning rituals become habits. And once habits enter our subconscious mind, we do them on autopilot and those very habits are what shape our lives.

4. It gives you time to think and plan. It gives you a chance to sit down with your thoughts, to pray to God, and to see if you are on the right trajectory. Are you going where you want to go? If you're not careful, your life purpose can be shaped not by God, but by the demands and expectations of everyone else. Getting up early gives you time to meditate, pray, and contemplate God's purpose for your day and week.

5. It gives you a psychological advantage. There's just something about getting up before the sun that gives you this intrinsic motivation and psychological advantage. Mike Tyson would get up at 4:30 every morning to go for a run. When he was asked why he did it, his response was, "Because I know for a fact there's no way my opponent is working as hard as me right now, and that's why I'm going to beat him." When you know you have accomplished more in the first few hours of your day before most people have even gotten out of bed, it gives you a sense of self-confidence and accomplishment.

How Do You Become a "Morning Person"?

Here are a few tips that will help the transition:

- *Have a compelling reason to wake up early.* Is it to be productive? To get a headstart? To have more personal time? To work on your goals? Knowing your why — a clear and compelling reason — will give you the added motivation.
- *Make a transition.* Wake up earlier by 15 minutes a day until you reach your goal. This will allow your body to adjust.
- *Place your alarm across the room.* I use my phone as my alarm system. When I was trying to establish a new routine of waking up at 5 a.m., I would place my phone on the

other side of my bedroom. This meant I had to get out of bed to turn it off. Once I'm out of bed, it makes it easier to start the day. After your body adjusts to the new rhythm, you won't need your alarm any longer. There are even apps that require you to take a certain number of steps before the alarm will turn off. That will really wake you up!

- **Don't hit the snooze button.** Don't hit the snooze button in the morning. The first action you do sets the context for the day. The snooze button is so dangerous because it trains your brain to procrastinate and actually makes you wake up feeling more tired. One guy on YouTube, Thomas Frank, shared a method he uses to force himself to wake up in the morning. He uses Buffer to schedule a tweet to go out at 6:10 a.m. that will give people $5 if he doesn't wake up on time to delete it. The tweet is pre-programmed to say: *"It's 6:10 and I'm not up because I'm lazy! Reply to this tweet for $5 via PayPal (assuming my alarm didn't malfunction). Limit 5 #sleepingin."*
- **Make sure you're getting enough sleep the night before.** Refer to the previous chapter on how to improve the quality of your sleep. No one can save you from tiredness or sluggishness if you simply don't sleep for enough time.
- **Connect with friends who want to wake up early.** My friend, Phillip Kelley, and I both wanted to establish this new habit. So we challenged each other to text at 5 a.m. The first person to text the other would win our little contest.

Establishing a Morning Routine

Henry Ward Beecher said, "The first hour of the morning is the rudder of the day." Have you ever heard someone say, "Man, I got up on the wrong side of the bed this morning"? What are they really saying? Something negative happened during the first part of their day that set the tone, trend, and trajectory for the next 24 hours.

> The first 20 minutes after you wake up are the most important minutes of your day.

Interestingly enough, this is proven by science. How you start your day will determine how you sustain that day.

Did you know that the first 20 minutes after you wake up are the most important minutes of your day?

Entrepreneur magazine writer Ahmed Safwan explains why:

> *The brain produces electrical patterns, often referred to as waves. Scientists have found a correlation between the frequency of brain waves and the body's state. When you first awake, your brain operates at around 10.5 waves per second. The range from eight to 13 Hz, or cycles per second, is the alpha stage. It's been called the gateway to the subconscious mind.*
>
> *Have you ever gone into a semi-daydreaming state while commuting? A few minutes pass, but you don't remember what happened. It's likely your brain entered the alpha state.*[2]

Interestingly enough, this is proven by science. How you *start* your day will determine how you *sustain* that day. The first 20 minutes of your day are when your subconscious mind is the most impressionable. Whatever you hear, read, and think about within the first 20 minutes of waking up, that will affect the spirit of your day.

So having this knowledge, how should that affect your morning routine?

Knowing that the first moments upon waking up are your most impressionable, here are some things you should probably avoid:

- **Avoid the News.** You don't need the latest crimes, murders, or scandals to dictate the trajectory of your morning.
- **Avoid Social Media.** seeing your friend's latest political rant probably isn't a great way to get your day started.
- **Avoid Email.** This will either be a mindless duty or if there are immediate emails you need to respond to, it can send your mind into a myriad of directions.

Instead, why not spend the first moments of your day engaging in these things:

- **Spend time in God's Word.** There's a reason why the Psalmist said, *"In the morning, LORD, you hear my voice; in the morning I lay my requests before you and wait expectantly"* (Psalm 5:3). Even King David knew the value of starting your day out with the Lord.
- **Visualize.** Think about the goals that you have for your day. Pray about the long-term goals and vision for your future. Where do you want to be in the Five Essentials of Life (Spiritual, Relational, Physical, Intellectual, Financial) a year from now? Five years from now? Spend some moments during the first part of your day praying and dreaming.
- **Practice Affirmations.** Steve Jobs (founder of Apple) was known for doing this. An affirmation or mantra is a personal statement that you live by and focus on. Maybe it's a promise God's gives you in His Word or a new habit you are trying to grow into. Instead of saying, "I want X," instead, declare by faith, "I am X."
- **Practice gratitude.** Of all the human thoughts and emotions we have, gratitude is by far the most powerful. Not only that, but when you focus on the positive, you'll see, discover, and create more of the same.
- **Exercise in the morning.** After you finish these other priorities, try moving your exercise routine to the morning instead of the afternoon or evening if at all possible. The reason is that exercise in the morning actually enables you to have more energy and focus throughout the rest of the day. Richard Branson claims exercising in the morning gives him four more productive hours in a day.

In my opinion, one of the best books out there that help you establish a solid morning routine is Hal Elrod's book, *The Miracle Morning*. It's become a best-selling book for a solid reason. Observing how he organizes the first three hours of his day has really inspired me to create my own morning routine.

Laura Vanderkam, author of *What The Most Successful People Do Before Breakfast*, discovered, in the course of researching dozens of people on how they spend their time, that most successful people devoted significant portions of their time in the morning to a task they found most important or loved to do. In her writing, Vanderkam goes on to suggest how people can become more productive morning people including such suggestions as making the to do list the day before; getting a good sleep; exercising; practicing a morning ritual, including meditation; eating a proper breakfast; avoiding morning meetings so the most important work can be done at highest productivity time; tackling the most important work first; and visualizing your ideal day.

> Most successful people devoted significant portions of their time in the morning to a task they found most important or loved to do.

Every morning you have two choices: continue to sleep with your dreams or wake up and chase them. When you wake up with determination you can go to bed with satisfaction. One man stated it this way: "You sleep to see your dreams. I get up early to work on mine." Make it your goal this year to create the life that you can't wait to wake up to. Always remember to fall asleep with a dream and to wake up with a purpose.

NEXT STEPS

What would be your motivation for waking up early?

What would a morning routine look like for you? Draft a morning schedule. What would you do and how many minutes would you allocate to it?

The INTELLECTUAL Essential

Invest in Yourself

"One hour per day of study will put you in the top of your field within three years. Within five years, you will be a national authority. In seven years, you will be the best in the world at what you do." —Earl Nightingale

Never underestimate the returns on an investment in yourself. It's an investment that offers minimum risk and a guaranteed big return. You will never go broke from investing in yourself. You and your personal growth are your most important asset. Your capacity to grow, develop, and improve yourself in these Five Essentials will be the engine of your wealth in all aspects of life. As Ben Franklin said, "An investment in knowledge pays the best interest."

One of the best ways that we motivate ourselves is through self-mastery. You must work on yourself continuously and never be satisfied with where you are.

The ability to invest time in you is the greatest ability that human beings have above animals. A dog can't be anything but a dog. But a human being has unlimited potential. By developing yourself, you can transform your life no matter where you are right now.

> You must work on yourself continuously and never be satisfied with where you are.

The Four Dimensions of Jesus' Personal Growth

When you look at the life of Jesus, you can see how He invested in his own personal growth. This serves as an example for us to follow as well. Beginning in Luke 2:40, we see that there were four dimensions to Jesus' growth:

First of all, Jesus had a **posture** of growth. Luke 2:40 says, *"There Jesus grew up, maturing in physical strength and increasing in wisdom, and the grace of God rested on Him."* Verse 52 says, *"And Jesus kept on growing —in wisdom, in physical stature, in favor with God and in favor with others."*

Notice those "-ing" words. Jesus was maturing, increasing, growing. It's a present perfect progressive tense describing an action with past, present, and future implications. He exhibited an active posture of continuous growth.

If you don't adopt a posture of growth, you will eventually become irrelevant to the world around you. Even if you're on the right track, you'll get run over eventually if you just sit there. Erick Hoffer observed: "In times of change, learners inherit the earth, while the learned find themselves beautifully equipped to deal with a world that no longer exists."

Secondly, we see that Jesus **prioritized** His personal growth. Luke 2:52 says, *"And Jesus kept on growing— in wisdom, in physical stature, in favor with God and in favor with others."* Notice the four areas where Jesus grew. They are part of the Five Essentials of Life:

1. Intellectual growth - *"in wisdom"*
2. Physical growth - *"in physical stature"*
3. Spiritual growth - *"in favor with God"*
4. Relational growth - *"in favor with others"*

Jesus *"kept on growing"* in these areas, but you will cease to "keep on growing" unless you make it a priority. All of these essentials must take precedence in your life. If you grow mentally but ignore your physical growth, you may die earlier than expected. If you grow socially, but neglect your relationship with God, those relationships will feel shallow and will not ultimately fill the void within your heart.

Thirdly, Jesus embraced **practices** for growth. In Luke 2:46-47, it says, *"After three days of separation, they finally found Him — sitting among a group of religious teachers in the temple — asking them questions, listening to their answers. Everyone was surprised and impressed that a twelve-year-old boy could have such deep understanding and could answer questions with such wisdom."*

Notice several key aspects about Jesus' practices of personal growth:
- Jesus had a place to grow (temple).
- Jesus had a people to grow with (the religious teachers).
- Jesus had a process to grow (asking questions and listening).

Sometimes, the reasons why we stay stuck where we are and fail to grow is because we don't put ourselves into a growth environment. If you're always the smartest person in the room, then one day you won't be the smartest person in the room. Put yourself in environments where you're asking questions rather than giving answers.

Fourth, Jesus knew the *purpose* of His growth. One day, Jesus was asking questions and listening in the temple and his parents lost track of him. When they finally found him, Jesus' response was: *"Why were you searching for me? Didn't you know I had to be in my Father's house?"*[1] At the heart of Jesus' growth was this understanding of his purpose in life. He knew his growth was important because it ultimately was preparation for the fulfillment of His mission. But when did the bulk of Jesus' growth occur? It was during the years when Scripture is predominantly silent about His life. We have a lot of information about Jesus' public ministry--about His birth, death, and resurrection. But the thirty years in between his birth and public ministry are almost silent. All we know about that time is what we read in Luke 2. During that season, Jesus was growing toward His purpose. I think there's a hidden lesson for us here. Personal growth in the hidden years is what God uses to prepare us for powerful impact in the public years. Jesus was intentional about His growth so He could be impactful with His purpose.

Tips for Personal Growth

The Book of Proverbs has a lot to say about investing in your own growth. *"Get all the advice and instruction you can, so you will be wise the rest of your life"* (Proverbs 19:20). Proverbs 18:15 says, *"Wise men and women are always learning, always listening for fresh insights."* You must determine to learn something new every day. Make it your goal that you won't lay your head on your pillow at night until you've learned and discovered something new. Maybe if we spent less time on social media we'd have more time to invest in personal growth. Are you spending more time watching television than you are working on yourself? My mentor used to teach me that if I change, everything will change for me; but if I don't change, nothing will change for me. So what are a few changes you can begin to make?

1. Bask in the company of like-minded people. When you surround yourself with other growing people, it drastically improves the speed and direction of your life. A recent study found that 70% of jobs are now found through networking. It's no longer about *what* you know; it's *who* you know. But you also pick up the traits, habits, and qualities of the people around you by osmosis. I agree with what Jim Rohn said: "You are the average of the five people you spend the most time with." The people we spend the most time with add up to who we become. There are people who are less advanced in their personal and professional life, and there are people who are more advanced than us. If you spend time with the people who are behind you, your average will go down, and with it, your success. But if you spend time with people who are a step ahead of where you are, you will become more successful than you are now. Take a look at the five people you spend the most time with. Do you need to make any changes?

> The people we spend the most time with add up to who we become.

2. Listen to less music, more motivation and instruction. Jim Kwik said, "If knowledge is power, then learning is your superpower." You want to read books and listen to podcasts that inspire you to become what God has ordained for you to be. I used to listen to music whenever I went to the gym or drove in my car. Not anymore. Today, I listen to YouTube videos that challenge and inspire me, podcasts that grow my knowledge and understanding, and sermons from other pastors that challenge me spiritually. Zig Ziglar used to talk about "the automobile university." The University of Southern California did a study that said that those who live in metropolitan areas drive a minimum of 12,000 miles per year. If you were to listen to instructional audio, or audio books during that commute time, you could earn the equivalent of two years of college education in just three years, simply by turning your car into an educational environment. That's the power of turning your drive time into your growth time.

3. Ask God to open your eyes for new opportunities to grow. Once you discover where you want to go; you grow your way into that role. At first, your dream might seem pretty daunting. Initially, your vision will always exceed your competency. That's why you have to grow yourself into that vision. As you begin to work on yourself, you will begin to expand your vision of yourself. And you will begin to see it reflected in all five of these dimensions of life. Jim Rohn said, "It's the set of the sails, not the direction of the wind that determines which way we go."

4. Find your unique factor. Sydney Madwed said, "If you want to be truly successful invest in yourself to get the knowledge you need to find your unique factor. When you find it and focus on it and persevere your success will blossom."

5. Find someone to coach you. If you want to grow, you're going to need to stand on the shoulders of those who are already where you want to be. Find a mentor or a coach that can invest in you. Offer to take them out to lunch and bring with you a prepared list of questions thoughtfully planned out. Mentors can help you climb the corporate ladder, put together a business proposal, or deal with office politics and negotiation. They will be your support system and your guide in this wild career journey on which you're about to embark. If you knew just how much money I spend personally on coaching services every year, it would probably shock you. I value direct and honest feedback from others. I need feedback on what's working and what's not working. Making these minor tweaks will put me months, if not years, ahead of just figuring things out on my own. I don't have enough time to make my own mistakes, I need to learn from the mistakes of others.

> Today, you get paid not for your time but for your value.

6. Grow your gifts as you use your gifts. If you have the gift of writing but you're not using it, you're going to lose the ability to write as well as you do right now. So whatever idea that you have, the longer that you sit on that idea, you're either creating or disintegrating. If you're not using it; you're losing it. Your skills are either expanding or diminishing every day. Whatever it is that you do, you want to have technical mastery over it. Part of self-motivation is finding something that gives you a strong sense of competence. You will become known for *that*. You will develop a reputation of being good at doing *that*. You set some high personal standards because you're not competing with anyone else.

Anthony Brevet said, "Nobody gets rich working for someone else. Invest in real estate, in your company, in your brand, in your education, or to promote yourself. Profits are better than wages." Today, you get paid not for your time but for your value. You don't get paid for how many hours you put in for your company but for the value add that you bring to the table. So what that means is this: If you want to be successful, don't seek success. Seek to become a person of value. Make yourself valuable and they will *pay for you*. As you hone in on your uniqueness and develop a gift in your life; they will pay you for what you offer.

Leaders Are Readers

Not all readers are leaders; but all leaders are readers. Did you know that if you just set aside 15 minutes a day to read, you'll read up to two dozen books a year? That means in a normal lifetime, you would read more than 1,000 books. That's equivalent to going through college five times!

I believe that reading is one of the best habits you can cultivate. It can fuel your creativity, relieve stress, and literally make you smarter. Not only that, but being an avid reader also improves your writing skills. So here are a few reading tips that can help you get the most out of what you read.

One tip that has proven to be useful is that I read most of my books electronically now. I still prefer to have a tangible, paperback book over an ebook, but there really are some clear benefits to Amazon Kindle. One is that Kindle allows you to highlight everything that you read and then access all of those highlights in one running list so you can see the best and most memorable content of any book in a single glance. Recently, I started purchasing the Audible version of a book along with Amazon Kindle. I literally play the audio version of the book and follow along in my Kindle. But if I need to get up and get a refill on my coffee, I'm still engaged in the book because I'm still hearing it. I can go back later and highlight a part that I thought was good and would like to refer back to later.

> The most important thing about a book is not what it teaches you but what it stimulates within you.

I would also encourage you to not just read a book but respond to it. You should practice active reading. Whenever you pick up a book, also pick up a pen to underline and make notes in the margins. Even when I'm reading magazines, I've got a pen in my hand. A book only becomes your book when you mark it up.

Remember that the most important thing about a book is not what it teaches you but what it stimulates within you. A.W. Tozer used to say, "One of the tests of a really fine book is while you're reading it, you have to put it down to start thinking." You take a moment to stop and process what you just discovered.

Real Learning Begins Outside the Classroom

As UCLA coaching legend John Wooden observed: "It's what you learn after you know it all that counts." How much have you invested in your education since you've graduated? Too many people graduate learning when they graduate school.

One of my coaching clients recently paid me $6,000 up front for executive coaching services. I could have used that money to make a down payment on a new car or take my family on a cruise. But guess what I did with that money? I invested 100% of it into more training, more web courses, more resources for my own personal growth. I invested it into growing myself because the more I grow, the more value I can add to others. It's only because of how I've grown up to this point that people pay me what they do to coach them in life, leadership, and business practices.

Your earning power will never exceed your learning power. Author and pastor Andy Stanley says, "In the early years of your career, what you learn is far more important than what you earn. In most cases, what you learn early on will determine what you earn later on."

Just because you're not in a classroom anymore doesn't mean that you should stop learning. Making time for continued development is key. I've earned a bachelors degree, two masters degrees, and a doctorate degree. But I have learned far more on my own since I've completed my doctorate than I ever did in my formal education years.

At the beginning of every year, I ask myself, "What does Brandon Park need to learn more about this year? Where do I need to grow? Which one of the Five Essentials do I need to take to the next level?" I write down on a piece of paper all of the ideas for where I would like to grow and develop. Then once that is done, it's amazing how the resources, training, or online webcourses start to be drawn to me like a magnet. I simply write down a list of courses, books, or training systems that I will participate in that year. At a set time every day (for me it's 6 am), I spend an hour going through that training. Once it's done, I note what I've learned and make any changes necessary, and I move on to the next training.

What Gets Scheduled Gets Done

> You don't get out of life what you want; you get out of life what you are.

John Maxwell said, "The secret to your success is determined by your daily agenda…you cannot change your life until you change something you do every day." Once again, you won't find the time, you have to make the time. You have to schedule your own growth or the tyranny of the urgent will always take precedent. Jim Rohn said, "Work harder on yourself than you do on your job."

You don't get out of life what you want; you get out of life what you are. Where you are at this point in your career is a reflection of you. Whatever you are producing in your life right now in this moment is a reflection of how much you've grown. That's why Jesus said you can judge a tree by the fruit that it bears. I can look at what you are producing and I can tell a lot about who you are and what you value in life. God wants us to bear not just a little fruit but "much fruit." In order to do that, you've got to spend time investing in yourself. In order to do something you've never done, you've got to be someone you've never been.

Tim Ferriss said, "Investing in yourself is the most important investment you'll ever make in your life." Make growing yourself a priority because at the end of the day, you are your longest commitment. The more you invest in yourself, the bigger the returns on your future success will be. It will not only improve your life but the lives of all those around you.[2]

NEXT STEPS

What are some things you would like to learn about this year? Make a list as things come to your mind.

Which tip for personal growth do you need to implement the most?

Remember that what gets scheduled gets done. When will you schedule time to invest in your personal growth? What time? How long? How many days per week?

Develop a Clear Vision

"Vision is the art of seeing what is invisible to others." — Jonathan Swift

We have an incredible imagination. Our eyes can take in 4 million bytes of information every second. The moment we take it in, our imagination processes it, and forms a 3D color picture and then immediately puts it into motion. The imagination is very powerful. We think in pictures. If I say, "Big Black Dog" You don't see the words, your imagination shows you that image. We are visually oriented. Every one of us in our imagination has a picture of ourselves, our family and our future. How we see ourselves is the way that we are going to become. You will never rise any higher than the image you have of yourself. You will never accomplish anything that you first do not see yourself accomplishing.

Walt Disney World in Orlando, Florida is the most popular tourist attraction on the planet. In 1998, forty-two million people went through the turnstiles at the Disney World theme park alone. It sits on 43 square miles. But what's sad is that even though Disney World was a lifelong vision of Walt Disney, he died before it opened. On October 1, 1971, during the Grand Opening Ceremony, someone turned to Mrs. Disney and said, "Isn't it a shame that your husband couldn't live to see this?" Her response was powerful. She said, "He did see it. That's why it's here."

Do you remember when you were a kid, what it was like to dream about your future? Growing up in south Florida, I had a hammock on my back porch where I would dream, sometimes hours a day, of what my future could someday look like. In many ways, I've accomplished many of those dreams I visualized as a kid there on my back porch. As kids we could barely wait to grow up and pursue the things that were in our hearts. We had those dreams for a reason. I believe that God will sometimes put a picture within our heart of what our future could potentially be.

When we're young we start off with big dreams. Yet one of the biggest problems that we have is that, as we age, our dreams tend to shrink to the size of our situation. It's a form of self-preservation really. We don't want to be disappointed or to feel as though we're not measuring up. Having small-minded goals is safe. Yet we need to heed the words of Albert Einstein who said, "Never give up on what you really want to do. The person with big dreams is more powerful than the one with all the facts." So periodically we need to be stretched. We need to learn how to dream bigger.

Why You Need Vision

Many folks today don't consider themselves to be "visionary" individuals. We all have our own unique proclivities and personalities, but we still need to have a vision for the future. Here are three reasons why:

1. When you make your vision clear; your fears become irrelevant. People typically set their dreams too low for several reasons. First, a vision makes us accountable either to ourselves or others. We don't like the pressure of people wondering if we'll deliver. Secondly, the fear of failure keeps our vision small. "What if I don't achieve this? I'll be embarrassed and it'll be a blow to my self-esteem." Thirdly the fear of criticism keeps our dreams small. Others may laugh at us or misunderstand our motives. Miracles start to happen when you give as much energy to your dreams as you do to your fears.

> Unsuccessful people make decisions based on their current situations; successful people make decisions based on where they want to be.

2. A man without a vision for his future, always returns to his past. When you get in your car to leave today, you'll likely need to put the car in reverse and back up. By doing so, you'll glance in your rear-view mirror to show you what's behind you. That look is important, but as you're traveling down the highway — please don't spend too much time staring in the rear view, because chances are you're gonna hurt somebody! In front of the rearview mirror there's a much bigger piece of glass called the windshield. Why is it bigger? It's because where you're going is a whole lot more important than where you've been. Unsuccessful people make decisions based on their current situations; successful people make decisions based on where they want to be. When people stay focused on their past, they get stuck. They can't see their way out of their circumstances, or their addiction, or their current lot in life. We need to stop looking at where we have been and start focusing on where God is taking us.

3. Vision is a preserver of life. Proverbs 29:18 says, *"Where there is no vision, the people perish."* Everybody needs a dream for life. It is a psychological necessity. If you're not dreaming, if you don't have a goal for life, if you don't have a vision, you're dying. Because you're either expanding or you're dying. We develop our dreams and then they develop us. Our dreams define us. Oliver Wendall Holmes said, "A mind once stretched by a new idea never returns to its original dimensions."

Back during World War II, enemies torpedoed a Navy cruiser carrying more than 1,100 crewmembers. As the ship sank into the frigid water, the crew floundered in the sea for five days. They were starving, drowning, and being attacked by sharks. The ocean current pulled nine of the guys away, splintering them off from the rest of the ranks. Seeing these men were beginning to lose their will, a young officer started asking them about their families and lives back home. He asked them to describe what they were going to do when they got back. He asked them what they wanted to accomplish and what difference they wanted to make. He had them envision how scared their spouses and children were; how their parents must feel not knowing if they were alive. He asked them to fight to stay alive, not just for themselves but for their loved ones back home. Finally a passing plane spotted the men in the water. Two-thirds of the 1,100 crew members perished. However, all nine inspired by that young officer lived.[1]

> Vision is the eye of faith to see the invisible and the decisiveness to make it visible.

What Is Vision?

I've enjoyed being a curator of definitions and quotations about vision over the years. Here are some of my favorites:

- Vision is a bridge from the past to the future.
- Vision is the eye of faith to see the invisible and the decisiveness to make it visible.
- Vision is the power that causes people to make huge sacrifices in order to become all they can become for God.
- George Barna said "Vision is a clear mental image of a preferable future imparted by God to His chosen servants and is based upon an accurate understanding of God, self, and circumstances."
- Vision is adopting an action-plan that will enable you to move forward in your life and work.
- Vision is the inward fire which enables you to boldly communicate to your peers what the future will be like.
- Vision is the dynamic that enables you to translate your faith and dreams into a new and personal walk with God.
- Vision is the God-given energy which will make you become a risk-taker.

To borrow the words of the great missionary William Carey, we ought to "Attempt great things for God and expect great things from God." We honor God by the magnitude of our faith. Vision is the God-given ability for you to catch just a glimpse of what God might do through your life.

It turns out, God is extremely interested in what you see through your spiritual eyes. Seven times in Scripture, God asks His people, "What do you see?" In other words, if you are always focused on your problems, what you *can't* do, always focused on your limitations, then that level of mediocrity is going to keep you right where you are. It's not because God doesn't want to increase you; it's because you've developed the wrong image on the inside.

The Bible says, *"Without faith it is impossible to please God."* Faith begins with stretching your imagination. Faith begins with visualizing the invisible. We cannot accomplish the impossible until we first see the invisible. Hebrews 11:1 in the Amplified translation says *"Faith is perceiving as real what is not revealed to the senses."*

> God may never give you a dream that matches your budget. He's not checking your bank account, He's checking your faith.

Have you ever thought about this? The plans that you have for your life and ministry may in fact be small in comparison to what God has in store for you. Ephesians 3:20 tells us that God is "able to do immeasurably more than all we ask or imagine, according to his power that is at work within us." That means if you can dream or imagine what your future could be like, it's already too small in the eyes of God. He's able to do "immeasurably more than all we ask or imagine." God may never give you a dream that matches your budget. He's not checking your bank account, He's checking your faith. Tony Hsieh, founder and CEO of Zappos said, "Chase the vision, not the money; the money will end up following you." The goal for your life should never be to become a success; but rather to become a person of value. Pray. Dream. Create a vision that makes you want to jump out of bed in the morning.

How to Dream Bigger

In Tommy Barnett's book, *Reaching Your Dreams*, he talks about how to find your purpose and turn your dreams into reality. Once you establish a relationship with God, you can begin to sort through your dreams to figure out which ones are from God. One of the most crucial questions Barnett talks about in his book is "How can I know which dreams in my heart are from God?" Here's the answer. You'll know it's God's dream if:

1. It is bigger than you. When we're kids, it's easy for us to dream big. "I want to become the President of the United States" was the aspiration of many a 3rd grader. But as we reach adulthood, we trim our dreams to manageable proportions so we don't get disappointed. That's the opposite of what we should do. Faith necessitates that we set higher goals, not lesser ones. God is the author of bigness, not smallness. The first test you can apply to your dream is, "Is it too big for me to fulfill without God's help?

2. You can't let it go. Can you let this dream go or does it keep bugging you? A God-given dream is a bothersome thing. It just keeps bobbing to the surface of your heart. If that's how your dream behaves, that could be an indication that it might be from God.

3. You would be willing to give everything for it. Are you willing to devote every ounce of your energy and every minute of your days to it? A dream inspires a devotion much like the kind of devotion a parent has for their child.

4. It will last forever. Many people pursue dreams that are shallow and temporal. They dream of fame, but fame never lasts. Yesterday's biggest star is today's trivia punch line. You can be a hero today and a zero tomorrow. The Bible says that there are only two things that will last for all eternity and that is truth and people.

5. It meets a need nobody else has met. The only way to minister to God is to minister to people. That's why Jesus said, *"When you've done it to the least of them, you've done it to Me"* (Matthew 24:40). Your dream must be built on human need. Will it help people? Will it improve lives? Alleviate human suffering? Does it fill a need that no one else is filling the way that you can fill it? If so, be assured that your dream is from God.

6. It brings glory to God. The most horrible thing in life is to realize that you've wasted so much of your life looking for ways to bring glory to yourself instead of bringing glory to God. Life is too precious to fritter away by building it on a crumbling foundation.

We all need to learn to dream one size too big. Great things can come from small beginnings when God is in them. Einstein said "Never give up on what you really want to do. The person with big dreams is more powerful than the one with all the facts." Tony Gaskins also said, "If you don't build your dream, someone will hire you to help build theirs."

The Art of Visualization

Doctors tell us that the part of the mind that plays the greatest role in achievement is that part of the mind that can imagine... that visualizes. There is a sense that what you see is what you will be. It's a fact of life: we produce what we keep in front of us. If you see your health, marriage, or job getting worse, that's exactly what you are going to produce. A lot of people want a better life; they want to get out of the rut that they're in, but they cannot give birth to something that they have not first conceived. You've got to conceive it on the inside through your eyes of faith before it can ever come to pass on the outside.

In 1995, Alvaro Pascual-Leone did a study that validated the importance of visualization. One group of volunteers practiced a five-finger piano exercise and neuroimaging revealed that it stimulated their motor cortex as expected. The other group of subjects didn't physically practice the five-finger piano exercise. Researchers told them to mentally rehearse it. They did the exercise in their mind's eye. And researchers discovered that the motor cortex was just as active during mental rehearsal as it was during physical practice. Researchers came to this conclusion: *imagined movements trigger synaptic changes at the cortical level.* In other words, the simple act of imagining something has just as much of a powerful neurological effect as performing the action itself. How you think and what you think about actually remaps your neural connections.[2] What you visualize, how you dream can literally determine the shape of your mind.

> We all need to learn to dream one size too big. Great things can come from small beginnings when God is in them.

The power of visualization was recently demonstrate by a new landmark study from Brian Clark at Ohio University. His research showed that sitting still, just thinking about exercise, actually makes us stronger. Clark and his colleagues recruited twenty-nine volunteers and wrappted their wrists in surgical casts for an entire month. During this month, half of the volunteers thought about exercising their immobilized wrists. For 11 minutes a day, five days a week, they sat in a chair, completely still, and focused their entire mental effort on pretending to flex their muscles. When the casts were removed, the volunteers that did mental exercises had wrists that were two times stronger than those that had done nothing at all![3]

Other researchers have also demonstrated links between the brain visualizing something and muscle development. Ten years ago, Guang Yue at the Cleveland Clinic reported that imaginary exercise increases the strength of finger muscles by up to 35%![4]

Jason Rogers, a former Olympic fencer said, "When you close your eyes and paint the full sensory picture of you achieving your goal, it's like giving your brain a practice round."

> How you dream can literally determine the shape of your mind.

Envisioning your success is vital. It enables you to focus on your goals and get your mind thinking positively. "The man who thinks he can, and the man who thinks he can't, are both usually right."

You can only materialize what you visualize. You must learn to see things as you would have them instead of as they are and keep that vision before you.

My youngest daughter Ainsley, is only eight years old but is already quite the track and field athlete. She gets her skills from my wife Carrie, who won two medals in the Junior Olympics when she was in High School. Carrie taught her to visualize the goal of where she wanted to land after her long jump and do whatever she could do to jump beyond that goal. Ainsley heeded that advice and advanced all the way to compete nationally at the Junior Olympics in Iowa and brought home the gold medal in the long jump after competing against seventy-five other kids from around the nation. Visualization really does work.

In his book, *The Miracle Morning*, Hal Elrod tells us how he visualizes each day:

> *Visualize your major goals, deepest desires, and most exciting, would-totally-change-my-life-if-I-achieved-them dreams. See, feel, hear, touch, taste, and smell every detail of your vision. Involve all of your senses to maximize the effectiveless of your visualization. The more vivid you make your vision, the more compelled you'll be to take the necessary actions to make it a reality.*[5]

Create Your Own Vision Board

In Habakkuk 2:2, God said, *"Write the vision; make it plain on tablets, so he may run who reads it."* There's great power that comes when you can write your vision and present it in a way that reminds you of your purpose and motivates you to take action.

A vision board is simply a poster board on which you post images of what you want to have, who you want to become, and what you want to accomplish. I have a vision board that I keep in my walk-in closet. It's a simple cork board that has pictures of the type of lake house I want to own someday, the number of books I want to write, my fitness goals (such as how much I want to bench press), how much money I want to give away in my lifetime, and specific strategies of how I want to multiply my impact and influence for others. I look over my vision board every morning when I'm getting ready for work and every evening before I go to bed. Every time I look at it, I get into that state of mind as if I've already acquired it. This one simple lifehack has enabled me to stay focused on my priorities and motivates me to keep going![6] As W. Clement Stone says, "Whatever the mind can conceive, it can achieve."

When I was working on my doctorate degree in seminary, our professor had us put together a document that outlined our vision for ministry in certain key areas. We were basically asked to dream big and to paint a picture with words of what kind of church we wanted to lead when we graduated. Because it was doctoral level work, it needed to look good. So I found a picture of a contemporary looking megachurch and decided to put that on the front cover of this vision project. I honestly forgot about it for six years. Then one day, the search team from this church in Kansas City asked me if I would pray about becoming the pastor of their church. Not being familiar with the name, I googled it and when the picture popped up, I was shocked. The church that was asking me to be their next pastor was the same church that I had put on my vision project six years earlier! God has a sense of humor. It's been my privilege to be the Lead Pastor of Connection Point Church. And who knows, maybe some of the dreams and visions you've been praying about for years will come true as well.

NEXT STEPS

Which definition of vision is your favorite? Write it out and reflect on it here:

Is there a dream you feel God has put in your heart? Write it down here and then go back through the six qualifications of determining if your dream is from God.

How might visualization and developing a vision board help you?

Determine Your Priorities

"We are often tired and imbalanced not because we are doing too much, but because we are doing too little of what is most real and meaningful."
— Marianne Williamson

Have you ever said: "I don't have time to do all that I want to do"? Let me give you an encouraging word today...*you're right*. According to *USA Today*, some experts got together to find out how much time was needed to do all that the average human being wants to do. They surveyed and factored in time for how much was needed for exercise, hygiene, work, commuting, household chores, eating, entertainment, spiritual development, and family time. When they added all those things together, they found that a human being needs 42 hours a day! If you are frustrated because you don't have enough time to do what you need to do, welcome to the human race. You may not have the time to do all that you want to do, but you do have enough time to do what you need to do. What you need to do is what God wants you to do. And if you capitalize on what you need to do, God will make sure you have the time to do it.

To change your life, you need to change your priorities. Steven Covey said it best: "You have to decide what your highest priorities are and have the courage — pleasantly, smilingly, unapologetically— to say 'no' to other things. And the way to do that is by having a bigger 'yes' burning inside."

Priorities will tell you everything you need to know about a person. It shows what they value. When something is important to you, you will always find a way to do it; when it's not, you'll find an excuse. Instead of saying, "I don't have time," try saying, "It's not a priority," and see how that feels. This is true about relationships. Nobody is ever truly "too busy." It just depends on what number you are on their priority list. If they want to find time for you, they will. The sooner you realize where you stand in somebody else's life, the sooner you realize where they belong in yours.

Prayers for Pondering Your Priorities

> Instead of saying, "I don't have time," try saying, "It's not a priority," and see how that feels.

Devoting a little of yourself to everything means committing a great deal of yourself to nothing. Robert J. McKain said, "The reason most major goals are not achieved is that we spend our time doing second things first." So here are five key questions for determining your priorities that I personally have turned into prayers:

1. Lord, why have you placed me where I am today? If you're employed, why are you on the payroll? Ask yourself if what you are doing right now is the most important thing that you've been hired to do. If your boss were sitting across from your desk watching you work, would you do anything differently? Here is a challenge for you: Make a list of everything you think you've been hired to do and give it to you boss. Then ask your boss to organize that work list according to what he determines are the most important priorities to him. What does he/she think is most important or least important? From that point forward, make sure you work the hardest and deliver the goods on those tasks that your boss considers to be the highest priority items. Become the best in your company on those deliverables — and you will be promoted.

2. Lord, where can I add the most value? There are usually only three things that you do that account for most of the value of your work. Which of your activities contribute the greatest value to your company? If you're not sure, ask the people around you. Everyone seems to know the most important things that other people should be doing.

3. Lord, what are my top 5% responsibilities? This is the question that seeks to answer, "What can I, and only I, do that if done well will make the biggest difference? Where can you make the most significant contribution? If you don't do it, it won't be done. Doing this task, doing it well, and doing it promptly can have a major impact on your life! Here's how the top 5% principle works: It doesn't matter whether you are an employer, an employee, or a student -- basically 80% of what you do, anyone can do! I know...that statement didn't exactly make you feel very valuable, did it? But it's true. Think of your daily schedule and the time you invest in answering the phone, checking your email, sitting and taking notes in a meeting, making the widgets, filling out the reports, and on and on. Basically, anybody can do 80% of what you do. Now 15% of what you do--anybody with some modicum of skill can do those things as well. This might include creating an Excel spreadsheet, using Adobe Photoshop, or wiring a three-way switch. With a little training, virtually anybody can have the skills that you do 15% of the time. Now, before you throw in the towel, quit your job, and give up on life, understand this. The 5% principle involves the 5% of things you do, that *only you can do*! Nobody else in the world can do this last 5%. You see, only I can be a husband to Carrie. No one else can do that. Only I can be Daddy to my son and two daughters. I'm the only father they will ever have. Only I can grow myself spiritually and professionally. I can't hire someone else to grow for me. There are certain things that only YOU can do and in the end when you stand before the God to give an account of your life — it is that 5% that you will be accountable for! God won't hold you accountable for whether or not your company made it into the Fortune 500. You won't be held accountable for how well your employees performed. But you will be held accountable for your 5% because that's what only you can do. And that's what I encourage you to invest in.

4. Lord, what is most fulfilling when I do it? As you reflect on your projects and tasks, which ones are deeply satisfying? In what areas are you the most fulfilled, faithful, and fruitful when you engage in them? What are the tasks that you love and would enjoy doing even if you weren't paid to do them?

5. Lord, what is important that I am ignoring? God frequently calls us to do things that seem uncomfortable, risky, and downright painful. Generally speaking, the people we find in Scripture who were called by God did not feel up to their calling. Whether it was Abraham's call to leave home, Gideon's call to lead an army, Esther's call to approach the King, or Mary's call to give birth to the Messiah, none of them responded, "Sure, I can do that." The first response to a calling from God is usually fear. Henry Blackaby writes, "Some people say, 'God will never ask me to do something I can't do.' I have come to the place in my life that, if the assignment I sense God is giving me is something that I know I can handle, I know it is probably NOT from God. The kind of assignments God gives in the Bible are always God-sized. They are always beyond what people can do, because he wants to demonstrate his nature, his strength, his provisions, and his kindness to his people and to a watching world. This is the only way the world will come to know him."

Our English word for *focus* comes from a Latin word that means hearth or burning center. When you think of life before electricity, everything in life revolved around the home fire. You socialized around the fire. You cooked around the fire. You did your laundry by boiling water around the fire. You would warm up your bath water by putting a pot of water on the fire. Focus. Hearth. Burning center. The very word means looking at the core of who we are inside our heart. What is it that drives us and is in touch with that burning center. That's where our priorities should lie. The more I know who I am in my "burning core" — the more I know what God wants me to do.

The Art of Saying "No"

Every "No" should be rooted in a deeper "Yes." In order to say "Yes" to your priorities, you have to be willing to say "No" to something else. If you have your "yes" rooted deeply, then your "no" becomes a lot easier.

We ought to say "No" to at least one thing each day so we can say "Yes" to something more important, spending more time on our priorities and less time on other things. Author Jim Collins of *Good to Great* suggests that we create a "stop-doing-list." It's tempting but naive to think that we can make more time for everything just by working more efficiently. If you are going to add something to your life, that means you have to subtract something else.

> Every "No" should be rooted in a deeper "Yes."

When I was in my 20s, I used to think that the great leaders were the ones who were great at *everything*. That's the perception we're sometimes led to believe due to what we see in books and movies. I set about trying to turn all of my weaknesses into strengths. For the first decade of my career, I just tried to get better at the things that I honestly wasn't good at. Then one day, God revealed something powerful to me: *My fully exploited strengths are of greater value than my marginally improved weaknesses.* Your weaknesses will never become strengths because compared to your strengths they will always be weaknesses. There are many things that you *could* do; but there are those few things that you *must* do. Learn to say "No" to the lesser things so you can say "Yes" to the greater opportunities and priorities before you. Only you can make it a priority to make your priorities a priority.

Your Priorities Are Your Calendar

Your priorities aren't what you say they are. They are revealed by how you live. You define what is important to you by what you dedicate your time to. The key is not to prioritize what's on your schedule, but to schedule your priorities.

The issue is not: Will my calendar be full but what will fill my calendar? The issue is not prioritizing our schedule but scheduling our priorities. You have to schedule your priorities or they don't happen. Time is like money in one way, and not like money in another way. It's like money in that it has to be budgeted. But here's how it's not like money. You can always make more money, but you can't make more time. You only have 24 hours of the day to work with, seven days a week.

> The key is not to prioritize what's on your schedule, but to schedule your priorities.

For instance, let's just say a missionary asks me to give him financial support in the amount of $100 a month. I could probably do that. But what if ten missionaries asked me to support them at $100 a month? What if a thousand missionaries asked me? At some point, no matter who you are, you run out of resources.

If someone asks you for money, here's what you have to decide: Where is it coming from? Is it coming from the housing budget? Is it coming from the car budget? Is it coming from the savings budget? Where is it coming from?

It's the same thing with time. If someone asks you to commit to something, if you commit to it, that time has to come from somewhere, and you have to decide, "Where am I going to take this time from? Am I going to take it from my family time? Am I going to take it from my study time? Do I have to take it from my rest?"

Whatever your priorities are, you're going to have to budget your time to fulfill those priorities. Maybe that's why Elisabeth Hasselbeck said "Nobody's life is ever all balanced. It's a conscious decision to choose your priorities every day."

Only A Few Things Are Necessary

Stress comes from not knowing what to do with your life. Jesus said something to a woman named Martha in the Bible. Martha had a visit from Jesus one day. As Jesus came to her home, she assumed He was hungry. Martha is so much like most of us. We live on assumptions. She assumed He was hungry. That's our problem too. We think we know what God wants us to do and that we can find the purpose for our life without asking Him. But vision is from God.

We must report to Him, submit to Him, and remain still until we are clear on the revelation of that vision.

Martha ended up cooking for God in the flesh, but He wasn't hungry. Then she became angry because other people like her sister Mary weren't joining her in her busyness. In other words, she tried to get other people involved in things that weren't God's will at the time. So then she came to Jesus and basically said, "Look, why aren't other people helping me? Send my sister to help me."

And the answer that Jesus gave her was a leadership answer. He said, *"Martha, you are so busy about many things."* That's probably what your life is like right now. You're busy about so many things. You're trying to do everything. You're trying to be everything to everybody. Then Jesus said, *"Only a few things are necessary"* (Luke 10:42). Defining and determining priorities is outlining those few things that are necessary.

Job 34:4 says, *"We should choose to follow what is right. But first we must define what is good."* Have you ever done that in your life? If someone were to ask you right now, "Name the five values that you're building your life on," could you list them? You can't build your life on certain values if you don't even know what those values are? If you don't figure out what's valuable to you, if you don't figure out what your priorities are, other people will be happy to determine them for you. And they'll be glad to fill up your life and schedule with their values, their priorities, and their issues. We have to decide what matters most, or we become victims of the loudest voices and the latest demands. Without a clarity of purpose and a proper sense of priorities, our lives will be shaped by the pressures around us rather than by a divine call.

Naming your priorities and actually aligning your activities around them may seem like a trivial task, but it can bring tremendous power into your life. The difference in hot water and boiling water is very small — only one degree. At 211 degrees, that pot on the stove is just very hot water. But with just one added degree of heat — at 212 degrees — you now have steam, power, and momentum. It's the small things, such as determining our priorities, that truly give our lives the powerful trajectory that we need.

Just like spinning plates at a circus, you can only focus on one priority at a time. And if you get too many going you're going to have plates crashing all over the place. I was once giving a talk on the importance of setting priorities. As each person was coming into the room, they were all given a paper plate and were wondering why we were passing them out. In the middle of the message, I encouraged them to think about the priorities that are in their life — the 5% of things that only they can do — and to write those priorities down on that paper plate. I encouraged them to put this plate somewhere where they could see it and be reminded about what those priorities are. For me, I keep my paper plate in my office drawer. So the next time I get a call asking me if I could take on this project, join this board, speak at this event, or schedule that appointment, I simply glance down and look at that paper plate. Does what I'm being asked to do fit within these priorities. If not, then my answer is simple: *"I'm sorry, but my plate is already full."*

> We have to decide what matters most, or we become victims of the loudest voices and the latest demands.

Bear Bryant was one of the greatest football coaches of all time. Shortly after he died, his family found a crumpled up piece of notebook paper in his wallet and it was obvious that he had carried this piece of paper in that same wallet for years. It was also obvious that he had folded it and unfolded it many times, but no one had ever seen it before. It said,

> "This is the beginning of a new day. God has given me this day to use as I will. I can waste it or use it for good. What I do today is very important because I am exchanging a day in my life for it. When tomorrow comes, this day will be gone forever leaving something in its place I have traded for it. I want it to be a gain, not a loss; good, not evil; success, not failure; in order that I shall not regret the price that I paid for it."

That's great advice from a football coach – We all agree that time is very, very short, and it runs out quickly. May God give us the wisdom to use our time wisely.

NEXT STEPS

What are the top five things you value in life?

What should be your top five priorities?

Looking back over what you underlined, highlighted, or noted in this chapter — what is your biggest takeaway regarding priorities?

Set Goals That Work For You

"Goal setting is the most important aspect of all improvement and personal development plans. Confidence is important, determination is vital, certa personality traits contribute to success, but they all come into focus in goal setting."
— Paul J. Meyer

I heard about a guy who was bragging to his friends about having thirty years of experience working at the same company. His manager however said, "You don't have thirty years of experience. You just have one year of experience that's been repeated thirty times." The old saying is true: "If you aim at nothing, you'll hit it every time." If you have no goals, you have no direction. No one just accidentally drifts to their chosen destination. You have to be intentional and clearly focused on what you want and why it's important and then pursue a plan of action that accomplishes your objective.

Nothing can add more energy to your life than concentrating all your energies on a limited set of targets. We are wired so that we are the happiest when we are pursuing something. Goals give you a new sense of energy, something to look forward to.

A goal is a statement of faith. It's saying, "I believe that God can do this through me." We have been given a great promise from Scripture: *"Ask and it will be given to you; seek and you will find;*

> **Nothing can add more energy to your life than concentrating all your energies on a limited set of targets.**

knock, and it will be opened to you." Give yourself permission to dream big and risk big. Jim Rohn says, "Don't set your goals too low. If you don't need much, you won't become much."

Don't Just Think It — INK IT

The weakest ink is better than the best memory. We have to write down our goals if we're ever going to see any traction. Napoleon Hill said, "Reduce your plan to writing... the moment you complete this, you will have definitely given concrete form to intangible desire."

Mark McCormick in his book, *What they Don't Teach You At Harvard Business School* tells about a Harvard study that was done between 1979 and 1989. In 1979, the graduates of Harvard University were asked, "Have you set clear, written goals for your future and made plans to accomplish them?" As it turns out, only 3% of the graduating class had any *written* goals and plans. 13% said they had goals but they were not in writing. The remaining 84% had no specific goals at all.

Ten years later, in 1989, the researchers found that the 13% who had goals (even though they were not in writing) were earning twice as much as the those who had no goals at all. But the most surprising finding was that they found that the 3% of graduates who left the Harvard MBA program with clear written goals were earning ten times as much as the other 97%.

The researchers made this determination. They said the difference lay not in intellect, skills, or abilities; it was the clarity of goals these students had for themselves when they graduated that made them succeed so dramatically.

What that means is this: It is entirely possible that if you have clear written goals, you can serve God with ten times the effectiveness as those who serve without goals. Outstanding high achievers have clearly written goals.

Something magical happens when you write down your goals. It changes the way you see your situation. When you set a written goal, your subconscious mind, that mind God put inside of you, starts to work toward the accomplishment of that objective. Put your goal on paper and make sure you have a place where you can view it and review it every single day.

How to Set SMARTER Goals

The reason why many people feel like setting goals doesn't work for them is because they've been doing it wrong. Goals don't motivate us unless they reach certain criteria and have a system that ensures their success. Michael Hyatt, former CEO of Thomas Nelson Publishers, teaches how to make goals more effective by using the acronym: S.M.A.R.T.E.R.[1]

S - SPECIFIC. The first attribute of SMARTER goals is that they are specific. Focus is power. You can drive the same amount of water through two pipes but drastically increase the force and pressure in one pipe by decreasing its diameter. That's what happens when we narrow our goals.

Saying "I want to lose weight this year" is not a goal; that's a wish. How much weight by when? Saying "I want to write a book" is just a dream; but not a goal. What kind of book? How many words a day will you write?

David Yongi Cho, pastor of the world's largest church in Seoul, South Korea once made a statement that challenged me. He said, "God doesn't answer vague prayers." Sometimes we pray things such as, "Lord, bless that family." What does that mean? What are we asking God to do exactly? How would you know if God answers that prayer? Remember, a goal is a statement of faith of something that you believe God can do through you. Don't pray vague prayers, and don't set vague goals. Be specific.

Saying, "I want to hire a personal trainer and workout four days a week for an hour each workout" is a specific goal. Saying, "I want to take an online course in how to write and publish a book and begin writing by the first of next month" is a specific goal.

M - MEASURABLE. This is important for two reasons. If you don't have some form of measurement, how will you know you've reached your goal? To say, "I want to earn more money this year than last year" is nice but how much more? There's a big difference between a cost of living adjustment and increasing your sales by 15%. Once you make a goal measurable, you've now established a criteria to know if you've been successful or not. But the second benefit to making measurable goals is that you'll be able to track your progress.

If your goal is to write a book, you can set milestones along the way. For example, this book you are reading is the fulfillment of one of my goals for 2018 — to write and publish a new book on the Five Essentials. One of the ways I made this goal measurable was by setting a subgoal of how many words I planned to write each day. Sticking to that schedule of writing 2,000 words a day enabled me to get this book completed on time. It's reaching those mini-milestones that really make the journey of achieving your goal so much more enjoyable. According to psychology professor, Timothy Pychyl, "We experience the strongest positive emotional response when we make progress on our most difficult goals."

A - ACTIONABLE. If you want something you've never had you've got to do something you've never done. Goals are action statements. Fundamentally, they are about what you are planning to do. So when you are writing out your goals, make sure that they are action oriented. Michael Hyatt suggests that it's best to use a strong verb in that goal that will prompt the action you want to take. Don't use words like "am, be, or have." You want a strong verb like "run, finish, or eliminate."

> Your goals need to be just out of reach but not out of reality.

Here's an example: Sometimes people's goals say something like this, "Be more consistent in saving." That's a state-of-being verb. That doesn't inspire anybody. But something like "Deposit 10% of my paycheck into my savings account on the firstt and fifteenth of each month" is actionable.

Another bad example is something like, "Be more health conscious." That's not actionable. Instead your goal could be something like, "Jog for 30 minutes five days a week."

R - REALISTIC. There's a reason why this component to setting SMARTER goals is further down the list. When you're first brainstorming your goals, you should try to suspend reality for a moment. Pretend that life is only a game and that anything is possible. If you had every skill, resource, and ability in the world, what would you do? What would you set out to accomplish? There will be a time later to eliminate the pipe dreams.

If you start your goal setting process with the question: "Is this realistic?" then chances are, you'll set the bar too low. According to Nobel-prize-winning psychologist Daniel Kahneman, "We are driven more strongly to avoid losses than to achieve gains." If this is your starting point in the goal-setting process, it triggers your mind to think in terms of avoiding loss and as a result we end up accomplishing less than what we might have.

After looking at the results of almost 400 studies, goal theorists Edwin Locke and Gary Latham concluded, "The performance of participants with the highest goals was over 250% higher than those with the easiest goals." In other words, we rise to a challenge, but we always hold ourselves back when it's easy.

Your goals need to be just out of reach but not out of reality. I tell my staff every year when we set goals to dream big and aim high. I say in staff meetings: "I'd rather aim for the moon and hit the picket fence than aim for the picket fence and hit the ground." Those who are worried about trying to do too much will usually succeed by not doing much. Michelangelo said, "The greater danger for most of us is not that our aim is too high and we miss it, but that it is too low and we hit it."

For a goal to matter, it needs to cause you some discomfort. If it doesn't challenge you; it won't change you. It's got to stretch you a bit. It has to be risky. But there's a difference between discomfort and delusion. Michael Hyatt says that what he likes to do is set a goal that is delusional and then dial it back a few clicks until it gets into the "discomfort zone." If you're not sure whether your goal falls into the "just out of reach but not out or reality" category, just ask your spouse or a close friend. Other people are usually better than we are at identifying our blind spots.

T - TIME-SENSITIVE. The fifth attribute of a SMARTER goal is that it includes one or more of five different time references: a deadline date, frequency, start date, time trigger, and/or streak target. Hyatt suggests that the best way to set goals is to break them down into two categories: Achievement Goals and Habit Goals

> A goal without a deadline will certainly be missing its sense of urgency or direction.

Achievement goals are focused on one-time accomplishments. It could be paying off your credit cards, running your first half marathon, or completing a big project at home or work. Deadlines are essential for all achievement goals. A goal without a deadline is not only unlikely to be accomplished but will certainly be missing its sense of urgency or direction. For example, "Increase sales revenue 20% is almost meaningless without a deadline." It could happen at any point over the next ten years. And here's another key thought about deadlines—don't set them too far out in the future. That might feel like the "safer" thing to do but distant deadlines discourage action. I used to do this and discovered that I kept telling myself, "Oh I have time. That's not due for another twelve months." The tighter the deadline the more focused and productive you'll be.

Habit goals are different than achievement goals as they don't help you meet a deadline but instead help you create a new behavior of regular, ongoing activity. It could be a daily prayer and meditation practice or meeting weekly for coffee with an accountability partner. Even though there's no firm deadline, the other time keys are just as critically essential. If you're setting a habit goal, make sure it has a *start date*. When are you beginning this new habit? Next, a habit *frequency* — how often are you going to practice this habit? After that, a time *trigger* — that's when you want to do the habit (ex: I will go to the gym as soon as I finish breakfast in the morning). Having a specific time of day that follows a previous event helps establish a new routine and keep you consistent. Finally, a *streak target* is determining how many times you plan to do the habit in a consecutive row. Just keep in mind that it takes anywhere between twenty-one to sixty-six days to establish a new habit.

E - EXCITING. A good goal is something that excites you. It inspires you. You get fired up just thinking about it. Joe Vitale says, "A goal should scare you a little, and excite you a lot." Having an external motivation might work for a little while; but it will likely burn you out in the long run. You need goals that are internally or intrinsically motivated.

Ayelet Fishbach and Kaitlin Woolley of the University of Chicago's School of Business asked people in a study to rate how much they enjoyed the New Year's resolutions that they set. They checked back a few months later and found that enjoyment was a key predictor of success.

The problem for many of us is that we set goals of what we think we should do based on what others expect or what we think would be good for us. Don't let your family's, colleagues', or society's ideals or expectations dictate your ambitions. The trick is to set goals that are not only personally important, but also personally inspiring. In fact, if your written goals are not from your true heart and inner ambition, your creative spirit will not work to produce them anyway.

Ask yourself tough questions: "Does this goal inspire me? Does it engage my heart? Am I willing to work hard to make it happen? Do I find this fun?

You should have goals that are so big, you feel uncomfortable telling small minded people.

R - RELEVANT. Effective goals have to be relevant to your life. This is all about alignment. Do you have goals set in each of the Five Essentials or is one major segment of your overall well-being totally ignored? Will your new weekend-gobbling hobby put an unwanted strain on your family? You need to set goals that are relevant to your actual circumstances and interests that align with your values.

When you're on the journey towards reaching your goals, here are two final thoughts to keep in mind. First, remember that discipline is the bridge between goals and accomplishment. What you practice in private will reap rewards in public. The department store founder, J.C. Penney said, "Give me a stock clerk with a goal and I will give you a man who will make history. Give me a man without a goal and I will give you a stock clerk." Goals keep you growing and thriving; but you need discipline to keep it going.

And secondly, don't give up on your goal when you get discouraged. Giving up on your goal because of one setback is like slashing your other three tires because you got a flat. You might need to make some adjustments or modifications along the way. That's okay. Be stubborn about your goals but flexible about your methods.

One day a high school freshmen started his first day at a men's-only boarding school. On the day he arrived, he hammered big brass letter "V" onto the front of his door. Everyone asked him what it meant as his name didn't have a "V" in it. But he would never comment about it. They would watch him touch the letter

> **Giving up on your goal because of one setback is like slashing your other three tires because you got a flat.**

"V" when he came back to his room and he would touch it again before he would open his door. When he moved rooms, he took his letter "V" with him. It wasn't until four years later that everyone knew why he had this peculiar practice—when he walked on stage to deliver his Valedictorian address, carrying his letter "V" with him in his hand. Never underestimate the power of a well-stated goal.

NEXT STEPS

What was your biggest takeaway from this chapter on setting goals?

Rewrite the SMARTER acrostic from memory and review each of the seven steps for setting SMARTER goals.

At the end of this book, I'll help you develop your own personal growth plan. But if you've thought of some goals you'd like to set, go ahead and jot them down here.

Time Management Principles

"Until we can manage time, we can manage nothing else." — Peter Drucker

Two women met for the first time since graduating from high school. One asked the other, "You were always so organized in school. Did you manage to live a well-planned life? "

"Yes," said her friend. "My first marriage was to a millionaire; my second marriage was to an actor; my third marriage was to a preacher; and now I'm married to an undertaker."

Her friend asked, "What do those marriages have to do with a well-planned life?"

"One for the money, two for the show, three to get ready, and four to go!"

Seriously, I believe that you need to have a well-planned life. The only way to manage time is to stay ahead of it. Once you know what your priorities are; it makes it easier to manage your time to align to those priorities. Managing your time without setting priorities is like shooting randomly and calling whatever you hit the target.

> **Managing your time without setting priorities is like shooting randomly and calling whatever you hit the target.**

Either you run the day or the day runs you. William Penn said, "Time is what we want most but what we use worst."

The Laws of Unmanaged Time

It's been said that "time flies" but the good news is that you're the pilot. If you want to become more productive, you've got to become a master of your minutes. But there are a few laws that govern our lack of managed time:

LAW #1 – Unmanaged time flows toward my weaknesses. I really believe that the majority of people spend the majority of their time doing things that they are second best at. Why? Because unseized time will flow in the direction of one's weaknesses.

LAW #2 – Unmanaged time comes under the influence of dominant people in my world. I don't know about you but I'm a people pleaser by nature! I love people and I hate to disappoint them. But I quickly learned when I was in my twenties and became the pastor of a little country church, that if I do not take control of my schedule there were about a hundred people in my congregation that would! I quickly learned that strong people in my world controlled my time better than I did because I had not taken the initiative to command the time before they got to me. Alec Mackenzie said, "Planning your day, rather than allowing it to unfold at the whim of others, is the single most important piece in the time management puzzle."

LAW #3 – Unmanaged time surrenders to the demands of all emergencies. So many of us are governed by the tyranny of the urgent. Not everything that cries the loudest should be the most urgent thing that we tend to. Elton Trueblood made a statement I'll never forget: "A public man, though he is necessarily available at many times, must learn to hide. If he is always available, he is not worth enough when he is available." You may not live a life in the public eye, but the same principle holds true for you as well. The world is full of disorganized people who have lost control of their time. A person can be gifted, can possess a variety of talents and enormous intelligence—but can wind up squandering it all because of an inability to seize control of their time.

Schedule the Big Rocks

In his book *7 Habits of Highly Effective People*, Steven Covey gave the "rocks in a jar" illustration that has become widely known. He took a wide-mouth jar and taught that if you wanted to put a bunch of big rocks (representing our priorities), some smaller pebbles (representing good things but not important things), and some sand (representing the things we do that waste our time) all into the same jar — the big rocks will never fit unless you put them in first.

A lot of us, fritter away our day on Facebook and Instagram, shopping online, driving through car lots to look at cars we can't afford, watching TV, or staring at our phones. These things occupy a tremendous amount of our time. They're not bad things, but they're also not getting us anywhere either.

Once you identify the big rocks (your priorities, the *Five Essentials*) those are the things that must get put on your schedule or they will never happen. William James said, "That which holds the attention, determines the action." In today's world, the key to true productivity is not to get more things done, but to get the right things done.

Here's what we need to remember: *Priority determines capacity*. It's what you put in the jar of your life first that determines your capacity. Once the big rocks are in, the lesser things (pebbles and sand) flow around them and fill in the cracks. But what is priority for you will determine the capacity of your life.

Ephesians 5:15-16 says, *"Therefore be careful how you walk, not as unwise men but as wise, making the most of your time, because the days are evil."* That phrase "making the most of your time" is an interesting phrase in the Greek. It's a word that means "to buy out of the market." It was a common word used to speak of buying something valuable in the marketplace. The word for *time* means "opportunity." Time (or *kairos* in Greek), means an appointed time in the purpose of God—a window of opportunity for God to act. The truth of the matter is, one year equals 365 opportunities. Every single day of the year, we should be doing the most to redeem the time and make the best use of it that we can. Zig Ziglar said, "People often complain about a lack of time when the lack of direction is the problem." Once you've got the big rocks in place, the direction for your day is set.

Top Ten Time Management Tips

Time management has been one of my greatest challenges as a leader and knowing how much I needed to grow in this area has helped me develop some new disciplines.

When I first encountered the book *The 90-Minute Hour*, I thought "That's impossible. How do you get 90 minutes out of a 60-minute hour?" But the author made a great point in that some people can get more done in an hour than other people do. That particular principle has really changed my perspective on time. The bottom line is we all have known people who can get more done in an hour than others. So in this chapter, I'm going to share a summary of what I believe are some of the best time management tips that I've tested and proven to helpful:

> Plan your week before you live your week, every single week.

1. Plan your week before you live your week. My leadership coach, Joe Calhoon, once gave me this advice when we were having lunch together: "Brandon, one of the greatest keys to success is to plan your week before you live your week, every single week."

You're envisioning, under God's direction, what He might have in store for you to do in the next 168 hours. If you break down the 168 hours in a week, they fall into three categories: 56 hours for work, 56 hours for sleep, 56 hours to do other things. Most people never fully optimize those 56-hour increments; yet its our greatest opportunity: sleep, work, life. People typically live their lives by default, rather than by design. They are reactive (just responding to what life throws at them) rather than being proactive and actually planning their day. We learned in earlier chapters that when it comes to money management, don't ask where your money went, tell it where to go. In the same way, when it comes to time management, don't ask where the hours went, tell them where to go.

Brian Tracy says, "You save 10 minutes in execution for every minute you invest in planning. This means that the very act of planning—thinking on paper before you begin—gives you a 1000% return on energy. This is one of the highest returns you can get from anything you do in life." Some of the most effective people that I know plan the next day before leaving the office the day before. At 4:45 p.m. today, take some time and plan out everything that you're going to do tomorrow. Put in your schedule those blocks of time to get those things done. Go ahead and pull all of the resources and file folders that you will need and put that folder on your desk for the next day. And remember to put in some margin for those unexpected things that come along the way as well. Plan your day before you live your day, every single day.

2. Develop a "Top Six List" of things to do. By focusing on just the Top Six items you must accomplish, you're bringing the 80/20 Principle to bear on your to-do list. The 80/20 Principle (also called the Pareto Principle) teaches us that 80% of your effectiveness will be found in 20% of your to-do items. You need to ask yourself, what are the top six things that I can to give me the most ROT – Return On Time. You may have twenty items on your To-Do List – but if you can accomplish just six of the most important ones – you will begin to feel and be very effective in your day.

3. Own the list. This may be the most important time management principle. You need to make a conscious effort to allocate your time. Proverbs 24:27 illustrates this: *"Finish your outdoor work and get your fields ready; after that build your house."* In other words, do the most important things first. In the day in which Proverbs was written, getting the fields ready first was critical because it meant food and income for the family. What good is a nice house when you don't have any food to eat or any income? So how do you decide what's first and most important?

Try this technique: Make a list of all the things you need to do today. Now ask yourself this question: "If I could only do one item on this list, which one would it be?" Mark that item as #1. Go back through the remaining items on the list and ask the question again. Mark that item as #2. Get the idea? Once the items all have a number, start with #1—and do it until it is completed. Cross it off the list, pause to feel the endorphin rush of accomplishment, and celebrate. Then go on to #2. Some of you are be thinking, "But what if I don't get to everything on my list?" To that concern, I would say two things: 1) You can take great satisfaction in knowing you accomplished what you deemed as being the most important, and, 2) You might need to practice giving yourself the gift of saying, "No."

4. Eat the frog. Brian Tracy wrote a book called *Eat That Frog: 21 Great Ways to Stop Procrastinating and Get Things Done*. It got its name from a quotation by Mark Twain, who famously said something to the effect of "if you eat a frog for breakfast, chances are that will be the worst thing you have to do all day." The point of that quotation—and the book—was that if you start your day by tackling your hardest but most important tasks, even if you don't do that much for the rest of the day, you will still have accomplished a lot. So this time management teaches that you make that "eat the frog" item the first thing on your list. Get it out of the way so you can move on to those other activities that aren't going to weigh on you that much. Sometimes "eating that frog" means having that difficult conversation with a coworker. Sometimes it means following up on something that you really don't want to do but you have to do it. Sometimes some of the most productive things that we have to do are some of the most unpleasant but unavoidable things. Some of you have so many frogs sitting on your desk and they're looking at you, croaking at you, and stinking up your office! *Eat the frog!*

5. Practice batching for time management. The idea of batching is that you dedicate blocks of time to similar tasks in order to decrease distraction and increase productivity. For example, anything that I need to do that involves creative planning, deep work, writing or studying — I do in the mornings from my home office. If I need to schedule meetings, my assistant schedules them in the afternoons — back to back — in 30-minute increments. I do all email correspondence for the day in one block of time, and all handwritten correspondence in another block. You get the idea. The problem with many of us is that we go through our day allowing distractions to dictate our activities. When you're in a constant state of reacting to needs (email, phone calls, text messages, random meetings)—that perpetual state of shifting gears and refocusing attention creates fatigue, stress, and decreased productivity. Remember this: Every time we become distracted, it takes an average of 15 minutes to regain our complete focus.

> Every time we become distracted, it takes an average of 15 minutes to regain our complete focus.

6. Use the Pomodoro Technique. One method for batching tasks works like this: 1.) You plan and prioritize all of the tasks that need to be completed by writing them down. 2.) You set a timer for 25 minutes and devote that time to a task or to a group of similar tasks. Larger tasks can be broken down into multiple blocks or "pomodoros" and smaller tasks such as responding to email or returning phone calls, can be grouped into a single block. After completing each Pomodoro, you put an "X" next to it and mark the number of times that you were distracted. 3.) You take a five minute break (giving yourself permission to check Facebook or go to the restroom), 4.) Begin another block of time (or "pomodoro"), 5.) Once you complete four pomodoros, take an extended 20 minute break. You've earned it! According to the Pomodoro website, you should see noticeable improvements in your productivity almost immediately and mastery of the technique in seven to twenty days.[1] You might be wondering what's up with the name "Pomodoro"? It actually means "tomato" in Italian. The inventor of the technique, Francesco Cirillo, initially used a tomato-shaped kitchen timer when he developed this technique.

7. Play instrumental music or white noise that helps you concentrate. Right now, as I'm writing this, I'm using a website that I recently discovered called *Focus@Will*. It's basically a website that streams instrumental music that is scientifically optimized to help you focus. There are even play lists depending on what your needs are at that moment—creative thinking, logical thinking, studying, etc. Scientists have discovered that depending on your personality type, there is a specific type of "music" that when engineered just right, puts your brain into a "flow state" making you hyper-focused and exponentially more productive. It's been proven to quadruple your focus and optimize your productivity. I highly recommend it.[2]

8. Arrive 10 minutes early. Getting to a meeting just 10 minutes early prepares you for the meeting that you're about to engage in and also lowers your stress levels. One of the most stressful things in our lives is this fear that we're going to be late to our next appointment or our next meeting. Just the thought that we may be late to something raises our stress level. When you are running late, not only does it make you stressed in *getting* to that activity, but it also takes you longer to get *engaged* in that activity. So you end up with a waste on both ends of the meeting — you're wasting time because you were late and you're wasting time because you're not really focused.

9. Start on time and end on time. Whatever activity you're involved in, it's important that you have a solid start time for that activity. Whether its a to-do list item or a meeting, it's important to have a solid start time. The reason why a lot of meetings drag on and on is because we don't start on time, often because we're waiting for people to arrive. By not starting on time, we've trained people to come in late. For every activity and everything on your schedule, you need to also have a fixed end time. There are some days where I might have seven or eight meetings on my schedule. The only way I can do that is that there are definite end times to each appointment. I've also started actually calendaring my to-do list items on my schedule by alloting a start and end time to those tasks in the time that I think it will take to accomplish them. You'll be amazed at how much more productive that will make you! Parkinson's law is the adage that "work expands so as to fill the time available for its completion." I've definitely known that to be true in my own life. If I have two hours to complete a project, guess how long it's going to take me? Two hours. If I have one hour to complete a project, guess how long it will take me? You guessed it. One hour. And chances are, it will be done with about the same level of quality because my focus is even more concerted.

10. Learn to pray this prayer: "God, what is the best use of my time right now?" The Bible tells us in James 1:5, *"If any of you lacks wisdom, you should ask God, who gives generously to all without finding fault, and it will be given to you."* God wants you to check in with Him throughout the day. He is able to literally direct the minutes of your day if you allow Him to. As Christine Caine says, "My job is to take care of the possible and let God handle the impossible." Our goal ought to be to do the best possible things at the best possible time. It's been said that if the devil can't make you bad; he'll make you busy. One anonymous author put it this way: "Beware of the barrenness of an overcrowded life." Don't be busy. Be productive.

> Time equals life. If you waste your time, you waste your life. But if you master your time, you master your life.

Let's say that implementing the lessons from this chapter, you learn a tip or two that will save you 10 minutes a day. This might not sound like much. But if you can save just 10 minutes a day, that means that at the end of the year, you will have two and a half extra days that you've saved!

But I believe these tools and practices are better than that. I believe I can save you 60 minutes a day in time management – would you believe that? If you were able to save an hour a day over the next year – you would get back an additional 15.2 days that you might have otherwise wasted! That's 15 days you'd get back in your calendar! You can thank me later.

We can do anything but we can't do everything. Time equals life. If you waste your time, you waste your life. But if you master your time, you master your life. I'd like to wrap up this lesson with a paraphrase of Psalm 23 as it relates to time management:

The Lord is my pacesetter, I shall not rush. He makes me stop and rest at intervals. He provides me with images of stillness to restore my serenity. He leads me in the way of efficiency to calmness of mind and this guidance is peace. Even though I have a great many things to accomplish this day, I will not fret for His presence is here. His timeliness, His all importance will keep me in balance. He prepares refreshment and renewal in the midst of my activity, anointing my head with the oils of tranquility. My cup of joyous energy overflows. Surely harmony and effectiveness shall be the fruits of my hours, for I shall walk in the pace of my Lord and dwell in His heaven forever.

NEXT STEPS

Where would you say you struggle the most in your ability to manage your time?

Look over the top ten time management tips, what are three that you plan to implement today?

How to Rewire Your Brain

*"If you realized how powerful your thoughts are,
you'd never think a negative thought again."*

The hardest part of life isn't keeping your body in shape but keeping your mind in shape. We can never get to the point where we neglect our mind. Instead, we need to train it as hard as our bodies. It's been said: Your mind is a garden, your thoughts are the seeds; you can grow flowers or you can grow weeds.

I was recently reading about how scientists have discovered more about the human brain in the last twenty years than in the last 2,000 years combined. Their biggest finding: *We have been underestimating our brain's capabilities.*

The average brain weighs just three pounds and yet it contains 100 billion nerve cells. Each nerve cell is connected to all the other cells with 10,000 individual connections. There are 5 trillion chemical reactions that are happening in your brain *every second*. This information is traveling at 268 miles per hour. It's no wonder why even though your brain is just 2% of your bodyweight, it uses up 20-30% of your total calories.

Dr. Duane Gish said, "The human brain is the most complex arrangement of matter in the universe." Some like to compare the brain to a highly sophisticated computer, but no technology can ever compare to its capabilities. It's the most influential organ in your body. It accounts for your ability to think, remember, love, reason, and imagine. Everything you see, hear, touch, feel, and smell is recorded on the lobes of your brain.

Your Life Follows Your Thoughts

Proverbs 23:7 says, *"For as a man thinks within himself so is he."* In other words, your life will move in the direction of your most dominant thoughts. Today, I want you to think about what you think about. If you can learn to control and rewire your brain, you can control your thoughts.

> Your life will move in the direction of your most dominant thoughts.

If we think negative, discouraging thoughts we will lead negative discouraging lives. If you want to experience God's best, you must be careful about what you allow your mind to dwell on. Most people don't realize that we can actually choose our thoughts. Just because a thought comes into your mind, doesn't mean that you have to dwell on it. We choose whether to hold onto that thought or ignore it. There's a difference between seeing a bird fly over your head and letting it build a nest in your hair. We can't allow negative, toxic thoughts to build nests within our minds.

What would you do if you went home today and found a rattlesnake in your house? Would you just leave it there while you sit down on the couch to watch the evening news? Or would you run, call animal control, or try to capture the snake yourself? Chances are you would do something to take action because you recognize that there is something dangerous in your house. The negative, toxic thoughts that enter our minds may not be rattlesnakes but they are equally as destructive. We need to have the same urgency in dealing with wrong thinking as we would with dealing with a poisonous reptile in our home.

What Enhances Brain Health?

According to Dr. Daniel Amen, there are several things that you can do that will enhance your brain health.

1. Positive social connections. Did you know that the types of people you surround yourself with can actually determine your longevity? Not only that but being around positive people rubs off on your attitude as well. Behavior as well as attitude is contagious. When you hang out with those who have healthy habits, you tend to pick that up as well.

2. New learning. Whenever you learn something new, your brain is making new connections. When you stop learning, however, your brain starts to disconnect itself. Learning something new each day staves off the potential of developing dementia or alzheimer's later in life.

3. Good brain diet. It's important to consume nutrients that will actually help your brain (such as avocado, turmeric, coconut oil, salmon, green leafy vegetables, walnuts, dark chocolate, etc.).

4. Sleep. One study showed how back in 1900, the average American got nine hours of sleep. Today the average is six hours. The problem is that with less than seven hours of sleep you start to lower the blood flow to the brain.

5. ANT killing. Dr. Amen uses the acronym ANT to describe "Automated Negative Thoughts." Scientists say that 75% of the mental, behavioral, and physical illnesses we have today come from our thought life. In his book, *Change Your Brain, Change Your Life*, Dr. Amen explains that every thought you have sends an electrical signal to your brain that can be recorded, analyzed, and visualized on a nuclear brain scan. Your thoughts literally possess physical properties that are tangibly real. And by allowing critical thoughts, blaming thoughts, condemning thoughts, anxious thoughts to run rampant in your mind—you are literally polluting your body. He says, "Every cell in your body is affected by every thought that you have." So if you want to change your life; change your thinking. If you want to change your health; change your mind.

> Your thoughts possess physical properties that are tangibly real.

Get Rid of Your Stinkin' Thinkin'

Romans 12:1-2 tells us that we must be *"transformed by the renewing of your mind."* So how do you do that? How do you renew, rewire, and reprogram your mind? You were made in God's image. Your toxic thoughts and occasional bad behavior is not who you are, but it is who you have become as a result of your stinking thinking. The good news is that if you have become something; you can unbecome it. If you've hardwired it in, you can hardwire it out. There is no thinking pattern that cannot be reversed.

When people make bad decisions or choices, those same bad decisions and choices get hardwired into our brains and literally alter the physical structure of the mind. You are the one who designs the landscape of your brain in either a positive or negative direction. Whatever you think about the most will grow into an ingrained thought pattern. You have literally "wired" those toxic thoughts into your brain and now you are living out that new reality. This is what the Bible refers to as a "stronghold." For some it could be lust, unforgiveness, anger, jealousy, or something else.

Yet recent discoveries in modern brain science have confirmed what the Bible has spoken of for thousands of years. The first discovery is that of neuroplasticity. Scientists used to think that the brain was fixed and unable to be changed. The good news is that you're not stuck with the brain you have. It can change and grow. If you make good decisions today, you can improve your brain's function within two months.

Neurogenesis is the second brain science discovery that works in our favor. This means that new nerve cells are birthed daily for our benefit. Sometimes people say, "I can't change this part of me. This is just who I am. This is part of my personality." That's only partially true. Yes, you've literally made it a part of your biology; but it did so because of your stinking thinking and bad choices. But God has designed your brain to follow the direction of your mind. We control our brain; our brain does not control us.

For every behavior we experience, our brain creates a neurological pathway. And as that behavior is repeated, those pathways become even more stable; and then deeply ingrained. Think of it this way: A single behavior or thought pattern maps out a "dirt road" in your mind. It creates a neurological pathway for thoughts to travel. But as you repeat those thoughts and thus repeat that behavior, your brain builds a paved road, allowing for increased volume and frequency of thoughts to move about. If you continue indulging in those thought patterns and behavior, before long, your brain has developed a neurologial pathway that looks more like an eight-lane-wide super interstate highway.

In order to change the behavior, we must first reprogram our brain. That involves the deconstruction of existing highways and that process does take time, but it works.

The Bible says that we are to do two things when it comes to our stinking thinking:

1. Take every thought captive. You have more than 10,000 thoughts that pass between your ears every single day. Yet the average person has 200 negative, toxic thoughts per day that are extremely damaging such as worry, jealousy, insecurity, lust, cravings for forbidden things, and so forth. Interestingly enough, depressed people have as many as 600 negative thoughts which is three times the average. You can't eliminate all of the troublesome things that go through your mind, but you can take them captive and reduce the number of negative thoughts. In 2 Corinthians 10:5 we read, *"We demolish arguments and every pretension that sets itself up against the knowledge of God, and we take captive every thought to make it obedient to Christ."* What does it mean to "take every thought captive?" I used to think it meant to "put it in a box." But in Scripture, the verb for "take captive" literally means "to take a prisoner with a spear." The word "spear" is literally embedded in the verb. It means to chase something with a spear. In other words, you're dealing with these negative, toxic thoughts in a violently aggressive way. Treat that negative thought as if it were a burglar trying to invade your home. What a powerful metaphor. God wants us to capture our stinking thinking and take it prisoner with a spear. But here's the key: you've only got about five seconds. You have to learn to say "No!" to every toxic, negative thought within five seconds, or you're allowing that thought pattern to once again take hold.

2. Commit to renewing your mind daily. W. Clement Stone said, "Keep your mind off the things you don't want by keeping it on the things you do want." Think of it this way: If you wanted to get all the air out of a glass, how would you do it? If you created a vacuum in the air, that's problematic because it's hard to do and the vacuum would shatter the glass. But in reality it's actually easy to get the air out. Just fill it up with water. So how do you renew your mind? You fill it with God's truth. Just trying to stop thinking wrong thoughts doesn't work. Those things have to be replaced with something else.

Over time, what happens is we develop an entirely new neurological roadmap, leading you to the life you were meant to live. Set your mind and keep it on the higher things. Don't go around thinking that your problems are insurmountable. That will keep you in bondage and defeat. Remember this: When you are negative, you are in agreement with the enemy. Instead of going around thinking about your problems and how impossible everything is, you need to cast down those thoughts and be thinking about how God is on your side. Instead of thinking about how big your problems are, start thinking about how big your God is. The bigger we make our God, the smaller our problems will become.

Cut Down the Tree!

Dr. Caroline Leaf, author of *Switch on Your Brain*, offers some amazing advice on how to rewire your brain. As a neuroscientist, she illustrates how God wants us to renew our minds. The nerve cells (neurons) in your brain look like little trees. As you're reading this book right now, your brain is processing at 400 billion actions per second. When we take things into our mind through our five senses we think about them and make thoughts about them. Those thoughts turn into literal physical structures within the brain. That's why scientists often refer to brain cells as "The Magic Trees of the Mind." Those 100 billion nerve cells can each grow up to 200,000 branches. That means we have the capacity for 3 million years of space to build memories! This is just what we know from our basic understanding of the human brain (and we're still discovering more!)

Because we can't see a thought--we can't tangibly touch it or see it--we think our thoughts are harmless. But no, they each exist as physical structures. Even as you're reading this book, you're enabling new thoughts and additional structures (trees) of your brain to change shape. But remember, God made you to be a neuroplastician which means you can literally do your own brain surgery. God designed us with the ability to change our own brain. It takes, on average, about twenty-one days to rewire a mental tree. That's twenty-one days to remove a toxic thought and replace it with a healthy thought. This might sound like a long time but there are 365 days a year or seventeen sets of 21 days. If you were to change seventeen things about yourself in a given year, I'd say you were accomplishing more than what most people do in a lifetime! (Interesting sidenote, twenty-one is an important number in the Bible. It took twenty-one days for Daniel to see a breakthrough!)[1] It takes 21 days for all the necessary protein changes to take place to create a new long-term integrated memory.

You've actually got about three different types of thinking when it comes to your brain:

1. Subconscious Thinking. This is where 90% of the action of your mind is. Thinking and thought building happen on this level and it operates at 400 billion actions per second.

2. Conscious Thinking. This is where just 10% of your mind action is. It operates at 2,000 actions per second. This is what you're consciously thinking about at this moment. It only operates when you're awake. So think of conscious thinking as "the movie screen" of your mind. It's what's currently playing.

3. Sensory Thinking. This would involve the information your brain is receiving from its five senses.

You see this played out whenever you learn something new. Let's take learning to drive a car for instance. When you were first learning how to drive, you had to think and process in your conscious mind every detail in the driving process: looking in the rear-view mirror, placing the transmission from reverse to drive, and many other tasks. But as you repeated that new learned behavior of driving a car, over time the process transferred over to your unconscious mind. That's why you can get in the car and have a conversation with someone. Your brain has automatized this new behavior into your subconscious thinking.

Caroline Leaf teaches us that our unconscious mind is filled with billions of these trees (good and bad thoughts). As we go through life, something might prompt or trigger us to bring up a thought from the subconscious mind to the conscious mind. Here's the thing: Once that thought moves into the conscious mind, it actually becomes malleable and changeable. This is why when you remember a past event, you actually remember the

> As you're reading this book right now, your brain is processing at 400 billion actions per second.

last time you remembered it, not the event itself. This explains why certain details in our memories sometimes shift.

> Once that thought moves into the conscious mind, it actually becomes malleable and changeable.

So when your toxic thought is in your conscious mind, you have the choice to either make it bigger or destroy it. Unfortunately, most people take that toxic tree of a thought and just add more branches to it. Someone hurt you and you start ruminating over and over in your mind what he said, or what she did. You've grown something that now has so many branches that it no longer reflects reality but rather is a reflection of your wrong perception of reality.

Or you can identify that toxic tree and say, "This is what I'm thinking and it's not good. I don't want this in my life. I'm replacing it with God's truth." When you do this, your brain sends a surge of neurochemicals — dopamine, oxytocin, serotonin, and others — and it literally starts attacking this thought, setting it on a chemical fire, and tearing it down. And then we can rebuild, in its place, a healthy new tree. This is how you rewire your brain within twenty-one days.

Abracadabra!

Your mind is always eavesdropping on your thought life. Your brain is like a supercomputer and your self-talk is the program that it will run. If you tell yourself, "I'm not intelligent. I can't ever remember anything," you're in reality dumbing yourself down as it becomes a self-fulfilling prophecy. Those thoughts become the unconscious programs for our mind.

Jim Kwik, an expert on learning and developing a super memory, gives this strategy for overcoming those irritating ANT's (Automatic Negative Thoughts). He uses the acrostic ABRA. That's a sound that magicians use when they perform a trick and it's a move you can implement as well, whenever you feel a negative, toxic thought come in:

A - Acknowledge. Don't just try to suppress it and not deal with it. If I were to say to you, "Do not think about a big pink giraffe." What are you going to automatically do? You're going to think of a big pink giraffe! Why? Because what you resist persists. When you fight for your limitations, you get to keep them. So you acknowledge that it's there and acknowledge that it doesn't belong there. That's when you bring that thought to the conscious mind to make it malleable and changeable.

B - Breathe In. When you breathe in, oxygen is good for the brain. But this means something much more. In the Bible, the Holy Spirit is called "breath." It's the word ruach in the Old Testament and pneuma in the New. Just as God breathed on Adam and gave him the breath of life, Jesus breathed on His disciples in John chapter 20 and said, *"'Peace to you! As the Father sent me, I also send you.' And when He had said this, He breathed on them and said, 'Receive the Holy Spirit.'"*[2] So you breathe in possibility, breathe in His power, breathe in God because *"greater is He who is in you than he who is in the world."*[3]

R - Release. Take that thought that you want to rid yourself of and exhale and release that thought. You release that hurt, release the anger, release those feelings of lust, release that limitation. Visualize it leaving you just as your breath is leaving your body.

A - Align. Align means to reset. So you align yourself with the truth. Whatever that negative thought was, say the exact opposite, make it positive and make it more empowering. You align to your true nature.

So next time you find a negative, toxic thought coming across the forefront of your mind, make it disappear like magic! ABRA: Acknowledge, Breathe In, Release, Align.

"The actions of men are the best interpreters of their thoughts."

In the game of baseball, they say that 98% of the game is mental. Isn't that also true about life? Ralph Waldo Emerson said, "Life consists of what a man is thinking about all day." What you think determines who you are; who you are determines what you do. That's why John Locke said, "The actions of men are the best interpreters of their thoughts." What consumes your mind controls your life. Only you can control the doorway to your mind.

NEXT STEPS

Write down three new truths you learned about the human brain. Remember that what gets written gets remembered.

Write down the ABRA technique in your own words:

A –

B –

R –

A –

Is there a toxic, negative thought that keeps pervading your mind? What's your strategy to deal with it based on what you read today?

Make Stress Your Friend, Not Your Enemy

"Just because we're in a stressful situation doesn't mean that we have to get stressed out. You may be in the storm. The key is, don't let the storm get in you."
– Joel Osteen

Is stress ever a problem for you? So many of us are all stressed out with no place to go. We're emotionally fatigued, physically drained, and spiritually defeated — and the reason is stress. The days are long and the nights are short and we feel as if we're the chief rat in the rat race.

I once read about a fighter jet that fired its own missile; but it was moving so fast that it overtook its own missile and shot itself down. I know a lot of people that do the same thing.

What exactly is stress? Stress is the gap between the demands that are placed upon us and our ability to meet those demands. On the one side, we have the responsibilities, demands, and opportunities of life and on the other side we feel our own inability, weaknesses, and lack of knowledge and energy. The gap lying between these is the stress factor.

> Stress is the gap between the demands that are placed upon us and our ability to meet those demands.

People today do so much to manage or escape their stress levels, whether it be prescription drugs, alcohol, or pornograhy, or even overeating. (Ironically, the word *stressed* spelled backwards is *desserts*).

There are actually two different types of stress:

1. Biological stress such as fasting, exposing your body to cold and heat, getting sunlight, exercise. If you apply these types of stress in the right way, they may inhibit your health in the short-term but your body will compensate by becoming stronger and more healthy in the long-term. To be healthy, you actually need biological stress to become more resilient, live longer, age better, be stronger, and avoid modern disease.

2. Psychological stress is what most of us think of when we feel "all stressed out and nowhere to go." Different parts of your brain are responsible for your feelings of stress. The amygdala is, the danger-sensing brain area that detects from your five senses that something isn't right in your surroundings and triggers the "acute stress response" which is basically "fight, flight, or freeze." The amygdala then sounds the alarm to another area of your brain, the hypothalamus, to create stress hormones. It turns out, God also gave us a "governor switch" that, when turned on, can actually prevent a negative stress response from happening in the first place. That's your prefrontal cortex. This area of your brain can calm down your amygdala so that your hypothalamus doesn't create stress hormones like adrenaline.[1]

> God will often give us more than we can handle so we can see how much He can handle.

So how do you develop your prefrontal cortex to keep your stress levels in check? Studies show that mindfulness meditation actually trains your prefrontal cortex for greater activation, so your amygdala can be controlled. Having a quiet time with God and practicing prayer, meditation, and mindfulness throughout the day are scientifically proven to reduce your stress levels.

Isaiah 40:31 says, *"Yet those who wait for the LORD will renew their strength; they will mount up with wings like eagles, they will run and not get tired, they will walk and not become weary."*

This is a promise from God but it comes with a stipulation. You must wait upon the Lord first and if you do, He will renew your strength. What's interesting is that the word for *renew* means "to change or to exchange." The Christian life is not only a changed life; it's an exchanged life. It would almost be like exchanging coats with another person. What that means is, we give God our weakness and in exchange for that, He gives us His strength. But in order for that exchange to take place, we have to wait upon the Lord. God will often give us more than we can handle so we can see how much He can handle.

Be Like the Buffalo

When storms brew on the Colorado plains, they typically move in from the west, many times building in strength and intensity as they travel eastward. Cattle and buffalo share the plains as their home, but their response to the impending storms is very different. Cattle will attempt to avoid the storms by running away from them. They scatter and run with the storm for a longer period of time, increasing panic in the herd as well as the chance of injury. Buffalo, however, will gather together, turn, and run directly into the storm, thereby reducing the duration of time in danger and increasing their chances of emerging unscathed on the other side.[2]

By nature, most people are like cattle. They want to escape stress and run away from it. But be like the buffalo. Change your mindset by embracing the challenges in front of you and run towards them, not away from them. Be proactive, not reactive.

Did you know that being on a personal growth plan, learning something new everyday, is one of the best ways to overcome stress? A study on stress and learning conducted by a professor and two PhD students at the Ross School of Business found that learning something new buffers stress by "building positive resources."

Another study put learning at the top of a list of eight strategies effective at restoring energy and vitality at work. Implementing the principles in the *Five Essentials* and having a personal growth plan can be one of the most important things you do to overcome stress. When we learn something new, we add to our skill set and also to our sense of self-efficacy. By making learning a regular habit, it helps transform not just our mindset but also our complete outlook on life itself.[3]

Bill Gates takes two "Think Weeks" every year for study and reflection. Beyond giving him a chance to catch up on important books of the year and take a look at the big picture, this habit sends a message to peers and colleagues.[4]

Ecclesiastes 10:10 says, *"If the ax is dull and its edge unsharpened, more strength is needed but skill will bring success."* If you've got a dull ax and you're chopping wood, it takes more energy. But if you have a sharp ax, it doesn't take as much energy. So, work smarter, not harder. Skill is the lubricant of success.

So instead of bemoaning how stressed out you are, ask yourself, "How can I learn and grow? What new skills do I need to develop?" Whether that growth is directly tied to what's stressing you out today or not, your new learning will feel like a vitamin B12 shot in the arm and propel you to chase the storms like a buffalo.

The Mind-Body Connection on Stress

Kelly McGonigal, a health psychologist, once did a Ted Talk about "How to Make Stress Your Friend." She said for years, we've been telling people "stress makes you sick," that it increases the risk for everything from the common cold to cardiovascular disease, and as a result we've turned stress into the enemy. However, it's not stress that kills us; it's actually our reaction to it.

Kelly pointed to a study which tracked 30,000 adults in the United States for eight years. They started asking people, "How much stress have you experienced in the last year?" And then they asked, "Do you believe that stress is harmful to your health?" Then they used public death records to find out who died. The bad news is that people who experienced a lot of stress in the previous year had a 43% higher risk of dying. But here's the key distinction: that was only true for the people who also believed that stress was *harmful* for their health!

> It's not stress that kills us; it's actually our reaction to it.

People who experienced a lot of stress but didn't view it as harmful were no more likely to die. In fact, they had the lowest risk of dying of anyone in the study; even lower than people who had relatively little stress!

Kelly makes the argument that changing how you think about stress can actually make you healthier. And science is proving her to be right. When you change your mind about stress, you also change your body's response to stress.[5] It actually produces a positive instead of a negative effect.

It's a pretty profound discovery—that your belief about stress can make a difference in your own life expectancy. The next time you feel "stressed," turn that feeling into a positive affirmation. "I'm grateful for this stress as it's making my body energized and more focused to meet these demands. With God's strength inside of me, I am more than able to meet life's challenges."

When God wants you to grow, he makes you uncomfortable. Why? Because every next level of your life will demand a different you. A cod fish company was shipping out fresh cod to fulfill orders, but when it got to the customer the cod fish had no taste. They thought about it for awhile and decided to place the fish in water in which it could swim. However, the cod fish just floated in the water and didn't swim around much. When the customers received the cod it still had no taste. Then someone came up with a new idea. They placed a different fish in with the cod, the cod's natural predator. The cod fish had to stay alert at all time and kept swimming around so it wouldn't get caught. As a result, the cod fish was very fresh and tasted great when the customer received it.

> When God wants you to grow, he makes you uncomfortable. Because every next level of your life will demand a different you.

Sometimes God may put predators in our lives to keep us going and to keep us alert and keep us from being stagnant in life. So stop thinking about how stressed you are and remember how blessed you are. So the key is to change your attitude about stress. If you can't handle stress, you won't manage success. Remember that most of your stress comes from the way you respond, not the way life is. Adjust your attitude, and all that extra stress is gone. A bad attitude is like a flat tire. You can't go anywhere until you change it. But once you do, you'll be able to get back on the road and headed towards your destination.

Tips on Managing Stress

There are many self-care ideas for how you can relieve stress in your life. Here are some that have really worked for me.

First, **learn to build margin into your life.** There's an interesting Scripture in the Gospels about Jesus. Mark 6:30-32 says,

> *The apostles gathered around Jesus and reported to him all they had done and taught. Then, because so many people were coming and going that they did not even have a chance to eat, he said to them, 'Come with me by yourselves to a quiet place and get some rest.' So they went away by themselves in a boat to a solitary place.*

What's interesting is that even when crowds of people were coming to Jesus and the disciples, He still pulled them away from the crowds to get some rest. It's a strange paradox that God has built into the fabric of life: When I slow down, I go faster! That's why we need to develop margin in our schedule. Do you know what margin is?

Margin is having some breathing room. It's keeping a little reserve that you're not using up. It's not going from one activity to the next with no space in between. I like this definition: Margin is the space between your load and your limit. When there is no buffer between our load and our limit, exhaustion is sure to take place. I think we all know what it feels like when our load is heavier than our limits! The average American spends 10% more than what they have in time, energy, and money. That's literally having a margin deficit! The truth of the matter is, most of us are far more overloaded than we can handle. So just as you would calendar your appointments, make sure that you are also scheduling some margin.

> S.T.R.E.S.S. = Someone Trying to Repair Every Situation Solo

Secondly, *evaluate what is stressing you out.* A couple of years ago, I went through a season of deep depression which came on the heels of a very stressful time in my life and ministry. I went through a lot of staffing changes, launched a new campus for our church, went through a rebranding process, and was trying to raise $12.5 million dollars all at the same time. I knew I wasn't in a good place. I was spiraling downhill on the inside but I didn't tell anyone. I've always adopted a "fake it till you make it" attitude by pretending that everything was going to be just fine. It wasn't until I had five or six people in the same week ask me, "Are you ok, because you don't seem ok?" that I knew I was really in trouble. That's when I realized that I couldn't wear the mask any longer and pretend that I was just fine. I saw my doctor and was treated for clinical depression due to a dopamine deficiency. I had also started to develop heart issues as well. But I vividly remember what the turning point for me was during that season.

A mentor of mine told me to make a list of everything that I was perceiving as a problem or a challenge in my life and ministry and put it on paper. A problem defined is a problem half-solved. So that's exactly what I did. I stopped after my list reached sixty-eight unique problems and challenges that I was currently facing. You would think that seeing a long list of sixty-eight issues would make me want to jump off a bridge. But it was actually a pretty cathartic moment for me. For the first time, I could get the issues that were swirling around in my head and be able to lay them all out before me. Dawson Trotman used to say, "Thoughts disentangle themselves when they pass through the lips and fingertips." Just the act of writing out my problems and frustrations and then giving them to the Lord was liberating. I also sensed the Lord telling me that if I could come up with a list of sixty-eight problems, then I should be able to also come up with a list of sixty-eight promises in His Word that can enable me to overcome those problems through His strength.

Thirdly, *vent your frustrations to a trusted friend.* Dave Willis once said that S.T.R.E.S.S. = Someone Trying to Repair Every Situation Solo. Don't try to carry those burdens alone. Find someone you can share them with and you'll be surprised how just verbalizing what you're internalizing will lift your spirit and lighten your load.

The last tip is by far the most important: *Learn to lay it down before the Lord.* I wonder how much of what weighs us down was never ours to carry in the first place. Stress can sometimes serve as an alarm clock that lets you know you're attached to something that's not true for you. It's been theorized that ninety of what's stressing you today will be irrelevant in a year. Don't lose sleep over petty things.

I have a little box I keep in my office that I call my "Trusting God Box." Whenever I am worried about something I can't change, I simply write that concern on a piece of paper and put it in the box. Once it's inside the box, it becomes God's property, His responsibility, not mine (it never was). From the moment I give my problem to Him, I'm not allowed to worry about it any more. If I find myself wanting to sit and worry about it, then I have to go to the box and physically take the concern away from God. And when I do, I'm visually and physically act out what is really happening on the inside—I'm choosing to stop trusting God! I want to challenge you to go home and find yourself your own "Trusting God Box" and leave it in God's hands once and for all. George Mueller said, "The beginning of anxiety is the end of faith, and the beginning of true faith is the end of anxiety."

When I was a teenager, my home church in south Florida was going on a mission trip to Montana. Our pastor took 150 people on this mission trip. We filled up an entire airplane. But could you imagine the logistics of leading a trip with that many people? As soon as the Pastor got all 150 airline tickets, he kept them in a safe place. I'll never forget when it was time to board the plane. Our Pastor stood between the attendant and each one of us. As each person passed, he would place our ticket in our hand and then we would give it to the attendant. Each person received their boarding ticket right when we needed it, just in the nick of time. What my pastor did for us, God in a similar way, does for you. God will always place Himself between you and the need; and at the right time, He will give you the ticket. Meet today's problems with today's strength. God promises to give us a lamp unto our feet; not a crystal ball into our future.

NEXT STEPS

In this chapter, it is said: "Every next level of your life will demand a different you." What are three things that need to change in order to take you from where you are to where you want to go?

In your own words, how can you make stress your friend instead of your enemy?

Which tip for mastering stress do you need to implement most today?

The **RELATIONAL** Essential

The Foundation of All Relationships

"We make loving people a lot more complicated than Jesus did." — Bob Goff

The most important phrase in the English language as well as any language is "**I love you.**" Love is not only the supreme quality in the universe but it's also truly the foundation of any healthy relationship. It's been said, "Love in your heart wasn't put there to stay; love isn't love until you give it away."

In Galatians 5:6, it says, *"If you are a follower of Christ Jesus ... All that matters is your faith that makes you love others."* God says what matters in life is not your accomplishments or your achievements or your fame or your wealth. What matters in life is one thing. All that matters is your faith that makes you love other people. He says if you miss that, you have missed the most important thing in life.

> **Choosing to love in spite of how you currently may feel is a higher level of love.**

In the Bible, love is not only taught as a command, but it's also a choice. We choose to love or not to love. A lot of people think love is somehow uncontrollable. We even use terminology that implies that it's accidental—*"I fell in love"*—like you would fall into a ditch. It's as if we have no control over our choice to love or not to love. It's a choice. As a matter of fact, choosing to love in spite of how you currently may feel is a higher level of love. It's giving a person what they need, not what they deserve, and that's exactly what God does for me and you. Karl Menninger once said, "Love cures people—both the ones who give it and the ones who receive it."

Love in 3D

> God will not bless a relationship He is not involved in.

If you wanted to find out the full meaning of the word "love" why not ask the greatest lover in all of human history, Jesus Christ Himself. In Matthew 22, Jesus taught "The Great Commandment" where He explains the three dimensions of perfect love. *"You shall love the Lord your God with all your heart and with all your soul and with all your mind. This is the great and first commandment. And the second is like it: You shall love your neighbor as yourself."*[1]

This single statement is the greatest explanation of love ever recorded. From the life of Jesus, we see that love is three dimensional: towards God, towards others, and towards self.

1. Love has an upward dimension. Jesus tells us that God deserves all of our love, not just a part of it. God is the absolute source of love; as 1 John 4:8 says, *"God is love."* When we love others, we are reflecting the love of God. If you grow in your love for God, your love for other people will grow even greater as well. This upward dimension of love supernaturally produces a love for others. C.S. Lewis said, "When I have learned to love God better than my earthly dearest, I shall love my earthly dearest better than I do now." The love of God is what allows us to love others. God will not bless a relationship He is not involved in.

2. Love has an outward dimension. In the great commandment of love, Jesus also calls us to love our neighbor. This can be difficult depending on who our neighbor might be in any given moment. C.W. Vanderburgh said, "To love the whole world for me is no chore; my only real problem is my neighbor next door." I remember in college, one of my professors said, "My wife and I are in a competition trying to out love each other." That's a game worth playing.

3. Love has an inward dimension. Jesus tells us that we're to love our neighbor as what? As ourselves. How you treat others is how you really feel deep inside. Brene Brown, author and TED talker, says it this way, "Because true belonging only happens when we present our authentic, imperfect selves to the world, our sense of belonging can never be greater than our level of self-acceptance." The relationship you have with yourself sets the tone for every other relationship that you have.[2]

Love in Action

Often dubbed, "The Love Chapter," 1 Corinthians 13 does not so much define love as describe it. It's almost as if Paul shines the concept of love through a prism and we see fifteen of its hues and colors. This is the full spectrum of what true love looks like. Each ray gives us a new facet of agape love. You'll notice that every single one of them is a verb (in the Greek even if not in all English translations). These are action words. Love must not only be articulated; it must be demonstrated. It's not just some vague concept or idea. You can see love working. Once again, we can see the three dimensions of love in this chapter. The first five attributes demonstrate how love has an *inward* perspective, the second set of five demonstrate how love has an *outward* perspective, and the last set of five detail an upward perspective. So let's dissect this concept of love and see where we might be succeeding and where we might need to grow in our love.[3]

> Love must not only be articulated; it must be demonstrated.

Love is PATIENT. The word for "patient" in the text is a word used to describe not how you respond to circumstances, but to people! It's a word that describes someone with a long fuse. The King James Version translates it as "longsuffering." If you simply reverse that word you can understand what it means to have patience. Longsuffering develops in your life when you "Suffer Long." God may sometimes bring people into our lives that quite frankly rub us the wrong way. I like to refer to them as "sandpaper" people. But even sandpaper people have a purpose. They can help smooth out our rough edges. Patience is the oil that takes the friction out of life.

Love is KIND. The word for kindness means useful serving, gracious, active goodwill that not only desires the welfare of a person but actively works for it. Just as patience will suffer anything from others; kindness will give anything to others. Kindness is the insignia of a loving heart. I once read a statement that was so powerful, it really spoke to me. It said: "You can really spot a real Christian not by how he treats his king but by the way he treats his servant." In other words, the litmus test of our love is not the way I treat those above me but the way that I treat those that are beneath me. How do you treat those who cannot further your agenda? Kindness is the ability to love people more than they really deserve. One thing that God is teaching me is that people will overlook the faults of anyone who is kind. You see, kindness has a sort of boomerang effect. The kindness that you spread today will be gathered up and returned to you tomorrow. Never forget that a human's greatest emotional need is to be appreciated. Demonstrate some type of random act of kindness today.

Love does not ENVY. Love does not have an inferiority complex, always wanting what others have and never satisfied with what they have. The word for "jealous" or "envy" in this verse means "to have a strong desire." One of the hardest battles we must overcome in this life is to fight off our tendency towards jealousy. There is always someone who is potentially a little better than you are. When love sees someone who is more popular, more successful, more beautiful, or more talented—it is glad for them and is never jealous or envious. A loving person is glad for the success of others, even if their success seems to work against his own.

Love does not BRAG. Love not only doesn't have an inferiority complex but it doesn't have a superiority complex either. Love is not braggadocious. It doesn't parade its accomplishments. It doesn't call attention to itself. You see, really, bragging is the flip side of the coin with jealousy. Whereas jealousy is wanting what someone else has; bragging is an attempt to make others jealous of what we have. Jealousy puts others down; bragging builds us up.

Love is not ARROGANT. This verb literally means "puffed up" and whereas bragging about yourself deals with your actions; arrogance deals with your attitude. This is an inner attitude of exalted opinion about oneself. It's having an inflated ego, an unrealistic idea of one's own importance. It's believing your own press. It's one thing for someone to praise and compliment you, but make sure that such praise only encourages your heart rather than inflating your head. A wise man once told me, "Praise is a lot like a good perfume or cologne. It's okay to sniff it, but it's not okay to swallow it." Do you know what EGO stands for? Edging God Out. There's no room for God in a head full of ego. Egotism truly is obesity of the head and the side effect is that the bigger one's head, the smaller one's heart. Neither an egg nor an ego is any good until you break it! D. L. Moody said, "I believe firmly that the moment our hearts are emptied of pride and selfishness and ambition and everything that is contrary to God's law, the Holy Spirit will fill every corner of our hearts. But if we are full of pride and conceit and ambition and the world, there is no room for the Spirit of God. We must be emptied before we can be filled."

> Egotism truly is obesity of the head and the side effect is that the bigger one's head, the smaller one's heart.

Love does not behave RUDELY. Paul is saying that love has manners. The verb for "behaving rudely" means to behave shamefully or disgracefully. Another way to put it would be to say that "love is tactful in its expression." How do you respond to the person who accidentally cuts you off on the highway? How to you treat the waiter or waitress when they make a mistake on your food order? Love does not behave rudely. Does the way you speak to your spouse and esteem them show what value they have in your heart? It's been said that if you ever see a man open up the car door for his wife nowadays, it means that one of two things is new: either the car, or the wife!

Love does not SEEK ITS OWN. This simply means putting the needs of others before your own needs. Love makes an effort to invest in others. Always remember that someone's effort is a reflection of their interest in you. Dennis Waitley wrote a book called *Empires of the Mind*. In that book, he says that there are approximately 450,000 words in the English language. Four hundred and fifty thousand words! BUT 80% of our conversations use only 400 words. And the most commonly used words in those conversations are these: "I," "Me," "My," and "Mine." So we all tend to think of ourselves first. It's a human tendency. Thus we tend to think in terms of others meeting our needs. But true love motivates us to look first to the needs of others. Sometimes the busyness of life keeps us focused only on our needs to the point that we can't even see the needs of others. That's why we have to realize that the quality of all our relationships is inversely proportional to the pace of our lives. The faster your pace of life the less quality you will have in your relationships.

Love is not easily PROVOKED. Other translations might say, *"Love does not become easily angered."* A frequent display of one's temper betrays an absence (or at least a severe limitation) of love. The word here used for provoked means to arouse to anger. In other words, love guards itself against being easily irritated, upset, or angered by things said or done against it. Here's what we have to understand: telling our spouse that we love them is not convincing if we continually get upset and angry at every little thing they say and do. Telling our children that we love them is not convincing if we often yell at them for doing things that irritate us and interfere with our own plans. Sometimes I hear people say, "I lose my temper a lot, but it's all over in a few minutes." So is a nuclear bomb! A great deal of damage can be done in a very short time. If you are the kind of person that is easily upset, a lack of love is the cause of it and an increase of love is the only cure. The German poet Herman Hesse gave one of the most thought-provoking statements that I've ever heard. He said, "If you hate a person, you hate something in him that is part of yourself. What isn't part of ourselves doesn't disturb us. We have a tendency to react negatively to the dark shadows in others that also reside in ourselves."

Love does not take into account a WRONG SUFFERED. One man said to his buddy, "Every time my wife and I get into a fight, she get's historical." His friend said, "You mean to say she gets hysterical?" He said, "No! Historical. She dregs up everything wrong I've ever done whenever we get into an argument." I counseled a woman once who brought with her a list, several pages in length, of grievances and issues she had with her husband. As I looked at that list, I thought about this Scripture. Love doesn't take into account a wrong suffered. That phrase is a bookkeeping term that means "to calculate or reckon as when figuring an entry into a ledger." The purpose of the entry is to make a permanent record that can be consulted whenever needed. In business, this is very important, but in relationships such bookkeeping is extremely harmful. This is the same Greek word that is used in Romans 4:8 to describe God's forgiveness of us. It says, *"Blessed is the man against whom the Lord will not count his sin."* That's how the forgiveness of God works. Our sin is blotted out. It is wiped away. Nothing is ever recorded for future reference. Love forgives. It's been said that true love does not forgive and forget, but rather remembers and still forgives. But resentment is very careful to keep a good ledger of wrongs, which it reads and rereads, hoping for a chance to someday get even. John Chrysostom said that a wrong done against love is like a spark that falls into the ocean and is quenched. Love quenches wrongs rather than records them.

Love does not rejoice in UNRIGHTEOUSNESS, but rejoices in the TRUTH. The only way to be angry and not sin is to be angry at nothing but sin. One translation of Proverbs 10:10 says, *"Someone who holds back the truth will cause trouble. But the one who openly confronts works for peace."* It's important to understand that every healthy relationship is built on two legs: confronting in truth and affirming in love. If you want to have a healthy friendship, if you want to have a healthy marriage--or anything else--you must have both of these in the relationship. If you only have one, you've got a one-legged relationship, and it isn't going to stand. It will fall over at anything. If you never take the risk to speak truth in love, you will always settle for a superficial, shallow relationship. Carrie and I were experts at this early in our marriage. We repressed the truth, we hid our feelings, we ignored issues, and swept everything under the carpet trying to just maintain the status quo in our marriage. But you can only sweep things under the carpet for so long until the mound under that carpet grows so much bigger and bigger that you can't help but trip over it. To have a strong marriage, you must be able to confront in truth and affirm in love. Because the truth often does hurt, we must speak it in love, and couch it in affirmations. Who do you need to have an honest conversation with?

> If you never take the risk to speak truth in love, you will always settle for a superficial, shallow relationship.

Love BEARS all things. The last four qualities of love are all very similar. The word here for bear means "to cover or to protect." Proverbs 10:12 says, *"Hatred stirs up strife, but love covers all transgressions."* We can measure our love for a person by how quick we are to cover up their faults. Parents are known to do this. When one of their kids misbehaves at school, they tend to put the very best face on it. "Well, Junior didn't understand what he was doing" or "She didn't really mean what she said." But when someone whom we *don't like* does something, our reaction is just the opposite: "Well, that's typical of John" or "What would you expect from someone like her?" Love makes the difference. This is not to say that we should minimize or compromise, but love does not expose or broadcast the failures and wrongs of others. It covers them and protects them. That's why 1 Peter 4:8 says, *"Love covers a multitude of sins."* During Oliver Cromwell's reign as Lord protector of England a young soldier was sentenced to die. The girl he was engaged to marry pleaded with Cromwell to spare the life of her fiancé, but to no avail. The young man was to be executed when the curfew bell sounded. But that night, when the sexton repeatedly pulled the rope, the bell made no sound. They couldn't figure out why so they sent a team of men to investigate. What they found was that this young man's fiancé had climbed into the belfry and wrapped her body around the clapper so that it could not strike the bell. Her body was smashed and bruised, but she did not let go until the clapper stop swinging. She managed to climb down, bruised and bleeding, to meet those awaiting the execution. When she explained what she had done, Cromwell commuted the sentence. He was touched by a love that "bears all things."

Love BELIEVES all things. The Amplified Bible puts it this way: *"Love is ever ready to believe the best of every person."* This means that you don't pre-judge and jump to negative conclusions about a person. In other words, love is not suspicious or cynical. If a loved one is accused of something wrong, love will consider him innocent until proven guilty. What we believe about a person makes all the difference in the world. If you believe something will work out, you'll see opportunities. If you believe it won't, you'll see obstacles.

> We can measure our love for a person by how quick we are to cover up their faults.

Love HOPES all things. The Amplified says: *"Its hopes are fadeless under all circumstances."* Love refuses to take failure as being final. The rope of love's hope has no end. As long as there is life, love does not lose hope. When our hope in someone becomes weak, we know our love is becoming weak. I was reading a touching story about a dog who stayed at the airport of a large city for over five years waiting for his master to return home. Employees and others fed the dog and took care of him over those five years, but he would not leave the spot where he had last seen his master. He would not give up hope that someday they would be reunited. If a dog can have that kind of love for his master and produce that kind of hope, how much more should our love make hope last? Chrysostom said, "Heat makes all things expand. And the warmth of love will always expand a person's heart."

Love ENDURES all things. This word for endure means "to remain under the load" and it was a military term used to describe an army that was holding onto their vital position at all costs! The idea here is that love endures everything without weakening. One translation says, *"there is nothing love cannot face."* Love has an incredible resilience that enables it to maintain itself under circumstances that would crush all other commitments. When the going gets tough, love keeps going. It will not throw in the towel and give up! Do you accept people just as they are, or do you attempt to change them into a person who will be a much more manageable object of your ideal love. Consider how hard it is to change yourself and you will understand what little chance you have to change others.

Love NEVER FAILS. True love cannot fail because it shares God's nature and God's eternity. What he is saying here is, "There is never going to come a time when love ceases." When Carrie and I got married, we both put into our wedding vows: "I will never leave you, I will never forsake you, I will never divorce you." Whenever a sea captain was heading into battle, where surrender was not even to be contemplated, he would order that the "colors" be nailed to the mast. By having the flags nailed up high there was no possibility of lowering them in the heat of the battle in order to raise a flag of surrender. My friend, if right now you feel like you are in a battle for your marriage, then nail the colors to the mast. Don't lower it to raise the white flag of surrender. Nail the flag of your marriage to the post of God's will for your life and always keep your mind focused, not on how you can get *out* of your marriage, but on how you can hold your marriage together, because that is what brings glory and honor to God!

Fill in the Blank

I want to encourage you to do something. Open your Bible and read 1 Corinthians 13 prayerfully back to God. But this time, insert your own name in place of the word "love" and see how you measure up. I have to ask the Lord, can I honestly say, "Brandon is patient... Brandon is kind... Brandon keeps no record of wrongs, etc"? Keep this description of genuine love before your eyes today and ask God to give you a measure of His grace and fill in the gap where your love might be lacking.

> Consider how hard it is to change yourself and you will understand what little chance you have to change others.

Here's a question I want you to consider: How do you know God loves you? The only way you know that God loves you is because He left His world and entered your world by sending His one and only Son, Jesus. That's the only way you really know God loves you. And God wants to enter your world today if you would invite Him in to do so. Perhaps this teaching on love has magnified a feeling of emptiness or loneliness on the inside of you. I once heard a person say that sometimes loneliness is God's cry for time alone with you. Give Him that time and bask in the overwhelming love that He has for you.

And remember, in the same way that we know that God loves us because He was willing to leave His world and enter ours; the only way you can really show how much you love somebody else is for you to leave *your* world and enter into *their* world. That's what love truly looks like.

NEXT STEPS

Think through 1 Corinthians 13's aspects of what love does. What are two or three actions of love that aren't usually true about you?

What's one action you can take this week to grow your impact and influence in the lives of others?

The Needs of Men and Women

"No one pushes to go to divorce court because their spouse is meeting too many of their needs. Met needs always produce the feeling of being loved, valued, and appreciated." — Mark Gungor

When God was creating the world, there was one thing that He said was not good about His creation, the fact that Adam was alone. So He created Eve to be the "helpmeet" to Adam. The word helpmeet means "a completer." It meant she was opposite to him and therefore complementary. My wife Carrie, and I are a lot alike, but we are also very different. The healthiest marriages are those that learn to appreciate the differences. God made us different that He might make us one. Differences don't have to divide us; they can actually unite us. God made men and women not to compete with each other but to complete each other.

Neither the male or the female is "better." We're just different. I know we live in a society today where people think they can "choose their gender" but that's a biological impossibility. Every cell in a woman's body is different from a man's. Women have the XX chromosome and men have the XY

> Differences don't have to divide us; they can actually unite us.

chromosome. Gender differences are not learned behaviors. They are literally encoded into every cell of our bodies by God Himself.

Men think logically with their heads; women think emotionally with their hearts. Men tend to be more goal oriented; women tend to be more relationship oriented. God built something in man that wants to take risks; women tend to be more interested in creating security. Men want to see the big picture; women prefer to see the details. Men tend to be more insensitive; women tend to be more empathetic. I'm not talking about strengths and weaknesses here because within each quality is an inherent strength and weakness. These are just observations.

> Our differences not only bring spice to a relationship but potentially sparks as well.

You've heard the saying, "Opposites attract" and that is certainly true. You are attracted, consciously or subconsciously, to people who have opposite character qualities from you. Opposites attract from a distance; but opposites attack up close. The very thing that attracted you to your spouse, if you're not careful, could end up irritating you. Our differences not only bring spice to a relationship but potentially *sparks* as well. We are different, but the difference is the dynamic!

Most problems in marriage are usually rooted in two spiritual causes: immaturity and selfishness. In other words, problematic relationships can trace every problem to a lack of understanding towards their spouse and a mindset (either conscious or subconscious) that says "What's in it for me?" as opposed to "What's best for our relationship?"

Not surprisingly, if you were to go into a divorce court and analyze the top two reasons why people today get divorced, you'd hear of incompatibility or irreconcilabe differences. Basically, that's just legal jargon for "immaturity" and "selfishness." Leo Tolstoy said, "What counts in making a happy marriage is not so much how compatible you are but how you deal with incompatibility."

Marriage doesn't have to end this way. Scripture tells us that a man is to cleave to his wife and the two of them become one flesh. God's mathematical formula for marriage is 1+1=1. There's no possible way that you can win in a war with your spouse. The two of you are one. If you damage him or her, you don't win; you lose. Any man who is at war with his wife is at war with himself.

A great relationship is about two things: first, appreciating the similarities; and second, respecting the differences. There are some things you can do to deepen the foundation of your relationship and one of the best things you can do for your marriage is to deeply understand and dedicate yourself to meeting your spouse's greatest needs.

The Needs of Women

William Harley wrote a book that has become a staple in marriage counseling: *His Needs, Her Needs*. After many years of counseling, Harley grew to understand the unique spiritual, emotional, and mental makeup of both men and women and how they differ significantly. His book has helped strengthen the marriages of millions of people.

Now I'm hesitant to share these top needs of men and women because they are generalities. Most men are stronger than most women (that's a generality) but there are some women who can beat up a lot of men (that's an exception). So when we talk about the differences between the sexes, we're talking about generalities.

> Intimacy to a woman means "into-me-you-see."

In 1 Peter 3:7 we read, *"Likewise, husbands, live with your wives in an understanding way, showing honor to the woman as the weaker vessel, since they are heirs with you of the grace of life, so that your prayers may not be hindered."*

Scripture says that men are to live with their wives *"in an understanding way."* In Greek, that word means that you're considerate and live with your wife according to knowledge. I know in some ways, I'll never fully understand my wife. And you'll never understand your spouse but we ought to dedicate ourselves to growing in that understanding. The primary emotional needs of women is intimacy. Intimacy to a woman means "into-me-you-see." That level of intimacy can be summarized into five uniquely related needs (according to William Harley):

1. AFFECTION: *"I need you to express your feelings for me in small ways."* You married the woman you love; now love the woman you married. A husband and wife were having marital trouble so they sought a counselor for help. After about an hour of venting their problems and frustrations about each other, the counselor got up from his chair, walked over to the wife, and planted a big kiss right on her lips! The counselor looked over at her husband, who sat there staring in disbelief. He then said to the husband, "Listen to me, now. Your wife needs that at least twice a week—every week!" The husband blinked, and scratched his head. "Well," he replied, "I guess I could bring her here on Tuesdays and Thursdays." That's an example of a husband who is hopelessly out of touch. Your wife wants you to honor her and cherish her and to demonstrate that through non-sexual affection. Closeness is more than just physical; it involves a spiritual and emotional connection.

2. CONVERSATION: *"I need you to talk to me."* One of the sexiest things to a woman is a man's ability to have a real, honest conversation. The ability to hold a good conversation has almost become a lost art form these days. Men especially, need to regain the art and ability to communicate well with their wives. Here's the interesting thing about men and women in how we speak: women share; men report. Women share their heart; men report "just the facts, Ma'am, just the facts." Husbands then should not just listen to what a woman says but pay attention to what she means. When Peter said, *"Live with your wives"* in 1 Peter 3:7, that phrase literally means "to be at home with." Peter would probably say to us today, "Guys, when you come home from work, just spend time with her. Get to how how her day went. See what's on her heart and mind."

3. HONESTY AND OPENNESS: *"I need to know what's going on in your life."* Women have the ability to take in all the details. In fact, she craves details. When she asks, "How was your day?" she wants more than just "it was fine." She wants to know what happened? Who was there at that meeting? What did you talk about? Wives often ask questions to get their husbands to open up to them because they equate openness with a deep sense of love. She needs to frequently hear her husband talk about what he is thinking, feeling, and dreaming about. She needs to feel like she can share herself without the fear of being judged and criticized or having him attempt to "fix the problem." This is why praying together as a husband and wife can be such a powerful thing. It's a beautiful form of openness to each other and to God. There are two hemispheres in your brain. Men tend to be left-brain dominant which is known for logic and reason. Women use both sides of their brain but tend to be more in touch with their right-brain hemisphere which explains her communication skills. The corpus callosum, the part of your brain that joins the two hemispheres together is thicker in women which explains why women tend to have greater intuition as they are concurrently using both sides of their brain; but the downside is that women also tend to have a more difficult time separating reason from emotion.

4. FINANCIAL SUPPORT: *"I need you to provide enough for us to live comfortably."* One of the chief concerns of women is security. This can be met in a variety of ways, but one of those is through financial security. Adam's job in the Garden of Eden was to dress and keep the garden. From the beginning of time, God made the husband's responsibility to be the provider and the protector. That's not to say that a couple can't both be in the workplace. But she needs to know that he is doing everything he can to earn enough to provide security and not spend too much to cause financial stress and hardship.

5. FAMILY COMMITMENT: *"I need you to be a family person."* She needs to be assured that you are a one-woman man. She shouldn't have to worry about your level of morality when you're away on a business trip. Don't look lustfully at other women. Let her know your plans. Keep your commitments to her and your family. Be a man that can be trusted and counted on.

Needs of Men

> "Your actions not only speak louder than your words but they also speak later than your words and longer than your words."

When you read 1 Peter 3, you'll notice that Peter gives six verses in dealing with the wife's role but only one verse to her husband. That seems pretty out of balance, but you've got to realize two things. First, in this situation, it was the wife who was the believer that Peter was talking to, not the husband. Secondly, the fact that she is the one who is following after Jesus means she is the one who is bringing spiritual maturity and selflessness to the table. The point that Peter is trying to make here is simply that *actions speak louder than words*. As a matter of fact Peter says, "Your actions not only speak louder than your words but they also speak *later* than your words and *longer* than your words."

Peter is saying that when a wife has a submissive spirit towards her husband and seeks to meet his needs as a kind and loving spouse, he will be motivated to reciprocate and meet her needs (and vice-versa). Peter says in vs. 2 that the husbands, *"may be won over without words by the behavior of their wives when they see the purity and reverence of your lives."* If your husband isn't living for God, you're not going to nag him into the kingdom. So quit putting gospel tracts in his underwear. Men learn far more with their eyes than they ever will with their ears. Your husband will respond to you by the way you act towards him, not so much by what you say.

According to William Harley, men have the following top five needs (not always necessarily in this order):

1. **SEXUAL FULFILLMENT:** *"I need you to have sex with me."* Any woman who's been married for more than 10 minutes knows that this is usually a man's number one need. There was a scientific study conducted recently on what days most men like to make love to their wife. For some reason they all began with the letter "T" – Tuesdays and Thursdays, Today and Tomorrow, Taterday and Tunday. Men express love to their spouse through sexual intimacy. He not only needs the physical release but he also needs to know that his wife desires him in that way. In his mind, how you respond to him in the bedroom communicates to a great extent just how much you love him. It's sad and disappointing how the devil has played a trick on so many couples today. The enemy will try to do everything he can to bring two people together sexually before marriage; but then he does everything he can to keep them away from each other after marriage. Learn to communicate love to your husband by meeting and desiring him in the bedroom.

> The enemy will try to do everything he can to bring two people together sexually before marriage...

2. **RECREATIONAL COMPANIONSHIP:** *"I need to play and have fun together."* Men want their wives to be their best friend. In today's world, it may be easy to leave a spouse; but it's not so easy to leave your best friend. Men crave recreational companionship. I recently saw a wife out fishing with her husband, not because she enjoys fishing; but because he does and she enjoys being with him. Realize that men communicate by sharing experiences, by sharing an activity. Women share experiences by talking about them. For your husband, just sitting together and watching TV or taking part in an activity that involves the both of you can build the relationship with or without any words being spoken. Wives can use this method to connect with their husbands and that will in turn encourage him to open up to his wife.

3. **ATTRACTIVENESS:** *"I need you to look good."* This may seem shallow but it shouldn't be. Men want to be proud of the woman that they've married. We can't always change everything about our bodies, but we need to be good stewards of them and play the cards we've been dealt with. Are you doing your best to look good for your husband? This isn't exactly politically correct to talk about these days, but politically correct or not, this need doesn't go away. Every husband wants to be married to a beautiful wife and there is nothing more attractive than a woman who is beautiful in her heart, beautiful in her spirit, and beautiful in her soul.

4. **DOMESTIC SUPPORT:** *"I need you to take care of the home front."* Men need a job, a purpose in life to keep them mentally healthy, but they also need a strong wife to help them achieve that purpose. Men often identify themselves by their work and they find their self-worth in their job. And when you take the stress off of them by taking care of many of their needs at home, they not only appreciate you for it, they love you for it.

> ...but then he does everything he can to keep them away from each other after marriage.

5. **ADMIRATION:** *"I need you to be proud of me."* A man wants his wife to admire him. I feel like I can conquer the world when Carrie admires me. Others may compliment my talents and abilities, but nothing means more to me than when Carrie gives me a compliment. It's been said that the way to a man's heart is through his stomach. I disagree. The way to a man's heart is through his ego. When you compliment him and through your words convey

how much admiration you have towards him, it fills his emotional bank to overflowing. Better yet, compliment him in front of others and he will never forget it. Men get their joy out of being successful, so wives, let your husbands know where you see how they are winning.

Affair-Proof Your Marriage

Did you know that you can affair-proof your marriage by understanding the needs of your spouse and how to meet them? Here's a key thought we must never forget: It's in those unmet needs that we find our greatest temptation towards having an extra-marital affair. When those top five needs go unmet, spouses become very susceptible to an affair. Why is that? Because needs may go unmet, but they do not go away.

I know a guy who fell into an emotional and sexual affair not too long ago. When I talked to him about it, I asked what it was that led to that point. He said that a woman at work was always admiring him, complimenting him, appreciating him. This was a need that was going unmet at home. And over time, without even thinking about it, the situation added to his underlying resentment towards his wife for not meeting that need. Even though this woman (by his own admission) wasn't as attractive as his own wife, he still fell into adultery because the mistress was meeting a need that was going unmet at home.

> The grass is always the greenest where you water it.

Now allow me to clarify — I am *not* saying that having an unmet need gives you license or an excuse to have an affair. But what I am saying is that William Harley's secret to affair-proofing your marriage works. Become a student of each other's needs and selflessly work to meet them to the utmost of your ability.

You may have heard that saying, "The grass is always greener on the other side of the fence." If that's true, make your grass so green that everyone else's lawn looks brown by comparison. The grass is always the greenest where you water it. Focus your attention on meeting and nurturing your spouse's needs. Become such an incredible lover and partner that your spouse would have to be an idiot to go elsewhere! Perhaps there would be far fewer marriages in court if there were more courting in our marriages!

Marriage: No Perfect People Allowed

Here's one last caveat to our whole discussion on meeting your spouse's needs. Your husband or wife, at best, will usually only fulfill 80% of your relational needs. Unfortunately, most people focus on the 20% that's missing, which leaves them feeling unhappy and unfulfilled. Maybe we start to wonder if we wound up with the wrong person. Maybe we start looking at other couples with envy wishing we could have a marriage like they have. Sadly, many will leave their current relationship in an attempt to go out and find that missing 20% in someone else. What they find is that the "new" person will also only fulfill about 80% of their needs as well, still leaving the same amount missing. If you want to have a happy and fulfilled marriage, then put your focus on the 80% that's right, wonderful, and beautiful about your spouse. When your focus is on that 80%, I think you might be surprised how you no longer even notice the 20%.

Rick Warren said "Marriage is a lifelong course in learning to be unselfish." A perfect marriage is simply two imperfect people who refuse to give up on each other.

When engineers built the Golden Gate Bridge in San Francisco, they made it in such a way that the bridge can actually sway up to 20 feet in the middle! It's pure concrete and steel all bolted together, but there is incredible flexibility there. There are also two incredible towers and all of the cables holding on to the bridge are affixed to those two towers. What is it that keeps that bridge up? 1.) The foundation and 2.) the flexibility.

What's true for a bridge is true for a husband and wife. You need a strong foundation (love for God and love for each other) and you need flexibility (appreciation of your differences). And may each of you always remember: It takes both sides to build a bridge.

NEXT STEPS

As a man/woman, how would you prioritize those top five needs for yourself? Share that personalized list with your spouse.

Which one of your spouse's needs do you feel you're best at meeting? Which need do you not meet as consistently? Would your spouse agree with that assessment?

Do you ever find yourself focusing on the "20% that's missing" in your marriage? What might happen if you put your attention more on the 80% of things you love and appreciate?

The Art of Listening

"We think we listen, but very rarely do we listen with real understanding, true empathy. Yet listening, of this very special kind, is one of the most potent forces for change that I know." — Carl Rogers

Have you had a conversation lately where you really don't remember what the other person was saying? Do you find yourself thinking of what you're going to say next rather than actually listening? It's been said that we should speak in such a way that others love to listen to us; but also listen in such a way that others love to speak to us. God created us with two ears and one mouth for a reason: We should listen twice as much as we speak. We have a biological challenge, too: We can listen about three times faster than anyone can talk! That means we have excess capacity in our brain that will wander off and entertain itself unless we take steps to intentionally manage it.

There's so much that you can learn when you just listen. When you talk, you are only repeating what you already know. But if you listen, you may learn something new. Did you know that if you scramble the letters in "listen" it also spells "silent"? Think about that for a moment. A person full of knowledge speaks; but a person full of wisdom listens. Mark Twain said, "Wisdom is the reward you get for a lifetime of listening when you would rather have talked." A wise person knows that there is something to be learned from everyone. Every single person on this planet is a master or an expert at something that I am not.

One of the most sincere forms of respect is actually listening to what another person has to say. The first duty of love is to listen. Sometimes what people need most is just someone to hear them out. No advice. No words. Just a shoulder and an ear. Listening is one of the loudest forms of kindness.

Three Levels of Listening

One of the most foundational relationship skills we can develop in this life is the ability to listen well. We need to learn how to become active listeners who have the ability to focus completely on what what people are saying and even what they're not saying. A leader who does not listen well will create followers who will feel marginalized and eventually stop talking. Andy Stanley says, "Leaders who don't listen will eventually be surrounded by people who have nothing to say." But regardless of whether you think you're a leader or not, you need to develop these skills. At its core, being a good listener is having the ability to shut out all distractions, both internal and external. But how do we do that?

"He who answers before listening - that is his folly and shame."

Think about the person you know who is the best listener. What is it that endears you to them? What character qualities and listening skills do they possess? I have a friend who listens so intuitively and attentively that he makes you feel as if you are the most important person on the face of the planet. I've often said to myself, "I want to be more like that." I believe once you can find an example like that to hold in your mind's eye and emulate, you're well on your way toward increasing your listening skills. But the first step to know where you need to go is to find out where you are. Chances are, you tend to gravitate towards one of these three levels of listening with most people never reaching the third.

Level 1 - Passive Listening. This is the kind of listening that pays attention in short spurts, tuning in and out of the conversation. You're aware that someone is speaking, but you're really only focused on yourself and what's going on inside your own little world. So Level 1 listening involves two conversations; the one with the speaker and the one going on in the head of the listener. Try this little exercise sometime: In the margin of this book, attempt writing the "Pledge of Allegiance" while singing "Amazing Grace" simultaneously. What happens? You really can't do both, can you? You have to stop singing to write or you have to stop writing to sing. That's exactly what's happening in our minds during this level of listening. We hear partially, but we're not really listening to what's being said.

Level 2 - Self-Focused Listening. At this level, you tune into the conversation, but really only on a shallow, surface-level basis. You're not perceiving the other person's intent, or the feelings and thoughts that their words represent. While you might be engaged in the conversation, you're still processing everything from your own point of view. You might even find yourself "reading your own biography" into the situations that the other person is talking about, or you'll be formulating your own responses of what you're going to say next, while they're still talking. You might even be tempted to complete the other person's sentences in order to keep the conversation moving at a steady pace or interrupt them periodically with your own advice, solutions, and similar stories from your experience. Proverbs 18:13 really speaks to the Level 2 Listener: *"He who answers before listening - that is his folly and shame."*

The book, *Listening for Heaven's Sake* describes several typical kinds of listeners who would all be considered Level 2 Listeners. They're described not by how they listen, but by how they engage in conversations.

- ***The Interrogator:*** This is the guy who simply wants the facts. He bores in with a barrage of questions until we begin to wonder if the bright light and rubber hose are coming out next.
- ***The General:*** Here's the person who likes to give orders, directions, and commands to help you out of the "mess" you're making of your life.
- ***The Pharisee:*** This is the perennial accuser, always ready to shake a finger at you. If you have a problem, it's your own fault. No question about it!
- ***The Labeler:*** This person seems to believe that if your problem can be categorized, labeled, and pigeonholed, everything will be just fine. The Labeler loves to use the latest buzzwords and jargon.
- ***The Prophet:*** This seemingly clairvoyant advisor delights in predicting a future of gloom or doom for you (or perhaps the opposite).
- ***The Historian:*** The lovable character is filled with stories of similar experiences and just can't wait to tell you all about them.
- ***The Quick Change Artist:*** The Quick Change Artist switches the subject smoothly, using your problems as a jumping off point.
- ***Dr. Deodorant:*** This "doc" just can't understand unpleasantness in any form. Fortunately for you, he has the solution. Just cover up the discomfort with sweet smelling words.
- ***Mr. Bumper Sticker:*** Most of Mr. Bumper Sticker's counsel and insight belongs on a bumper sticker. He goes through life spreading cliches and proverbs like Johnny Appleseed spread seeds.
- ***The Robber:*** He knows exactly how you feel before taking the time to listen to you. He literally robs you of an opportunity to speak for yourself and steals emotions from you.

The lesson we can learn from a Level 2 Listener is this: How you respond to someone in a conversation is a clear indicator of your listening level. This type of listening commits one of the most basic communications faux pas out there — we do not listen to understand; we listen to reply. We have to retrain ourselves to not listen with the intent to reply, but with the intent to deeply understand.

Level 3 - Intuitive Listening. This is an all-encompassing, 360-degree active listening. You are fully aware of the entire environment surrounding the conversation, including the prompting of the Holy Spirit. This is listening with the whole heart, going beyond just the facts and words to noticing their non-verbal cues and what they're communicating (or not communicating) through body language. This type of listening is fueled by curiosity. When you are genuinely focused on the other person's life and interests you will be intensely curious, always wanting to know more, to probe deeper, and to understand them more fully. Curiosity naturally results in questions that will enable the person you're talking with to more fully explore his own life, values, dreams, and goals. Even if you're wiser and more experienced, when you are listening at this level it takes you off the pedestal of being the expert and places you on equal ground with the other person.

> We have to retrain ourselves to not listen with the intent to reply, but with the intent to deeply understand.

This is one of the reasons why life and leadership coaches get paid thousands of dollars for their skills. They've been trained to listen intuitively to their clients and to ask powerful questions based on the verbal and non-verbal feedback they're observing. That's why life coaching has grown dramatically over the last decade. It helps people to process through the challenges they're going through. Cheryl Richardson says, "People start to heal the moment they feel heard."

How to Be an Active Listener

Here are seven tips to take your listening skills to Level 3 - Intuitive Listening:

1. Focus on being interested, not interesting. Most people do just the opposite. When they go to a party or a social event, the chief concern on their mind is, "How am I coming across to this person? Am I interesting to them? Do they like me? What can I do or say that will give a good impression." Ironically, it's been found that the less you think of yourself, the more that others think of you. Your focus should be to become deeply interested in them; and by doing so, it endears you to them. Focus on eliminating those internal and external distractions. The quieter you become, the more you can hear. Rachel Naomi Remen said, "The most basic and powerful way to connect to another person is to listen. Just listen. Perhaps the most important thing we ever give each other is our attention...a loving silence often has far more power to heal and to connect than the most well-intentioned words."

2. Ask powerful questions. Over the years, I've been studying the power of questions. Here's what I've discovered: those who are the most successful in life seem to be the best at asking really good questions. The best listeners are also the best questioners. People absolutely love to be around those individuals who ask good questions because it shows that they really have a love and interest in them and who they are as a person. As a Leadership Coach, I've become a curator of questions. Here are some of my favorite conversation starters when meeting someone new:

- *Do you know what your name means?*
- *Where did you grow up?*
- *What do you do for a living?*
- *What is your dream job?*
- *What do you like to do in your spare time? Hobbies?*
- *Where do you see yourself five years from now?*
- *What's the best piece of advice you've ever received?*
- *Who do you look up to?*
- *What's your most embarrassing moment?*
- *What are you really passionate about that makes you get out of bed every morning?*
- *What is your biggest regret?*
- *What are some of your goals? Short-term/long-term?*

3. Tune in with all your attention. Nothing will make people lose respect for you quicker than if they feel like your focus is always somewhere else when they're talking to you. So next time you're in a conversation, make sure you're really engaged. Jim Elliot, a missionary who was killed in the jungles of Ecuador, once wrote this prayer in his journal: "Lord, wherever I am, help me to be all there!" I've begun to make that my prayer as well, so that when I am with another person, I value them enough to be fully present in that moment.

4. Communicate you are listening with a nod or a sound. Let people know that you're tracking with them and actually paying attention. Make sure that your body language communicates your interest in what they're saying. Maintain an open body posture (crossing your arms may communicate judgement or dominance). Avoid extreme facial expressions (regardless of whether they're favorable or disapproving), and nix the foot tapping and other fidgety habits that signal impatience.

5. Paraphrase what the speaker says. This is repeating back to the person what you heard them say. Once you've listened and absorbed, you can use validating questions to make sure you heard them correctly. Start by succinctly repeating back what you heard: *"So what I hear you saying is ___. Is that right? Let me summarize what I heard you say: ___. Did I miss or misinterpret anything?"* Then, ask clarifying questions about anything you don't 100% understand: *"When you say revenue, what specific revenue are you referring to?"* or *"Can you repeat that? I want to make sure I heard you correectly."*

> The best listeners are also the best questioners.

Harper Lee, in the book *To Kill a Mockingbird*, made a potent observation: "People generally see what they look for, and hear what they listen for." We hear others through our own filter. Paraphrasing back to them what you *think* you heard will either confirm that you heard them correctly or give them an opportunity to clarify what they said.

6. Maintain eye contact. Intuitive listening is not just hearing their words, but understanding that people communicate powerfully with just their facial expressions and eye movements. Typically, when people look up and to the right, they are either lying or tapping into their imagination. When they look up and to the left, they are remembering or recalling something, tapping into the memory part of the brain. However, be sure you get to know their natural movements, because this can be reversed for left-handed people. And this is *not* a fool proof method so never read too much into the direction of eye movements. Here are some other guidelines observed in people:

- Looking to Their Right = Auditory Thought (Remembering a song)
- Looking to Their Left = Visual Thought (Remembering the color of a dress)
- Looking Down to Their Right = Someone creating a feeling or sensory memory. (Thinking what it would be like to swim in jello.)
- Looking Down to Their Left = Someone talking to themselves.[1]

7. Turn off all distractions. It truly is impossible to listen to anyone and do anything else at the same time. It's also disrespectful when you're engaged in a conversation and look down at your phone to check a text message. Do yourself and the person you're talking to a favor and turn your phone upside down so you won't be distracted by any notifications.

The Still Small Voice

As important as it is to listen deeply to others, there's another voice that we need to learn to tune into and that's the voice of God. People often look for God to speak through big or dramatic ways, but Scripture tells us that God speaks through a "still small voice."[2] He speaks to us primarily through Scripture, but He also speaks through impressions (ideas He puts into our minds), through other people (godly friends and gifted teachers), as well as through special circumstances (open and closed doors)

> God speaks to those who take time to listen, and He listens to those who take time to pray.

Did you know that right now, in the very room where you are reading this book, there is music playing in every genre imaginable. There are reporters giving updates and used car salesmen offering commercials. All of this is happening right now in the very room in which you sit but you're totally unaware of it. Why? Because unless you have a device such as a radio or a digital TV antennae, you will not be able to pick up the frequencies of AM and FM radio or digital television programming. Those radio waves and frequencies are flowing through your room and even your own body even though you're totally unaware. If you can understand the principle of how radio and TV frequencies work, that's a good analogy of how things operate in the spiritual realm. God is always talking to us through the Holy Spirit. But unless we are tuned into His frequency, we never hear His voice. Jesus said, "My sheep hear my voice, and I know them, and they follow me." Practice the art of listening to God. Sometimes God stays silent until we're ready to listen. So right now, would you stop and pray this prayer sincerely to God: "Lord, if there's something you want me to know about You or do for you today, speak to my heart. I'm ready, willing, and open to hear from you and to do whatever it is you're telling me to do." God speaks to those who take time to listen, and He listens to those who take time to pray.

NEXT STEPS

Review the three levels of listening. Which level would you say is your "default setting?"

What needs to change in order for you to become a Level 3, Intuitive Listener?

Which one of the listening tips speaks to you the most?

How to Resolve Conflict

"Peace is not the absence of conflict. It is the ability to handle conflict by peaceful means." — Ronald Reagan

Relationships are harder nowadays because conversations become texting, arguments become phone calls, and feelings become status updates. If there was ever a time when we needed to maximize our conflict management skills, it would be today. Max Lucado says, "Conflict is inevitable, but combat is optional." The good news is that you can learn how to mitigate conflict to reduce the friction that is bound to happen in all of your closest relationships just by gaining some new tools in your toolbelt. Abraham Maslow says, "If the only tool you have is a hammer, you tend to see every problem as a nail." So we need to develop some new tools in learning how to manage conflict.

In Matthew 5:23-24, Jesus said, *"If you are offering your gift at the altar and there remember that your brother has something against you, leave your gift there in front of the altar. First go and be reconciled to your brother; then come and offer your gift."* That Scripture reminds me of two truths. First, it's far easier to remember those who have hurt us than it is for us to remember when we've hurt other people. Louis C.K. Reminds us, "When a person tells you that you hurt them, you don't get to decide that you didn't."

The second truth that Scripture teaches us is that it's up to us to take the initiative. When it comes to confrontation, one of the most important things you need to do is to make a conscious effort to initiate connection anytime you think you may be in conflict with someone. If you just think you can "sweep the issue under the rug" and not deal with it, it will only grow like a cancer and begin to rot the very binding that holds your relationship together. Don't wait for them to come to you; you need to go to them!

The Four T's of Managing Conflict

In Romans 12:18 it says, *"If possible, as long as it depends on you, live at peace with everyone."* That means that sometimes, conflict is outside of our control. But as long as it depends on you, properly respond to the conflict by tempering your behavior so you don't make the problem worse. Here are four "T's" to remember next time you find yourself in a confrontation with someone:

First, TOTAL PICTURE.
An old man entered a restaurant and walked up to a bus boy and asked, "Do you have anything that will cure hiccups?"

Without a word, the bus boy picked up a wet rag and slapped the man across the face with it.

The man, shocked by what just happened, said "Hey! Why'd you do that?"
The bus boy said, "Well, you don't have hiccups anymore, do you?"
The old man said, "I never did…I wanted something to cure my wife, she's out in the car!"

Are you the kind of person that jumps to conclusions long before the problem has been laid out before you? That's actually a pretty common occurrence for anyone who has a strong personality. But that just means that you have to be even more proactive to retrain your brain to follow a process that will keep you from hammering people with your predisposed judgments.When someone is sharing his or her point of view with you, you need to listen, ask questions, listen again, ask more questions, listen some more, and then finally respond.

> The reality is, most of us only hear about 20% of what is being spoken whenever a conflict is taking place.

The reality is, most of us only hear about 20% of what is being spoken whenever a conflict is taking place. So make sure you fight against the tendency to be preparing your own "rebuttal" while they are speaking. If you will just calm yourself down and listen empathetically to what's being said, you will be more likely to respond appropriately.

Keep in mind that a conflict is usually never about the surface issue at hand. Its underlying root is usually about a person's unsaid, untreated, and unhealed wounds. Most of the difficult people in your life are difficult because they have had a lot of difficult people in their lives. They have some baggage. And most of the time, they have no idea what they're doing.

When Jesus was being crucified, He said, "Father forgive them…"Why? "Because they don't know what they're doing."

It was the religious people who killed Jesus, and they thought they were doing the right thing. And most of the difficult people in your life think they're doing right and justified in their actions and attitudes because of the dysfunctions they've grown accustomed to along the way.

People's emotional difficulties are hard to see and that's why they're hard for others to accept. We can accept physical difficulties a lot better. Why? Because we can see them! If a person is blind, you would never say, "Oh I'm not going to be around you anymore." If a person only had one leg you wouldn't say, "Oh, I can't be at your house and watch you hobble around on one leg!" Heaven's no! You would understand them and empathize with them. But we don't treat emotional difficulties the same way we treat physical ones.

Always remember this liberating truth: By their fruits you shall know them, but by their roots you shall understand them and not judge them. That's why we need to get as much of the total picture as possible when dealing with conflict.

The second "T" is TIMING.

Did you know that most arguments actually occur right before mealtimes? The reason is your blood sugar is low, which in turn makes you a little more "moody." Because of this, you probably should avoid having tense conversations right before dinner. Knowing when to act is just as important as taking the right action. The timing of when you handle a confrontation is just as important as what you actually do and say. It seems to me the most common cause of bad timing in relationships is selfish motives. We lash out at our spouse when we're in the heat of the moment or when it's on our mind, but really that's a sign of immaturity. Think of the timing of small kids when they get upset. It's often poor because they're only thinking of themselves.

> The timing of when you handle a confrontation is just as important as what you actually do and say.

Examine your motives to be certain that they're not self-centered and then ask yourself these questions:
1. Am I ready confront? That's a pretty easy question to answer, because it's really a matter of whether or not you've done your homework.
2. Is the other person ready to hear? If you have laid a relational foundation and the two of you are not in "the heat of the battle," then the answer may be yes.

The third "T" is TONE.

People often respond to our attitudes and actions more than our words. Many petty conflicts actually turn into all-out-wars because people use the wrong tone of voice. Proverbs 15:1 says, *"A soft answer turns away wrath, but a harsh word stirs up anger."* Haven't you found that to be true? Try this experiment: The next time someone says something to you in anger, respond with gentleness and kindness. I guarantee that will tone down or soften his attitude.

When we get upset, what's the first thing we do? We raise our voices! I heard about this country boy from east Tennessee who met a group of girls from an Ivy League school. With his southern accent he asked, "Where do ya'll go to school?"
One of the girls said, "Yale."

This country boy took a deep breath and said, "WHERE DO YA'LL GO TO SCHOOL?"

Now understand, when you get into an argument, you don't need to YALE! Show some respect.

The other extreme coping mechanism that people fall into when in conflict is stonewalling or giving the other person the "silent treatment." Husbands and wives especially can be experts at this.

You can never allow any conflict in your marriage to shut off the lines of communication. When you do that, it's just like shutting oxygen off to the brain! Pouting and silence have never once solved the tension in a relationship.

I heard about a couple that had a big fight and they went into the silent pout. They didn't speak to each other for two solid weeks. Finally, one day they were driving through the countryside and there was a pasture where a bunch of mules were grazing in the field. The husband looked over at his wife and broke the silence by asking, "Relatives of yours?"

Without even a blink she said, "Yes…in-laws."

Don't fall into the passive aggressive trap of giving the person you're upset with the silent treatment. Not only will it leave the issue unresolved, it's likely to make it worse.

The fourth "T" of conflict management is TEMPERATURE.
When tempers flare, people are prone to dropping bombs when using a slingshot will do. The size of a problem often changes based on how it is handled! We don't need to make a mountain out of every mole hill. There's no need to get all bent out of shape about things that ultimately don't matter. I like how Winston Churchill put it, "You will never reach your destination if you stop and throw stones at every dog that barks." I stopped explaining myself when I realized that people only understand things from their level of perception. If they are unwilling to be open-minded enough to expand their perception, then there's not much else I can do. So you don't have to attend every argument you're invited to. Be selective in your battles for sometimes peace is better than being right.

> I stopped explaining myself when I realized that people only understand things from their level of perception.

We need to realize that if the reaction is worse than the action, the problem usually increases. But if the reaction is less than the action, the problem usually decreases.

One man said to another, "Does it bother you that your wife gets the last word." He said, "No, I'm just excited when she gets to it!"

That's why I try to follow a self-imposed guideline that I call the Reprimand Rule: "Take thirty seconds to share feelings—and then its over."

Anytime we let a little thing create a big reaction (one that lasts longer than thirty seconds) we are using a hammer to beat the other's head. I once read somewhere that 10% of conflict is due to a difference in opinion, but 90% of escalating conflict is due to the wrong tone of voice. Don't let your tone get out of hand.

We need to understand that actions are remembered long after words are forgotten. When you graduated high school, can you recall the message the commencement speaker delivered at your graduation. Probably not. But you do remember graduating. Can you recite your wedding vows from memory? Unlikely. But you do remember exchanging your wedding vows with your spouse. My point is that the way you treat people during a conflict will be a lifelong memory that will stay with them longer than the words that you choose.

Connect During the Conflict

It's been said, that nine times out of ten, an argument ends with each of the contestants more firmly convinced than ever that he is absolutely right. "A man convinced against his will is of the same opinion still." But it doesn't have to be this way. It's not only possible to connect with the person you're in a disagreement with but also help them to see your point of view and reconcile the argument.

In his book, *How to Win Friends and Influence People*, Dale Carnegie gives some tried and proven methods for dealing with conflict without arousing resentment:

STEP #1 – Begin with praise and honest appreciation. It is always easier to listen to unpleasant criticism after we have heard some praise of our good points. Beginning with praise is like the dentist who begins his work with Novocain—the patient still gets a drilling, but the Novocain is pain killing.

STEP #2 – Call attention to people's mistakes indirectly. Charles Schwab was passing through the steel mills one day when he came across some of his employee's smoking. Immediately above their heads was a sign that said, "No Smoking." Schwab didn't point to the sign and say, "Can't you read?" He walked over to the men, handed each one a cigar and said, "I'll appreciate it boys if you will smoke these on the outside." They knew that they had broken a rule and they admired him because he said nothing about it and gave them a little present to make them feel important. Simply changing one three letter word can spell the difference between failure and success in changing people without giving offense or arousing resentment. Many people start their criticism with praise followed by the word "but" and then ending it with a critical statement. For example, little Johnny brings home his report card and his parent says, "We're really proud of you Johnny for bringing your grades up this term. But if you had worked harder on your algebra, your grade would have been a lot better." Johnny might have been encouraged until he heard the word "but" and then he would have wondered if his parents were sincere when they praised him. But if you just change the word "but" to an "and," it makes all the difference in the world. "We're really proud of you, Johnny for raising your grades this report card, and by continuing those same hard-work efforts your algebra grades can be up with all the others." Why should you call attention to people's mistakes indirectly? Because (as Galileo said) "You cannot teach a man anything; you can only help him find it within himself."

> "It's us against the problem, not us against each other."

STEP #3 – Talk about your own mistakes first. It isn't quite so bad to listen to a person criticize you if they too begin humbly admitting they have made the same mistakes. You want to be careful to guard against the perception that somehow you think you're superior to them.

STEP #4 – Tell what's bothering you using "I messages." "I messages" are a tool for expressing how we feel without attacking or blaming. By starting from "I" we take responsibility for the way we perceive the problem. This is a big difference compared to "you messages" which put others on the defensive and close doors to communication. When a wife yells at her husband and says, "You've left the kitchen a mess again! Can't you ever clean up after yourself?" that's only going to escalate the conflict. Now take a look at how differently an "I message" comes across: "I'm annoyed because I thought we agreed you'd clean up the kitchen after using it. What happened?" When you make these "I" statements it's important to avoid put-downs, guilt-trips, sarcasm, or negative body language. A key thought you need to remember in conflict resolution is this, "It's us against the problem, not us against each other." "I" messages enable us to convey this.

STEP #5 – Ask questions instead of giving direct orders. I worked under a manager who always gave suggestions rather than orders. She never said, "Do this" or "Don't do that." Instead, she would say, "You might consider this..." or "Do you think that would work?" She would always give people the opportunity to do things themselves. A technique like that encourages cooperation instead of rebellion. People are most likely to accept an order if they have had a part in the decision that caused the order to be issued.

STEP #6 – Use encouragement – make the fault seem easy to correct. Carnegie says, "Tell your child, your spouse, your friend, or your employee that he or she is stupid or dumb at a certain thing, has no gift for it, and is doing it all wrong, and you have destroyed almost every incentive to try to improve. But use the opposite technique—be liberal with your encouragement, make the thing seem easy to do, let the other person know that you have faith in his ability to do it, that he has an undeveloped flair for it— and he will practice until the dawn comes in the window in order to excel."

STEP #7 -- Praise every improvement. Be "hearty in your approbation and lavish in your praise." Jess Lair said, "Praise is like sunlight to the warm human spirit; we cannot flower and grow without it. And yet, while most of us are only too ready to apply to others the cold wind of criticism, we are somehow reluctant to give our fellow the warm sunshine of praise."

How to Make a Friend Out of an Enemy

Someone has well said that the best way to defeat your enemy is to make a friend of him. According to studies, it's actually easier to turn an enemy into a friend than you realize. This phenomenon was first observed by Benjamin Franklin and was proved much later scientifically by Jeker and Landy in 1969.

> The best way to defeat your enemy is to make a friend of him.

Ben Franklin once made a claim that he could easily turn an enemy into a friend with one simple act – asking them for a favor.

That's right – not performing a favor for them but asking the person you're at odds with to do a favor for you actually changes the dynamics in your relationship entirely. This works for three reasons:

1. It's the concept of cognitive dissonance. When you ask someone for a favor, you force that person to justify their actions to themselves. They're not even consciously aware of it, but on a subconscious level they're trying to process through, "Why did I just do this for him? Why would I do something like that? What does this say about me and how I feel about him?"

2. Asking someone to perform a favor for you is a subtle form of flattery. Imagine you are asking your nemesis at the office to help you with a report. The implication isn't that you're lazy or stupid. Rather, you're recognizing their prowess and ability as a whole. You recognize that they are so skilled at what they do that you're willing to risk embarrassment and ask them for their advice. In a way, you are submitting to them and admitting that you would like their help.

3. Asking someone for a favor is just more interaction between you two, whereas there was previously zero. You likely avoid people you don't like. You start developing faulty stereotypes and perceptions about them so when you do actually interact, you realize there's more there than what you previously perceived before.

Now one key thought to remember is that if you're asking an "enemy" for a favor you want to keep in mind the three-minute rule. Ask them for a favor that wouldn't take them any longer than three minutes to do. You don't want to infringe on their time or burden them unnecessarily. This works in all areas. Asking someone to do a small favor for you makes you more likable, regardless if they like you or hate you.

Let Go of the Rope

Whether a conflict has been resolved or not, you still need to forgive and move on with your life. I can think of many people who have said or done things that have terribly hurt me in the past. Not a single one of them has asked for my forgiveness. You see, I could wake up every day, bitter towards those people, angry with them, upset with them—but I don't.

How do you get to that place where you choose to forgive? Can I just share what works for me? Maybe it will work for you as well. I just spend some time meditating on the fact of how much God has forgiven me. I focus over and over again on how much God's grace has been poured out in forgiveness over my own sin and mistakes. And when I start to stack up the list of sin after sin after sin, all of a sudden I see that God has forgiven me an incredible amount and it becomes much easier to forgive those who have sinned against me. Colossians 3:13 says, *"Bear with each other and forgive whatever grievances you may have against one another as the Lord has forgiven you."*

How do you know if you have truly forgiven someone? It's simple really.
- You no longer bring up the offense to the *person*.
- You no longer bring up the offense to *others*.
- You no longer bring up the offense to *yourself*.

We've all seen, even if only in a picture, a bell in a bell tower. These enormous bells hang up high and have a rope attached to them. To ring the bell, the rope must be pulled down a few times. After the person pulling the rope lets go, the bell will still keep swinging and ringing for a little while longer until it slows down and eventually stops.

Forgiveness is the act of letting the bell rope go. It means that you choose to no longer hold on to the offense from that person. But a lack of forgiveness is when you constantly pull the rope. Every time something triggers your memory, you mull it over in your mind and it's our constant pulling of the rope of wrongdoing that prevents us from ever getting over it.

If you choose to let go of the rope, you're still going to hear the ring of the bell for a little while longer. Those feelings of resentment and heartache may still ring in your ears temporarily. But if you just keep your hands off the rope and leave it alone, the ringing in your mind of what that person did will eventually slow down and stop.

To heal a wound, you need to stop touching it. What's true for the body, is true for the spirit as well. If you want to forgive someone, you have to let go of the rope of offense.

The fact of the matter is, every person you are close to will eventually disappoint you, hurt you, anger you, and let you down at some point. We are all human--and no matter how hard we try, we often fail. To maintain long-lasting relationships, you must be one who is able to forgive. If you are unable to forgive, you will be in bondage all of your life. Nothing will isolate you from other people like unforgiveness!

But having a conflict with someone you love and care about can actually be a tremendous opportunity for growth. Just as when a bone is broken, it is stronger in the place of its brokenness after it has healed, so a relationship can emerge much stronger once it comes out through the tunnel of tension and confrontation.

I was reminded of a line in Edwin Markham's poem "Outwitted" that really speaks to the power of love in resolving conflict:

He drew a circle that shut me out--
Heretic, a rebel a thing to flout.
But love and I had the wit to win:
We drew a circle that took him in.

NEXT STEPS

Is there someone you're currently not at peace with whom you need to go and make things right?

Write down three takeaways from today's lesson. What is it about conflict management you need to remember the most?

Is there anyone you need to forgive and "let go of the rope?"

Making and Keeping Friends

*"The older I get the more selective I am of who is in my tribe.
I would rather have four quarters than a hundred pennies."* — Unknown

Somebody once said that God gives us our relatives, but thank heaven we can choose our own friends. Friendships are so important and yet culture today seems to put a shallow priority on them at best or completely disregard their importance at worst. Yet the friends you choose will greatly determine the quality and direction of your life. Those closest to you will determine your level of success or failure.

> The friends you choose will greatly determine the quality and direction of your life.

In the 1960s, Jack Warner, who was the last of the five living Warner Brothers sold his stock in Warner Brothers for 640 million dollars. A reporter asked him, "How many friends do you have in the world?" His response is heartbreaking: "I don't have a single friend in the whole world." There's an example of a man who was very rich financially but extremely poor relationally.

Everybody wants friends. Loneliness is rampant in our society. It's the number one emotional problem. So how do we increase the quality of our friendships? The key to having great friends is being one yourself.

According to a survey, the qualities most sought after in a friend are:
- Trust
- Shared Interests
- Being there for you when you need them
- Laughing together
- Enjoying each other's company

We should be friendly to everyone, but that doesn't mean we should have everyone as a friend. Proverbs 12:26 says, *"The righteous should choose his friends carefully, for the way of the wicked leads them astray."* When you do a word study on that word choose it's the Hebrew word tur which refers to a man searching out land. What that means is the wise person always explores and evaluates prospective friendships, and selects them carefully as if he is investing in real estate.

The Book of Proverbs, has a lot to say about making and keeping friends. Here is a list of seven marks of real F.R.I.E.N.D.S.

Fight For You

Those who are your true friends are deeply committed to you. Proverbs 18:24 says, *"A man of many companions may come to ruin but there is a friend who sticks closer than a brother."*

Notice that it says "a man of many companions." Does that mean it's wrong to have a lot of friends? No. The point is we need to focus on quality, not quantity when it comes to having friends. You can't be committed to everybody.

> A friendship should add great things to your life; but it will also cost you something: time, energy, and commitment.

A friendship should add great things to your life; but it will also cost you something: time, energy, and commitment. That's really the reason why many have no friends. They're not willing to make that kind of investment. I believe there are two major hindrances to being, having, and developing friendships: *time and self-centeredness.* The gravitational pull of human nature is toward self, not toward others. Sometimes people say "I don't have time to develop any strong, close relationships with others." Then quite frankly, you're out of the will of God. God wants you to have friendships that will encourage you spiritually and in all the other Essentials of Life.

One of the disgraceful marks about American culture today is that people do not want to make a commitment to anything or to anyone. This is why many people never join churches, won't take ministry responsibilities in a church, live together before they are married, and divorce one another over a small rift. We live in a society where commitment is out, and convenience is in.

In Bible times, people took their best friends seriously! They would enter into covenants with each other. That "covenant" meant they made an agreement that they would be true and loyal friends the rest of their lives. (See the example of David and Jonathan in 1 Samuel 20.)

Sometimes people will say, "Well, so-and-so was criticizing my friend, but I'm not going to get involved. I'm just not going to take sides." No, a real friend takes your side. They stand with you through thick and thin. They are consistent, even when it's inconvenient, even when you don't deserve it, and even when it comes at a great personal cost to them. A real friend fights for you.

Chuck Swindoll says that in the military, if they were on the front lines of the battle field, they were always taught to dig a hole that was big enough for two. You need someone there alongside you when you fight those battles.

Reflect You

The Bible says in Proverbs 27:19 (Living Bible) *"A mirror reflects a man's face. But what he is really like is shown by the friends he chooses."* The kind of friends you choose says a lot about the kind of person you are; it's like looking in a mirror. Do you know why it's so important for you to choose the right kind of friends? Because you will become like those you spend the most time with.

> The kind of friends you choose says a lot about the kind of person you are; it's like looking in a mirror.

Author and speaker, Charlie Jones, said "The difference between who you are today and who you will be in five years will be the people you spend time with and the books you read."

Jim Rohn says, "You are the average of the five people you spend the most time with." Think about who your "fave five" are? You show me your friends, and I will show you your future.

Think of yourself as a magnet. If you take a magnet and pass it over the top of some metal shavings, those shavings will jump up and cling to the magnet. The magnet doesn't even have to physically touch the metal shavings. It just has to be in close proximity to them. In the same way, you and I are like a magnet and we will attract to our own character and personality the traits and qualities of those we spend the most time with. That's why 1 Corinthians 15:33 says, *"Bad company corrupts good character."*

Warren Buffett says, "It is better to hang out with people better than you. Pick out associates whose behavior is better than yours and you will drift in that direction."

There are four kinds of people in your life: people who add, subtract, divide, or multiply. Every relationship will affect you in some way — either for good or for bad. Those who do not increase you, inevitably will decrease you. Each relationship nurtures a strength or a weakness within you. So when choosing friends, always remember the Reciprocity Rule of Human Behavior: Over time, people come to share, reciprocally, similar attitudes toward each other.

Intimate with You

One of the best definitions of friendship I've ever come across is this one: Friendship is a relationship where I can be transparent and open, without fear.

To maintain a friendship, you must be honest and transparent. Genuine friendship is built on trust. And trust is built on openness, honesty, transparency, and vulnerability.

Life is too short to go through it without vulnerability. If a friendship is when someone has access to the information that is you, then a best friendship is when you hand over the key to the vault. That is, you let the person know you at the deepest and most vulnerable level.

You invite them in to know your dreams, your vision for life, your core values, your hurts, your secrets, your sin struggles, your heartaches. Those are not easy things to let others in on. And it's risky. But they are essential for having close friends. When you hand over the keys to the vault, you are saying, in essence: I am entrusting you with myself.

The best friendships are those that deepen that attachment through mutual vulnerability. In other words, both parties are vulnerable and open. This is important because, without vulnerability one person becomes the counselor and the other person becomes the counselee, which is not the true nature of friendship. Friendship is always a two-way street of both give and take.

So you take the initiative to look for ways to build vulnerability into the relationship. Put all your cards on the table, face up. Ideally, your best friend knows all your flaws and wounds. The more a person knows your real self at a deep level, the more whole you become.

This is why Scripture teaches us to *"Confess your sins to each other, and pray for each other so that you may be healed."* (James 5:16). As long as our secret sin struggles remain in the dark, they still retain power over us. But once they are brought to the light, that sin begins to lose its grip. This is really the root of sexual addiction especially since it flows mostly from loneliness, powerlessness, and past hurt. Your own healing from your own baggage will be greatly accelerated by having close friends you risk being vulnerable with.

Encourage You

I can tell a lot about a person by what they choose to see in me. True friends are constantly looking for ways to encourage you. Paul said something pretty striking in 2 Corinthians 6:12. He said, *"We are not withholding our affection from you, but you are withholding yours from us."* I think all of us can relate. We've all been there where a friendship feels like it's a one-way street. A friendship that is only one way is really no friendship at all.

There are two kinds of relationships you can have: ones that replenish you or ones that *deplenish* you. In a friendship that involves no sacrifice or initiative on your part, you are not replenishing your friend but deplenishing him. Remember this important truth: A friendship is only as strong as the neediest friend. If you're always helping me, but I do not help you, in time you will grow weary of me! But when you help me and allow me to help you, we strengthen one another and the relationship grows healthier and stronger as a result.

> There are two kinds of relationships you can have: ones that replenish you or ones that deplenish you.

It's also important that you listen carefully to how a person speaks about other people to you. This is how they will speak about you to other people. Anyone who is a gossip to you will likewise be a gossip about you. Don't invest yourself in a friendship like that. Find better friends. People with purpose, goals, and vision have no time for drama. They invest their energy in creativity and focus on living a positive life.

After spending time researching this topic, I've come to the conclusion that at the DNA level, a friendship must have three elements: knowing, liking, and presence. They may seem simple, but they're the three components that are universal in any relationship:

1. Knowing means you have objective information about this person. You know facts about them. Where they live. Their hobbies. Their faith. Their likes and dislikes.

2. Liking means you want to spend time with each other. You're drawn to each other's presence. When life happens, for either good or bad, you want them to know about it, and you want to know about their life as well.

3. Presence. Friends spend time together—plain and simple. This is how knowing and liking actually happen. You've got to actually hang out on a regular basis. It may be a phone call, a lunch, an evening, a bike ride, a vacation. The more time together between two good friends, the better the relationship.

A lot of times, (men especially) will say that their spouse is their best friend and that's the way it should be. However, one of the best things you can do to make your marriage greater is for each of you to have best friends. This is not just a positive suggestion; it is a necessity for several reasons. Your spouse can't meet every emotional need that you have, and you can't meet his or hers. We weren't designed to have just one person meet all of our relational needs. You don't dump the entire truckload of hay on one horse. God designed us to be in community.

> Some people aren't loyal to you; they're loyal to their need of you. Once their needs change, so does their loyalty.

So look for ways to encourage your friends. One of the greatest joys in my life is the "No Purpose Phone Call." It's when one of my friends calls me during the day for just a few minutes, just to ask what's going on. There's no agenda, no project, no push. That "No Purpose Phone Call" is what gives me a boost – kind of like an afternoon cup of coffee. It's amazing the good that happens when you talk to someone you truly and simply like. Proverbs 19:22 says *"Friendliness bears fruit for a man."* Encouraging and enriching the lives of others leaves you feeling encouraged and enriched as well.

Need You

When I say that genuine friends "need you" I'm not talking about being a codependent, needy person. But genuine friends place you as a priority in their life. Proverbs 4:23 tells us that we are to guard our hearts and to make sure that anyone we let into our life really deserves to have a place there to begin with.

One guy said, "I don't have time for part-time people in my life." Some people aren't loyal to you; they're loyal to their need of you. Once their needs change, so does their loyalty. It's been said that time decides who you meet in life, your heart decides who you want in your life, and your behavior decides who stays in your life. Make time for those who make time for you. One recent survey showed that when it comes to relationships, 85% of people don't want perfection, they just want effort.

Every person is like a Lego block. You only have so many points of connection until you're maxed out. Robin Dunbar, a leading expert in social networks, did extensive study on how many "friends" you can have and he came up with a formula known as "Dunbar's Number." That number is 150!

According to his research, he identified that 150 is the maximum limit of the number of people we can have meaningful relationships with at any one time. That breaks down into four categories:

Best friends or intimate friends — This can be three to five maximum. This would obviously include your spouse or romantic relationship (boyfriend, girlfriend). These are your BFF's. The group that is within your inner circle. These are the people that you have regular contact with, a deep commitment to developing one another, and with whom you feel the freedom to be completely open and vulnerable. Evidently, God has so wired up our brains to where we only have space for three to five meaningful relationships in that inner-circle.

Good friends – You have relational space for up to fifteen good friends but this is including the five intimate friends we've already talked about. These are people you would consider to be your "good friends." You may share life goals with these people and you have the freedom of asking personal questions.

Close friends – You can have up to thirty-five close friends (or fifty total if you include the previous two categories). With your close friends, you have semi-regular contact, some common interests, and the ability to ask questions about their life.

Acquaintance friends – This number is all encompassing and makes up for the remainder to total 150 in all. These are the folks that you have infrequent contact with in life, shallow interaction, and mostly superficial connections.

Dunbar explains that these layers are the result of the time we invest with people.
- We spend 40% of our time with our closest three to five people.
- The next ten get 20% of our time.
- The remaining 135 get the balance of our time.
- After 150 people, we have almost nothing left to give.[1]

I have met thousands of people but one real friend is worth a thousand acquaintances. I read somewhere that an acquaintance is someone you chat with about politics, casual friends are people you argue with about politics, but best friends don't talk about politics because they have more important things to talk about in life.

Can you be popular and not have any close friends? Sure. Your social life can prevent you from having any deep relationships. You're so busy impressing everybody on a superficial level that you don't know anybody in depth. You need to be committed.

Proverbs says, *"Some friendships don't last, but some friendships are more loyal than brothers."*[2] Loyal means you're committed. They need you and you need them. How many committed friends do you have? More importantly: Who are you committed to? Who knows that you are committed to them?

Robin Dunbar also confirmed through his research something that you've probably known for a long time. He studied what strengthens relationships and what prevents friendships from decaying.
- For WOMEN – Talking keeps friendships from decaying. (No surprise there).
- For MEN – Doing stuff together is what keeps friendships from decaying. (Hunting, fishing, sports, gym, hobbies, etc.)

Like anything in life, the more focus and energy you put into your friendships, the more you'll see their potential and value. The less focus and energy you exert, the less good you will receive, and over time, that friendship will deteriorate.

So you can be proactive and take initiative to be intentional about improving your friendships, or you can be passive and go with the flow and let things happen and lose that relationship. Friendships will either improve or diminish, depending on how proactive you are.

> Inconsistency and a lack of intentionality is what destroys friendships.

Inconsistency and a lack of intentionality is what destroys friendships. Proverbs 17:17 tells us, *"A friend loves at all times, and a brother is born for adversity."* Notice that it says, *"all times."* A friend can be counted on to be dependable. A friend is in your corner when they see you're cornered. A friend walks in when everybody else is walking out. They stand with you through thick and thin.

Develop You

Ike Reighard says that there are four types of friends that every person needs:

The Developer. Your best friend will always be the person who brings out the very best in you. According to Billy Graham, he wouldn't have made it as an evangelist if he had to minister alone. When he was first getting started in his ministry, Billy met his staff and best friends: Cliff Barrows, George Beverly Shea, and Grady Wilson. These three men protected him, strengthened him, counseled him with their wisdom, and corrected him when he needed it. He is convinced that without these friends he would have burned out within a few years after his first groundbreaking crusade in 1949[5]. Developer friends will bring the gift of encouragement to your life and bring out the very best in you

The Designer. This is someone who is a friend to you in a mentor-type capacity. We tend to think of a mentor as a personal, hands-on coach. Jesus was a master mentor. He ministered to thousands, trained hundreds, equipped twelve, and had an intimate friendship with three men (Peter, James, and John). The designer mentors us in any area where we need a model to follow and an example to learn by.

The Disturber. We need friends who will help us shake up our status quo and call out the greatness that is on the inside of each of us. Disturbers ask us difficult questions, forcing us to take a closer look at motivations and ambitions. They know when we're retreating back into our comfort zones and they call us out to greater effectiveness. God uses disturbers in our lives to become the object of greater force that breaks inertia and propels us to greater achievement.

The Discerner. In a lifetime of relationships, perhaps only a handful of people are willing to play this vital role because it requires mutual vulnerability. The Discerner type of friend makes a great accountability partner as they're able to bring the gift of spiritual insight into our lives. They know how to speak the truth in love. They know how to exhort and rebuke, seeking to keep their friend on the right track.

Straightforward with You

A true friend will level with you. He or she will shoot straight with you. They'll tell you the truth, even when it's painful. This is very important because all of us have blind spots. We need people who can tell us where we're blowing it! In life, you want a friend that is both like a mirror and a shadow; a mirror doesn't lie and a shadow never leaves.

> In life, you want a friend that is both like a mirror and a shadow; a mirror doesn't lie and a shadow never leaves.

Proverbs 27:6 reads, *"The wounds of a friend are trustworthy, but the kisses of an enemy are excessive."* The sad thing is, most of us never have a friend at that level and that's why we don't grow spiritually. We don't have anybody who says, "I care enough to tell you, you're blowing it! You're heading down the wrong track." Have you ever given anyone in your life the freedom to speak into you in that way?

Proverbs 24:26, *"An honest answer is the sign of a true friendship."* Friends are candid. They don't keep secrets. Even when it's painful they tell you the truth.

When it comes to being straightforward with your friends, though, make sure you abide by these three rules:
1. You compliment in public but you correct in private. Don't ever offer a constructive word of criticism when someone else is around to hear it. That's embarrassing and you friend will resent you for it if you do.
2. You correct when people are up not when they are down. When your friend is in a good place, he can handle a gentle rebuke. But you never kick him when he is down. Correct when they're up and comfort when they're down.
3. You never correct a person until you've proven that you're open to correction. Never rebuke your friend until you've proven that you're open to rebuke from them about an area in your life where you have a blind spot, a need. You have to earn the right to speak into someone's life in this way.

If you would like to measure a relationship to determine whether or not it really qualifies as a friendship, here are the two questions you should ask of the other person:
1. Can I trust him enough to be totally honest with me?
2. Can I trust him enough to be totally honest with him?

Only a true friendship expects and can survive mutual honesty. Yet 95% of people replied in a recent survey that honesty was the number one thing they wanted in a friendship.

So just to review, how do you make and keep good F.R.I.E.N.D.S.? Remember that a true friend is someone who will...
Fight for you
Reflect you
Intimate with you
Encourage you
Need you
Develop you
Straightforward with you

If you were another person would you like to be a friend of yours? I want to just quickly say that to have friends, you must take the initiative to make friends. Proverbs 18:24 truly is the cardinal rule of friendship: *"A man that has friends must show himself friendly."* The Bible teaches very clearly that the way to have good friends is this: The type of friend I am is the type of friend I will attract. Don't be passive--be active, even aggressive in reaching out to people and befriending them. Don't wait for someone to come to you--you take the responsibility, the initiative, to go to them. Friendly people never have a shortage of friends!

NEXT STEPS

Who would you consider your top three to five friends in your inner circle?

How would you rate your practice of investing in those individuals?

What are three things you need to do different in order to increase the quality of your friendships?

The Science of Likability

"All things being equal, the likable person wins. But all things not being equal, the likable person still wins." – John Maxwell

John D. Rockefeller was the first billionaire in the history of the world. At one time, the company he started, Standard Oil Company, controlled and marketed 90% of the oil produced in America. Today we have Exxon, Mobil, Amoco, and Chevron, because of this man's vision and ingenuity. For the vast majority of his life, he was by far the richest man in the world. Even today, the name Rockefeller is associated with wealth. Yet he made this incredible statement: "I will pay more for the ability to deal with people than any other ability under the sun."

John D. Rockefeller said the most important abilities that anyone can possess to achieve success are people skills. According to a report by the American Management Association, an overwhelming majority of the 200 managers who participated in a survey agreed that the most important single skill of an executive is the ability to get along with people. They rated this ability as being more vital than intelligence, decisiveness, knowledge, or job skills.

When I teach on this topic, I often ask people to describe the best and worst leaders they have ever worked for. People inevitably ignore innate characteristics such as intelligence, extroversion, attractiveness, and so on, focusing instead on qualities that are completely under the leader's control: approachability, humility, and positivity. These words, and others like them, describe leaders who possess emotional intelligence. TalentSmart research data from more than a million people shows that leaders who possess these qualities aren't just highly likable but outperform others by a large margin. Becoming a more likable individual is completely under your control, and it's a matter of emotional intelligence (EQ). Unlike innate, fixed characteristics, such as your intelligence (IQ), EQ is a flexible skill that you can improve with just a little effort.

Why Is Likability so Important?

At least two major reasons make likability critical:

1. It is the precursor to all relationships; and relationships are the precursor to success in any area of your life. We do business with people we know, like, and trust. If people don't like you, they won't buy from you. If you sell something someone else sells, why should a customer buy it from you rather than them? Increasing your likability is one of the best ways to separate yourself from the herd.

2. The fastest way to influence others is by being likable. This is not to say that being likable is more important than other values, but when we decide to show a genuine interest in other people, they tend to be interested in us. So likability can become the gateway to influence.

W. Clement Stone said "Little hinges swing big doors." You may be doing a lot of big things right, but there are these little hinges that swing big doors and make all the difference. Here are a few of the "Laws of Likability."

The Law of First Impressions

Unfortunately, first impressions–however unreliable–really are lasting impressions. To win people over, work hard to make a strong, positive first impression with everyone you meet.

> Becoming a more likable individual is completely under your control.

It's important to realize that there are really three aspects to how we present ourselves to others: verbal (the actual words you use), vocal (tone of voice), and visual (body language and facial expressions). These make up the total picture of how we communicate with others. In his book *Silent Messages*, psychologist Albert Mehrabian contends that "total liking" equals 7% verbal liking (what we actually say), 38% vocal liking (how we use our voice in saying it), and 55% facial liking (not your attractiveness but how you smile and how animated you are when you speak). So here are a few things you should pay attention to in order to beef up your first impression:

Eye contact. The eye is truly the window to the soul. When you make eye contact with people and hold it, you not only come across as more likable but also as more confident, competent, and intelligent.

A smiling face. It takes only fourten muscles to smile but it takes seventy-two muscles to frown (no wonder some people feel worn out). The expression you wear on your face is more important than the clothes you wear on your back. There was a department store manager that was asked what he was looking for when hiring somebody. He said, "I would rather hire a sales clerk who had never even finished grade school but yet had a pleasant smile, rather than hire someone with a PhD who had a somber face." In Job 29:24 it says, *"When I smiled at them...the light of my face was precious to them."* Your smile brightens the lives of all who see it.

> Research shows that people decide whether or not they like you within seconds of meeting you.

A firm handshake. Avoid the "dead fish" handshake at all costs. Research shows that people decide whether or not they like you within seconds of meeting you. A firm handshake communicates enthusiasm and competence as well. When I met my father-in-law for the first time, there was something that he said impressed him about me. He said jokingly, "If you didn't have a firm handshake, I'm not so sure I could have let you marry my daughter." I'm glad my own dad taught me the importance of a firm handshake.

Call people by their name. Strangers are just that, strange, but a friend is known. We're admonished in 3 John 14 to *"greet the friends by name."* Why? Because a person's name is to them the sweetest and most important sound in any language. In college, I had two friends in my dorm. One was from Nigeria and everyone called him "Dammy"— but I learned to call him by his full name Adedamoela Onafowokan. Another friend was from Russia – Artom Anatolovich Mirskov. Both of those guys made repeated comments on how impactful it was when someone actually took the time to learn, and pronounce properly, their name. Remember the sitcom *Cheers? "Where everybody knows your name, and they're always glad you came. You wanna be where you can see, our troubles are all the same. You wanna be where everybody knows your name."* People gravitate toward those who remember and call them by their name. It's a sign of respect and thoughtfulness.

A genuine compliment. If you really want to make a great first impression, practice the "thirty-second rule" of speaking something positive about a person within the first thirty seconds of meeting them. It might be what they're wearing, their hair, the uniqueness of their name, etc. Always remember that relationships grow fast and strong in an atmosphere of affirmation. If you see something beautiful in someone, speak it.

The Law of Curiosity

One of the best selling books of all time was written by a man named Dale Carnegie: *How to Win Friends and Influence People.* In that book, he says, "You can make more friends in two months by becoming interested in other people than you can in two years by trying to get other people interested in you."

The best conversationalists have this cadence going on where they ask you a question, allowing you to give an answer. Then they repeat the process. If you want to be well-liked by others, learn the skill and art of asking good questions. People will love to be around you because it shows that you really have an interest in them and who they are as a person.

Have you ever left a conversation that was totally one-sided? You probably left thinking, "Wow, that entire conversation was all about him!" How did that make you feel? I call that a lack of conversational generosity. We hate it when others can't stop talking about all of their own thoughts and ideas, but we're blind to how often we do this ourselves.

The author of *The Jungle Book*, Rudyard Kipling said,
> I keep six honest serving men.
> They taught me all I knew;
> Their names are What and Why and When,
> and How and Where and Who.

He's talking about the power of asking questions.

Proverbs 20:5 says, *"The purpose in a man's heart is like deep water, but a man of understanding will draw it out."* Think of the heart of every person you meet like a deep well. Good questions invite people to open up about themselves and divulge their thoughts and feelings on a wide variety of topics.

> If you want to make the maximum impact, become genuinely interested in other people.

Are you genuinely curious about people Friendships develop from open exchanges of interest. When you initiate a conversation, put the entire focus on the other person. People love to talk about themselves and like those who listen to them do it.

Many years ago, the New York Telephone Company made a detailed study of phone conversations to find out which word was most frequently used. What would be your guess? It's none other than the personal pronoun "I," which was used 4,000 times in 500 telephone conversations. That suggests we should talk to others about their favorite topic: themselves.

If you want to make the maximum impact, become genuinely interested in other people. Remember that people you talk to are just as consumed with what is going on in their lives as you are consumed with your own life.

The Law of Energy

When it comes to your relationships, you are like an elevator. You will either lift people up or take people down. We always tend to gravitate towards people who make us feel good and we're repelled from people who don't.

Whether you realize it or not, you emit positive or negative energy, and other people receive it. If you exude positive energy, which many people describe as "good vibrations," you will affect others in an upbeat way. You will make other people feel energized and buoyant. Of course, your positive energy must be totally authentic.

To find out what kind of energy you emit, ask at least five people from different areas of your life to comment. Some useful questions include "How would you describe my mood?" or "How would you describe my personality?"

Psychologists once asked a group of college students to jot down the initials of the people they disliked. Some of the students taking the test could only think of one person. Others listed as many as fourteen. The irony that came out of this bit of research was this: those who disliked the largest number of people were themselves the most widely disliked. You will find that the more likeable you are the more likely you are to like other people and to be liked by them.

This illustrates the principle that who we are determines how we see others. Not too long ago, I went out to lunch with a pastor. As we ate he began to talk about all the people in his congregation. He had a problem with this ding-a-ling deacon and that ding-a-ling choir member. I'm thought to myself, "How can you lead people when you don't like or respect them?" He didn't last long in that church and we should not be surprised.

Ephesians 4:29 give us this word of advice: *"Do not let any unwholesome talk come out of your mouths, but only what is helpful for building others up according to their needs, that it may benefit those who listen."* Are your words, your countenance, your energy level building people up or are you taking them down?

A traveler coming through a small town asked an old man seated by the road, "what are the people like in this town?"

The man asked, "Well, what are the people like where you came from?"

"Horrible" the traveler said, "They're mean, untrustworthy, detestable in all respects."

"Ah, well, you'll find them to be the same in this town too.

Scarcely had the first traveler gone on his way when another stopped to ask about the town he was going into.

The Old Man said, "Well what are people like in the town you came from?"

He said, "Oh they were fine people: honest, industrious, and generous to a fault...I was sorry to leave."

The Old Man responded, "That's exactly the kind of people you'll find here."

The way that people see others is a reflection of themselves. If I am a trusting person, I will see others as trustworthy. If I am a critical person, I will see others as critical. If I am a caring person, I will see others as compassionate.

Another important thought to consider is that we assign people the characteristics that they make us feel when we are around them. If someone makes you feel angry when you are around them, you think they are an angry person and a jerk. If someone makes you feel insignificant when you are around them, you think that person is a loser and you despise them. But if you make me feel confident and strong when I'm around you, I think *you* are a confident and strong person. If you make me feel like a million bucks when I'm around you, then I think you are priceless.

The Law of Similarity

People are most comfortable with those they resemble. Something that allows you to make a bond immediately is the discovery of similarity. When a person discovers that they have something in common with you, they automatically feel close to you.

You do this in two ways:

1. You can search for similarities. President Teddy Roosevelt was known for doing this. If he knew he was going to meet with someone the following day, he would find out what their interests were and he would study up on their interests the night before he met them. Today, this is easy since mostly everyone is on social media such as Facebook, Instagram, or LinkedIn. You can simply scroll through their page and discover commonalities with other people you want to get to know. We search for similarities in other people instinctively. When you meet someone new what are some of the first questions you ask them? Where are you from? Where do you live? Where do you work? Where did you go to school? Why do we do this? Because we instinctively seek out similarities to establish common ground. In 1971, Donn Byrne scientifically proved the value of this effort. He found that we are more drawn and attracted to people who show greater degrees of similarity to us. The more similarity, the more attraction. We like people who are similar to us in background, opinion, and attitude.

2. You can create similarities. Did you know that you can not only search for similarities, but you can actually create them? The way you do this, thereby increasing your likability factor, is by mimicking their body language, tone of voice, rate of speech, and overall manner of appearance. This technique is called mirroring and it's been shown to produce feelings of positivity. If someone leans forward while speaking to you, do the same when it is your turn to speak. Remember to handle mirroring intelligently, subtly, and appropriately.

The Law of Giving

A terrific way to increase your likability is to give people something of value. I'm not necessarily talking about a monetary gift. It could be a card or text of encouragement or just providing emotional support to someone who's going through a critical juncture in their life.

Scripture teaches us that when we give we also receive (Luke 6:38). That's the traditional quid pro quo. But likability champions don't focus on what they might get when they give to others. Instead, they simply give with joy. This is not the natural human tendency. The majority of people only care about others to the extent that this person is needed in their life.

Let's face it--because we're born with a sinful nature, we are selfish, self-centered, and self-focused by default. Have you ever seen a baby take a swig from their bottle and the pass it to a friend to see if she'd want some too? Do toddlers love to share their toys or do they want *all* of the toys to keep to themselves? Because this is our natural inclination, it takes intentional effort to go outside of ourselves and to *"look to the interests of others"* (Philippians 2:4). Arel Moodie says that the number one key to increasing your likability is to make people feel special. Think of the people you believe are the most likable in your life, the people that everyone loves to be around.

Now ask yourself, how do you feel when you are around them? How do you think other people feel when they are around this person? They feel special. The most likable people you know have this effect on others; but the good news for you is that this is learned behavior. You can do it too.

So here are some suggestions of things you can do to give to others. This things don't cost anything but show those people how much you value them.

- You can pass along a blog post or an article about subjects of interest to them.
- Offer helpful advice or provide special favors.
- If someone is in sales, send them a potential lead or refer him/her to someone who may want to buy their product or service. Look for ways to make valuable introductions for others.
- Sending clients an email just to see how things are going builds your likability because it shows you care. If you do this only once a day during your work week, you'd have 260 people who like you more by the end of a year. Please, do not end the touching-base email with, "If you ever need more widgets, give me a call" or anything similar. They already know what you sell. At the very least, what you do is probably in your email signature. Your goal should be only to give.
- Play "phonebook roulette" by randomly swiping through your contacts and reach out to someone you haven't spoken to in a while. Just send them a text that says, "Hi NAME, I was just thinking about you and wanted to let you know I really appreciate just having you as a friend. You make the world a little bit more awesome. I just wanted to check in on you and see how you were doing." Send that message to however many people God lays on your heart. It's that simple. You're not expecting anything back from them.
- If you find out that someone has a particular interest or hobby, you can find a small gift on Amazon or a cool YouTube video and just send it to them. Just say, "Hey NAME, I remember how much you loved X and I just happened to come across this cool Y and had to share it with you.
- The bottom line is: When you go out of your way to be a giver and make people feel special — *your likability factor will soar!*

Not Everyone Will Like You

You won't be the cup of tea for everyone you meet and you must learn to accept that. The Pareto Principle, also known as the 80/20 rule, was proposed by Vilfredo Pareto, an Italian economist who noticed that statistics rarely broke down into even 50/50 dynamics. Instead, they more often broke down into 80/20 categories. For example: 80% of your company's profit is coming from 20% of its products.

How does this apply to our topic of likability? Your personality isn't going to connect with everybody. Your work isn't going to please everybody either. If you write a bad song, give a bad sermon or write a bad book, you're likely going to get a lot more than 20% of people not liking you. But just know, even if you're perfect and you "hit it out of the park," there will still be 20% of the population noticing your flaws.

> When you go out of your way to be a giver and make people feel special — your likability factor will soar!

You can create the most beautiful work in the world and one in five people won't like it. Just go to Amazon and read the reviews of *Grapes of Wrath*. How could anybody not honor that accomplishment? Turns out exactly 20% didn't think it was a five-star book, while 80% thought it was great.

What happens with most people is that we end up listening to the 20% and we end up living for them in order to gain their approval. It's just never going to happen, so why waste your time? You likely still have 80% of people who are ready and willing to move with you.

> People need hope now more than ever. Every person you meet has some form or type of insecurity.

We can get ourselves into trouble when we seek to win the approval of others. That's why Paul said, *"Am I now trying to win the approval of human beings, or of God? Or am I trying to please people? If I were still trying to please people, I would not be a servant of Christ."*

Our goal should never be to earn people's approval but to influence them for good. Make it your mission to never let a day go by that you don't give a word of encouragement, compliment, or act of kindness toward someone else. People need hope now more than ever. Every person you meet has some form or type of insecurity. So view every person you meet as if they have the words "Encourage Me" stamped to their foreheads.

When it comes to relationships, nothing is more basic or vital than likability. The way likability works could not be more straightforward: Give and you receive. When you get right down to it, likability is pure common sense. Give people reasons to like you and they will; don't and they won't.[1]

NEXT STEPS

What are three aspects of likability that you feel like you excel in?

What are three aspects of likabililty that you can begin to improve in?

Working Your Networking

"Networking is not about hunting. It is about farming. It's about cultivating relationships. Don't engage in 'premature solicitation.' You'll be a better networker if you remember that." — Dr. Ivan Misner

If you've ever been to Redwood National Park in California, you know how enormous those trees can be. They are actually the largest living things on earth. Some of those trees are 300 feet tall and more than 2,500 years old! But you will never see just one redwood tree all by itself because they are unlike any other tree. A palm tree, for example, may grow to be thirty feet tall with a tap root extending thirty feet deep into the ground. But for the giant redwood, for every foot in height, the roots go out horizontally three feet. Then each tree's root system interlocks and intertwines with the root systems of the other trees, resulting in one massive network. The reason those trees can go so high is because of the strength of their network.

What's true for a redwood is true for you. You need to intertwine and interlock your life with others if you ever want to reach new heights. There's an African proverb that states: "If you want to go fast, go alone. If you want to go far, go with others."

The business community describes this concept as *networking*. I used to hate the concept of networking with others in my field. There was something about it that just seemed so

> *"If you want to go fast, go alone. If you want to go far, go with others."*

presumptuous and uncomfortable to me. All that smarmy schmoozing seemed like nothing more than a business card collection contest. I never liked the idea of wanting to promote myself and honestly I never felt like anyone would really care to know what I do for a living. The whole thing seemed rather pointless to me. But then I realized how flawed my perception of networking really was. It turns out, successful networking is really the complete opposite of what I thought that it was. Networking is not about collecting contacts; networking is about planting relationships. True networking occurs when there's an understanding that everyone in the room has equal value. In its purest form, it's about people enjoying other people, communicating passions, and connecting with others who share those passions.

Building the right network can open new doors to future success in your life and business. Professional networking today is crucial to your success. Nearly all of today's artists, songwriters, producers, and similar professions got their big break due to their professional network. Your network creates your net worth. In fact, some have speculated that your network *is* your net worth. Robert Kiyosaki said, "The richest people in the world look for and build networks, everyone else looks for work."

How to Become a Master Networker

Having organized a monthly networking meeting myself, I've noticed that there are some that excel in their networking skills while others feel like they lag behind. So here are some helpful tips I've learned from friends and mentors who are "jedi masters" at networking:

> Be the 1% who seeks to add value to others first and foremost.

Seek to add value to others. The one networking tip that can truly pay off with massive dividends is this one: *gift first*. Keith Ferazzi says, "The currency of real networking is not greed but generosity." This is a lot easier said than done. Most of us are only turned into one station: WIFM - What's In it For Me? You are naturally a taker. You are selfish and self-motivated. It's part of our nature to look at those in a room and wonder who you could benefit from? As a leader, when I'm contacted by someone, 99% of the time, their communication is what *they* need and what *they* want from me. My challenge to you is to be the 1% who seeks to add value to them first and foremost. Darren Hardy told a story about a man who introduced himself and discovered what Darren was working on. Remarkably, this new contact found ways to assist Darren in unsolicited ways. Darren said that all the value he contributed made some sort of psychological deficit in his mind, so he went out of his way to bring value back to him. "Come to think of it," he said, "I did feature him in my publication, endorse his book, show up at his events… all of which I probably would not have done otherwise." He goes on to say, "This is an example of the law of reciprocation in action. If you do for others, they are psychologically compelled to want to do for you. This is not saying you give to get. The opposite is true in fact. You give with no agenda or no direct or immediate agenda."

Figure out how you can be useful. Take an interest in them first. Focus on them and what they want, not what you're after. And this is an important tip to remember. Please don't ever ask the question: "How can I help you?" It sounds nice, but it actually puts the burden back on them to try to figure out a way for you to help them. That's awkward. Figure it out yourself. Listen intuitively to what their needs are or what projects they're working on and find a way to add value. Instead you can close by saying something like,

"If you need anything, please reach out to me or connect via LinkedIn or Facebook" and give them your business card. "Supporting another's success won't ever dampen yours." Brian Tracy says, "Successful people are always looking for opportunities to help others. Unsuccessful people are asking, what's in it for me?"

Think people, not positions. Never dismiss anyone as unimportant. Don't ever make the mistake of discounting people due to their titles. "Everyone reading this knows people who are smart, ambitious, motivated, and interesting," Andrew Sobel says. "Some of those people, in eight or ten years, are going to be influencers. They may even be CEOs." It's a lot easier to get to know someone and form a connection early in that person's career, he explains. "It's not that easy to break into the inner circle of fifty- or sixty-year-old executives. It's a lot easier to build up that equity early. So think about who in your network seems to be going places and is really interesting and make a strong connection. Even if they don't become an influencer, it'll be an interesting relationship."[1] When you genuinely treat others as valuable, they will in turn treat you as a person of value. You can learn something from virtually anybody. Everyone that you will ever meet knows something that you don't. Be like a sponge thirsty for new insight. Look for that "something."

> When you genuinely treat others as valuable, they will in turn treat you as a person of value.

Get outside the sphere. In his TedTalk, "Networking is not Working," Doug McColgin says, When you network within your industry, you meet people with the same educational background, the same work-specific vocabulary and the same kind of experience. We eventually form a closed "Worksphere" of people from our organization and our trade associations. It gets easier to talk to anyone within this "Worksphere,: and harder to mix with outsiders. Once we mingle with outsiders, though, we tend to "see things we already know about in a brand new light."[2]

Bring all your cards. Always have business cards handy as they're an effective way to leave your name behind so people remember who you are. Don't wait for the person you just met to ask for your card. They might not think of it. Just offer them one of yours and let them know that it's okay to reach out. If they give you their card in return, now you have a solid, repeatable connection.

Follow up. After you initial encounter with someone new, life and busyness tend to get in the way. But it is possible to put a strategy and schedule together to remedy this problem. Darren Hardy has one of the best practices I've seen. He calls it his "3-15-5-1" strategy. On Sunday he plans out his entire week and schedules three chunks of time when he will reach out to his contacts and find ways to make deposits into those "relationship accounts." He has no agenda besides making deposits and watching his relational equity grow with interest. So here's how his 3-15-5-1 strategy works: He schedules three in-person meetings by practicing the "never-eat-alone" principle. This could be during breakfast, lunch, dinner, or coffee. He schedules fifteen written communications (this could be cards, texts, or emails). He schedules five phone calls with those he wants to keep in touch with. And he puts on his schedule to send out a gift to one person per week. He carves out a certain percentage of his budget for "gift giving" and he sends it out throughout the year.[3] It's important for you to continue to build a serious relationship with those you do serious business with. People walk away from business deals all the time; but seldom do they walk away from relationships.

Be generous. Andrew Sobel says, "You have to have a generous spirit. The greatest networkers I know genuinely like to help others. They're always doing it. And if they ever do need anything, people will fall all over themselves to help them." Proverbs 19:6 says, *"Many will seek the favor of a generous man, and every man is a friend to him who gives gifts."* The thing about generosity is that it tends to have a boomerang effect. It always comes back to you. That's why Zig Ziglar said, "You can have everything in life you want, if you will just help other people get what they want."

Buy first. You would never walk into Apple Headquarters seeking to do business with Tim Cook while carrying a Dell computer and an Android phone, would you? If you are wanting to meet some Big Kahuna you should at least be a customer for the products that they sell; show up for the events they put on, and/or donate to the causes they care about.

Don't ask before you give. I recently had a friend from college ask me for a recommendation letter for a job he was pursuing. I write a letter of recommendation for someone almost every week so this was not an unusual request. But what was unusual is that this "friend" hadn't responded to my emails or text messages countless times. I hadn't heard from him in years--not until he needed something from me. Needless to say, that really left a bad taste in my mouth. Before you ask a favor from anyone, make sure you've invested in that person. If you're not making regular deposits into that relationship, you haven't earned the right to make any withdrawals to ask for a favor.

Others first. Matthew 7:12 says, *"In everything, therefore, treat people the same way you want them to treat you, for this is the Law and the Prophets."*

How to Introduce Yourself at a Networking Event

A lot of times people attend networking events and they don't even know where to begin. Maybe they're a little shy or introverted and it's already difficult for them to walk up and introduce themselves to someone they don't know, let alone to try to figure out what to say.

You likely either gravitate towards the same people you already know (which kind of defeats the purpose of a networking event) or you're afraid that telling people what you do won't garner the reaction you're looking for.

"Hi, I'm Jane Doe. I'm a web and graphic designer." Well, what do you think of when you think of web and graphic design? Do you create apps? Do you design t-shirts? Introducing yourself by starting with your job title can stop conversations before they even start. Or worse, they can elicit the wrong assumptions.

According to Maya Elious, "The best way to introduce yourself is by the value you bring to your clients." She says that a more effective introduction would be, "Hi, my name is Jane Doe. I help entrepreneurs strengthen their brand identity so they can reach their ideal target market."

Notice what she did there. She combined two important components of a good networking introduction: Result + Benefit
- Result = strengthened brand identity.
- Benefit = reaching ideal target market.[4]

Lisa Nichols is known for articulating the SNAAP technique (Super Networking At Accelerated Pace) for making an unforgettable impression in sixty seconds. The key is making your language clear, concise, powerful, and quick. The benefit is that it not only elevates the path of connection between you and the other individual but also increases the value of the contacts that you get. Once again, you speak more to the results that you create in the world versus the process.

When you meet someone new at a networking event, most people want to tell you about what they do. But if you want to increase your USP, Unique Serving Proposition, don't tell me what you do, tell me the results of what you do. And you always end with a question. People's listening will naturally shift and I'll show you how that occurs. When someone asks you what you do for a living, your response should be based on three questions:

1. **What are the results?** What are the results of what you produce in your work?
2. **What's in it for me?** This speaks to how what you do might directly impact or be beneficial to the person you're talking to or at least beneficial to someone they might know.
3. **Who do you know?** Remember to always wrap it up by asking a question. This is a natural disruptor. And even if the person you're talking to isn't a viable contact for you, they might be able to give you a referral for someone else within their own sphere of network who is.[5]

Sallie Krawcheck sums this relationship building practice well: "Networking is the number one unwritten rule of success in business." That's why it's believed that 80% of business opportunities are filled through networking. Your next job is no longer just based on what you know but who you know.

Ultimately, the golden rule of networking is to heed the words of Jesus: *"Treat others the same way you want them to treat you."* Paul also says in Scripture that we are to *"do nothing from selfishness or empty conceit, but with humility of mind regard one another as more important than yourselves."* May God give us the grace to add value to others through our own network of influence.

NEXT STEPS

Look through your contacts and pick five people that you're going to "make deposits" in this week. Find out what they are working on and seek to add value to them. What resources, books, or seminars are you aware of that might be useful to them. What ideas, thoughts, or words of encouragement could you offer them that would be helpful?

1. _____   4. _____

2. _____   5. _____

3. _____

The SPIRITUAL Essential

Becoming God's Friend

"People in India are physically hungry. People in America are spiritually hungry. That makes people in India better off, because Americans don't realize why they are starving." — Mother Theresa

If we meet these Five Essential needs God's way, each can be a doorway to spiritual growth and victorious living. If, however, we ignore these needs or attempt to meet them outside of God, then those same needs can quickly escalate and become problem areas in our lives.

John Ortberg says "God's primary will for your life is not the achievements you accrue; it's the person you become." Growing closer to God is not the result of "trying harder," but letting God love you. That's what we call surrender.

The bottom line is we all have a void in our heart that only a relationship with God is meant to complete.

When I say… *"I feel so empty."*

God says… *"I created you with a longing in your heart that only I can fill"* (Psalm 90:14).

> Growing closer to God is not the result of "trying harder," but letting God love you. That's what we call surrender.

Science says that we need at least 4 basic elements to survive:
1. Water
2. Air
3. Food
4. Light

Compare that with what the Bible tells us Jesus said about Himself:
1. I am the Living Water — John 4:1-30
2. I am the Breath of Life — John 20:21-23
3. I am the Bread of Life — John 6:25-29
4. I am the Light of the World — John 8:12

Science was right. We need Jesus to live.

Ted Dekker made a correlating observation that I've found valuable: "'Where is God? Where can I find Him?' we ask. We don't realize that's like a fish swimming frantically through the ocean in search of the ocean." But if God's presence is everywhere, why don't we always sense His presence with us?

Let me ask you a question: How close are you to God? The answer is simple. You're as close to God as you want to be. How impersonal God seems is a measure of the distance you have put between yourself and God. While there are times when we really want to have a deeper friendship with God, oftentimes we're not willing to pay the price. James 4:8 says, *"Draw near to God and He will draw near to you."* That verse contains both a precept and a promise. The precept is you draw near to God. The promise is God will draw near to you. He is always more eager to meet us than we are to meet Him, but we must initiate the first step.

Foundations of Friendship

When you think about it, developing a friendship with God is no different than becoming friends with anyone else here on earth. Genuine friendship is built upon four foundations. If you want a real friend or if you want to be a real friend, it means that you must invest in these four things:

1. Time Spent Together. Two people will never grow in their friendship with one another if the parties never make any effort to hang out. We will never achieve that closeness we desire from God unless we make the effort in devoting time to be with him. We have to make the choice to "draw near to God" before He will draw near to us. Why? Because we are the ones who moved. We are the ones who get distracted from our walk with Him. Do you feel like you are "too busy" to spend time with the Lord each day? Then you are saying the immediate demands of your schedule are more important than enjoying that deep, satisfying communion with God.

2. Two-Way Communication. If you want to build a friendship with somebody, it involves actually communicating with them. Communication is not just a one-way monologue. How would you like it if you were trying to talk to someone but could never get a word in? You know how it feels when you try to have a conversation with someone like that. Likewise, prayer is not a monologue; it is a dialogue. Prayer doesn't just mean you recite your wish list to God and go about your business. It means that you share your heart with Him but then remain still long enough to hear His voice. God speaks primarily through His Word, so try interacting with the Spirit by praying as you read Scripture. As you meditate on His Word, ask Him questions: Lord, what are You trying to say to me? How does this apply to my life?

3. Vulnerability. It's very rare to find a friend you can truly and completely be yourself with. They say if you can find two to three friendships like this over a lifetime, you are a very blessed individual. An important factor in genuine friendship involves our willingness to be open, honest, and transparent about the deepest issues in our lives. The depth of any friendship is limited to the extent of our transparency with that other person. The same is true in our friendship with our Heavenly Father. God wants us to expose every area of our life to Him. Although the natural response is to shrink back from such vulnerability, we have to remind ourselves that God already knows us inside and out. Despite that knowledge, He still loves us more than we can ever comprehend.

4. Shared Interests. Think about it. Your closest friends are people who you genuinely enjoy being around because you both like to do the same stuff. If we're going to grow in our oneness with God, it means we must learn to share His interests. We need to learn to love what He loves. We have to start caring about the things that He cares about. God is always attentive to our concerns, but do we care about His desires and purposes? Are you more interested in the Lord or in what He can give you? When our prayers are focused only on ourselves, when we neglect His Word, and when we are "too busy" for God, it communicates an unspoken message to Him: "I'm not interested in you."

You are in total control of the closeness you have in your friendship with God. But if you truly desire to be closer, then you must choose to do the things that foster a good friendship! We never grow closer to God when we just live life. It takes deliberate pursuit and attentiveness.

It's important for us to realize that in any relationship, intentionality is necessary to achieve intimacy. If you're married, chances are you and your mate didn't simply drift to the altar. You drew near to one another as you got acquainted and spent time together. You went on dates. You talked on the phone. And when you weren't on the phone or on a date, you wished you were. Most marriages start off with a high level of passionate intimacy, but it's also common that as the years go by, you can find yourself starting to drift apart emotionally. When that happens, the main reason is because one or both parties are no longer intentional when it comes to investing in that relationship. God is waiting on you to draw near to Him, and when you do, He will draw near to you.

> You are in total control of the closeness you have in your friendship with God.

What Does It Mean to Have God as a Friend?

There's a principle of friendship that says over time you become like those you spend the most time with. That's our goal as disciples of Christ: to become like Him (Romans 8:29).

There are some great Scriptures about what it means to have God as a friend:
- James 2:23 – *"'Abraham believed God, and God counted him as righteous because of his faith.' He was even called the friend of God."*
- In John 15:15, Jesus said to His disciples, *"No longer do I call you servants, for the servant does not know what his master is doing; but I have called you friends, for all*

that I have heard from my Father I have made known to you."
- James 4:4 – *"Don't you know that friendship with the world is hatred toward God? Anyone who chooses to be a friend of the world becomes an enemy of God."*
- Exodus 33:11 – *"The LORD used to speak to Moses face to face, as a man speaks to his friend."*

Scripture says that the Lord spoke to Moses like a man speaks to his friend. There are really only two ways you can know God: casually or intimately. You can either know about God or you can really know God. The Bible says that the Israelites knew the works of God, but Moses knew the ways of God. Psalm 103:7 says, *"He made known his ways to Moses, his acts to the people of Israel."*

Moses and God

Moses' friendship with God fascinates me. After Moses helped free God's people, the Israelites, out of Egypt, they were wandering in the desert for a period of forty years. Moses had some intense pressure on him as he led hundreds of thousands of nomads out in the desert, but he was also marked as a devoted friend of God.

Moses knew God in a way the rest of the people didn't. He understood God's ways. The rest of the people only saw the acts or the works of God. That describes many Christians today. There are Christians who know what God does, but they don't know who God is. They don't know God as an intimate friend.

When you read the Bible, you see that the Israelites were an unstable people. They were constantly pushing the panic button, always in a frenzy, always worried, constantly complaining. Why? The writer of Hebrews put it this way: *"They always go astray in their heart; they have not known my ways"* (Hebrews 3:10). You see, the Israelites were fine as long as the works of God kept coming their way in their favor! But when God was no longer doing what they wanted Him to do, they panicked! The point is, if all you ever do is see the works of God, as long as the sun is shining, you'll be fine marching in the parade, but when difficulties come, you'll start questioning your faith. You've known God's works, but you've never come to understand God's ways.

There's one more thing I want you to see about Moses. Exodus 34 says, because Moses was spending so much time with God and basking in His presence, he did not know that the skin of his face shone with the radiance of God's glory.

The people of Israel would see Moses coming down from the mountain and his face would shine so brightly that the Bible says Moses had to put a veil over his face. I think the lesson here is that your intimacy *with* God will increase your influence *for* God. When you spend time seeking God's face, the radiance of His glory will begin to show up on your face. People will know that there is something different about you.

After a while though, Moses drifted away and wasn't spending much time in building his friendship with the Lord. As a result, he lost his glow, but he continued to wear the veil. He didn't want anyone else to know that the glow was gone.

As a kid, I used to have a lot of glow-in-the-dark toys. They're fun to play with because you can expose them to a light source, and then go in a dark room and watch them glow. But we all know what happens if you leave those toys in the dark too long. They lose their glow. If we don't spend time "re-charging" ourselves spiritually in the light of the presence of God, we too will lose our glow.

That's why the New Testament says, *"And we all, with unveiled face, beholding the glory of the Lord, are being transformed into the same image from one degree of glory to another"* (2 Corinthians 3:18).

How Can We Grow in Our Friendship with God?

There are many ways to grow that friendship, but here are some foundational practices we can develop:

Communicate with God daily. Prayer is simply communicating with God. Don't worry about the words that you use, because God knows your heart. Don't worry about whether you're sitting, standing, or kneeling. The main thing you need to know is that God wants to hear from you. I have three kids, whom I love with all my heart. When they want to speak to me, I couldn't care less about the position of their hands or the formality of their words. What I am drawn to is the genuineness of their hearts, and the same is true of our relationship with God.

Learn about God daily. When I was a kid growing up, I hated reading. It's ironic that God called me to be a writer as an adult. Maybe you're not a person who reads much--that's ok. I'd encourage you just to read a chapter a day in the Bible, which doesn't take much time at all. Through the Bible, we begin to learn things about God we never knew. Someone once said that the Bible is like a vast ocean, shallow enough that a little child can play with no fear of drowning, yet so deep that scholars can swim in it and never touch bottom. The more you learn about God through His Word, the more you crave to know more about Him. If prayer is speaking to God, then spending time reading the Bible is God's opportunity to speak to you. Many times, I've learned that if there's something I'm praying about, the answer can be found in the section of the Bible I'm reading that day.

Become part of a local church. God has intended the church to be a microcosm of what the Christian life is all about. Being a part of the "Body of Christ" means that you have a place to worship corporately with other believers, be equipped in the Word, and be empowered to serve in ministry. Getting involved in a church is vitally important. Since we live in an ever-increasingly busy world, we have to be intentional when it comes to protecting and prioritizing our time in being a part of a local church.

Find some Christian friends on the journey. I've discovered my most significant "spiritual growth spurt" when I found some friends who would help me along in my spiritual journey. There's nothing greater than knowing that you have the support system of a small group standing with you, praying for you, encouraging you, and sharing their insights from God's Word with you. Proverbs 27:17 says, *"As iron sharpens iron, so one man sharpens another."*

Michael McAfee says, "Don't ask God to guide your steps if you are not willing to take a walk." Life's most exciting adventure is intimacy with God. God wants to be your best friend, and He wants you to continually grow in your relationship with Him. The Christian life is like riding a bicycle; you're either moving

Life's most exciting adventure is intimacy with God.

ahead or falling off. I hope you will take the principles from today's lesson and begin your own exciting adventure. Meet with God today. He's looking forward to building a friendship with you.

NEXT STEPS

On a scale of 1-10 (1 being as far away from God as you can get and 10 being as close to God as you can get on this earth), how would you rate your friendship with God today?

What do you think your next step needs to be today to go to the next level?

Seek Him First

"Instead of fitting God into your schedule, try to plan your schedule around God. Make Him your life, and everything else will be put into perspective."
— Allison Marie

The last of the Five Essentials, *Spiritual*, is not only the most important but the highest priority. Think of it as the central gear that turns all the other gears. Our devotion and discipline to our spiritual life will determine the quality and direction of our relationships, our intellectual ability to grow and set new goals, our physical health, and our financial standing.

Just think of your life like a wheel. You have the center of the wheel, the hub, which serves as the core and then you have the spokes that come out from the hub. The spokes of life include your relationships, your family, your finances, your work, your dreams, your goals. Right now, you're building your life around something. Just as the earth orbits the sun, something is going to be your center, your very hub, the thing that has a gravitational pull on you causing you to orbit around it. So, what is it? Is it work? Goals? Family? Finances? Or might it be your relationship with God? What is your life revolving around right now?

The center of your life is critical because a solid center means a solid life. A faulty or a weak center produces three negative effects in your life:

Frustration — When you have a faulty center, your life will spin out of control. All of your other priorities (the other four essentials) will likewise spin out of control as everything will be out of balance. Building your life around the wrong center is like driving your car through a thick fog; you don't know where to turn and you end up making some very poor decisions.

Fatigue — When you have a faulty center, you feel worn out all the time. Not only does the hub of the wheel provide stability, but the hub is also the power source for the entire wheel as well! Power emanates from the hub to all the spokes, not the other way around. I took my kids not too long ago to a county fair and we rode this ride called "The Gravitron." It basically looks like a flying saucer. You get inside and everyone stands up along the outer edge. As it starts to spin, the centrifugal force causes your body to "stick" to the wall while the floor drops beneath you. What amused me most during the ride was watching the operator controlling it. He was sitting in the very center eating a donut, perfectly at peace, when everyone else was screaming. I think that's an adequate picture of our lives when troubles come. You can always tell whose life is centered on God because when trouble hits, they are at peace while everyone else is falling to pieces. Maybe the fact that you feel like you're spinning out of control right now is evidence that you've moved away from your relationship with God being your center.

Fragmentation—Having your spiritual life aligned means that you're able to better focus. I don't think I've ever met anyone who said they wanted to waste their life, but let's face it, it's easy to get distracted nowadays isn't it? I see this in a lot of people as they move from one activity to the next activity with their priorities all out of alignment. They don't even understand why they're doing what they're doing. God wants us to live a life that is focused, balanced, and purposeful.[1]

Seek Him First

Matthew 6:33 is really the verse that I built this entire book on. It says, *"But seek first his kingdom and his righteousness, and all these things will be given to you as well."* I want to encourage you to commit this verse to memory and meditate on it often. This one Scripture alone has really helped to change how I view my life. It's God's promise to help us with our priorities. The context of this verse is within Jesus' greater teaching on what we should do with the worries and concerns we have in life. Jesus says, *"Do not worry about your life, what you will eat or drink, or your body, what you will wear."* When the Spiritual gear is in the center and God is first; the Lord promises to not only balance life's demands but also to meet your needs. When He is at the hub, all the other spokes simply fall into place. He sees us through. He meets all of our needs. We don't have to worry about a thing. God says, "Let me simplify your life. Put Me first."

Stop and think about this for a second. It's an astonishing invitation. Jesus is saying, "If you follow me, you can safely stop worrying about anything. People who don't know God at all are the ones who run after these things and worry about them, but your Father in heaven knows you need them, and He will care for you."

Bob Briner writes:
> *In many ways, the entire life and ministry of Jesus was about setting priorities and adhering to them. When He said, "Let the dead bury their own dead," Jesus spoke to the need not to be distracted from the real and most important goal, even in those emergency situations that claim our attention (Matthew 8:22). And perhaps His most famous and*

telling statement of all, "Seek first the Kingdom of God and His righteousness, and all these things shall be added to you" (Matthew 6:33), brilliantly sums up the entire message of Jesus. In other words, get your priorities straight and everything else will fall into place.

When Jesus said, *"Seek first the kingdom of God,"* He was telling us what our number one priority ought to be. The word "seek" means "to actively pursue" or "to go after." It's in the present tense which means we should continually, at every moment, be seeking first the rule of God in our lives.

James Merritt says, "King Jesus is not interested in being the first runner-up in your beauty contest. He is not interested in being Vice President in your corporation. He is not interested in being second in command of your army. He wants to be the King on the throne of your heart, not a co-partner in a duplex."

Sacred vs. Secular?

One of the biggest misconceptions that Christians have today is that their faith is just one compartment in their life. They open the "God box" on Sunday when they go to church, and then put God back on the shelf while they do their own thing Monday through Saturday.

When I was writing this book, I had a few people ask me, "Why would a pastor write a 'secular' book on finance, and relationships, and physical health. Aren't all those 'secular' topics?" That line of thinking precisely illustrates the dichotomous mindset that plagues Christianity today. If you're

> One of the biggest misconceptions that Christians have today is that their faith is just one compartment in their life.

a believer, *everything is spiritual*. How I conduct business, how I invest, how I work out, what foods I eat, how I grow in my capacity to learn, all of those things are spiritual undertakings when I do them through the strength of my faith. Do you know what the problem is with many of us? Our faith is something tacked onto our lives instead of being our foundation. Jesus said in Matthew 6:24, *"No man can serve two masters..."* You can't serve both God and yourself. You only have one master at a time.

Your preeminent goal should be to know God powerfully, passionately, and personally. When you get the Spiritual gear turning, everything else will flow out of that.

You might say, "But wait a minute. I've got other things to do! I've got a job. I've got to rest. I've got to have recreation. I've got to have friends. I can't just narrow my interests to one thing." Understand that when you bring your life into a burning focus on seeking first *"His kingdom and His righteousness"*, all of these other things contribute to the main thing.

We like to neatly divide life up into the secular and the sacred. People have said to me things like this: "Well, you know Brandon, what I would really like to do would be to just get out of this job and serve God full-time!" I hope you will allow this truth to resonate within your heart. If you are a Christian living in the power of the Holy Spirit, you already serve God full-time! I don't care what you do or where you work—if it is an honorable occupation—you're already in full-time ministry. Your work is to be the temple of your devotion and the platform of your witness.

> **Every job is a sacred job. Every task should be an outflow of our spiritual center.**

Even though we tend to divide up life into the secular and the sacred, that concept is not found in the New Testament. In the Old Testament, they had priests and then the rest of the people. But in the New Testament, we're all priests. In the Old Testament, in order to encounter God, they had to go to the temple, but in the New Testament, we can encounter God anywhere because His Holy Spirit lives inside of us. In the Old Testament, certain holy days were to be set aside as sacred; but in the New Testament, every day is a holy day. Every job is a sacred job. Every task should be an outflow of our spiritual center.

The Kingdom of God

When Jesus said, *"Seek first the kingdom of God,"* there obviously must be a kingdom to seek. But what exactly does that mean? The reality is, this teaching on the kingdom of God was the very heart of Jesus' life message. This phrase is found sixty-one times in the gospels and eighty-five times in the New Testament altogether. Jesus even said that the reason he came to earth was to introduce the kingdom of God. *"I must preach the kingdom of God to the other cities also, because for this purpose I have been sent."* Even in the Lord's prayer, He taught us to pray, *"Your kingdom come"* (Matthew 6:10).

So this raises a big question: Is the kingdom of God something we'll enter into later in the future or is this something we can experience right now in the present? And the answer is *yes*! We just saw where Jesus says to pray, *"your kingdom come"* (that's future) but in another instance, Jesus said, *"the kingdom of God is within you"* (that's right now!)

The kingdom of God does not indicate an actual territory as much as it is a sphere of influence. Think about it this way: Every kingdom has a king and every king has a throne.

Imagine that your heart is a throne and someone or something is going to sit on that throne and rule your life. You cannot make Jesus the king of your life until you abdicate yourself as the one who is sitting on the throne of your heart. In other words, you cannot pray "*Your* kingdom come" until you first say "*my* kingdom go."

Not only are we to seek the kingdom of God but also we're to seek *"His righteousness."* In other words, not only are we to be seeking God's control over us, but we're to be seeking God's character within us. If God is ruling over you, then His righteousness will be within you because your character is simply an outward expression of whatever is controlling you on the inside.

Today you can visit Buckingham Palace where there Queen of England resides. Everyone in London always pays attention to the flagpole over Buckingham Palace because if the colors of the monarchy, the royal flag, are flying from the top of the building—it lets the people know that the queen is at home.

Did you know that joy is the flag that will fly from the castle of your heart when Jesus is the king on the throne of your life?[2] God has called you to be the light of the world, but you won't shine that light until you plug into the Power Source. We're never going to make a difference in this world until the world sees a difference in us.

> Your character is simply an outward expression of whatever is controlling you on the inside.

All These Other Things

The last part of that verse is the part that we all like to key in on: *"But seek first his kingdom and his righteousness, <u>and all these things will be given to you as well</u>"* (emphasis mine). Here's another way to say it, "If you make it your top priority to be involved in what God is doing and have his goodness increasingly fill your life, everything else will be taken care of." The way to have it all is to make sure you're aiming past the target, pursuing the most valuable thing.

We often hear the call to discipleship only through the lens of sacrifice (looking at what we are losing). But Jesus rarely spoke this way. He promised people that what initially looks and feels like a sacrifice will pay off in the end.

Are we saying that we ought to use Jesus for our personal gain? Are we simply talking about "marrying him for his money?" Is this somehow tied into "prosperity theology" where I rub my Bible three times and a new car appears in the driveway? Absolutely not.

I don't pursue God to get more; I pursue God because there is more. If you chase Jesus as hard as you chase the things you think you want; you'll wind up with more than you'll ever need. I need God to consume me more than my life currently does. Never hold on to anything tighter than you're holding on to God.

Psalm 37:7 teaches us that God always gives His best to those who leave the choice with Him. When we give God our desires, we get to see Him at work.

I love how Andy Stanley puts it: "If you are 'seeking first' his kingdom where you are, then where you are is where he has positioned you."

Carlo Carretto said, "We are the wire, God is the current. Our only power is to let the current pass through it." God wants us to be a mind through which Christ thinks, a heart through which Christ loves, a voice through which Christ speaks, and a hand through which Christ helps.

It's a Bird... It's a Plane...

Superman has always been my all-time favorite superhero. Growing up as a kid, I had all the movies and collected all the comic books. I even had Superman pajamas complete with my own little red cape. Part of what made me so fascinated about Superman was that during the day, he seemed like your average, ordinary guy. As Clark Kent, he worked for the local newspaper and was always getting into conflicts with his boss while also failing to get the attention of Lois Lane. He seemed so typical, like any regular reporter.

But should this average, typical guy happen to pass by an empty telephone booth, he could dash in with that black suit, those thick glasses, and that slicked back hair, emerging with the blue suit, red cape, and massive letter "S" across his chest to stand for his heroic title: *Superman*.

He was "faster than a speeding bullet, stronger than a locomotive, and able to leap tall buildings in a single bound." Superman was incredible! But what was it that gave him the power to fight the evildoers of Metropolis?

It was because Superman knew that he was *not of this world*. If you know the story, Superman was originally from the planet Krypton. He was able to draw upon his strength from his real home up there and live it out down here. He drew upon his power from up there and displayed it down here.

Friend, I want to remind you that the Jesus Christ says, "*You are not of this world...You were bought with a price – therefore honor God with your body.*" And as one of God's children you have the strength and the power of His Holy Spirit living, residing, and dwelling within you. God wants you to draw upon the strength that is *up there* and live it out *down here*. He wants you to draw upon the power from up there and display it down here.

> As one of God's children you have the strength and the power of His Holy Spirit dwelling within you.

When you show up to work, it ought to be as if you have a giant "S" written across your chest. It won't stand for *Superman* but it will stand for *Saved*. It won't stand for *Superwoman*, but it will stand for *Servant of the Most High God*.

When this world looks at you, may they be able to say, "It's a bird... no...It's a plane...no. It's those *Super, Sanctified, Spirit-filled, Sold-out*, and fully *Surrendered Saints*" who are ready to make an impact on their world for the glory of God.

NEXT STEPS

Based on how you've lived this past week, what would you say is your "center" that you've been orbiting your life around?

What does seeking first "the kingdom of God and His righteousness" look like in your life?

How to Pray with Power

"Bold prayers honor God, and God honors bold prayers. God isn't offended by your biggest dreams or boldest prayers. He is offended by anything less. If your prayers aren't impossible to you, they are insulting to God."
— Mark Batterson

Do you feel like your prayers get answered? Do you sometimes pray and wonder if God is even listening, let alone willing to answer? Maybe you're longing for a closer walk with God. You want to really know Him in a way that is meaningful and life changing and to have a prayer life that is real. Prayer is one of those subjects that seems so difficult and elusive, but it doesn't need to be. You can learn to pray with power to an all-powerful God.

> Think of prayer like a two-sided coin. There are two purposes to prayer: to converse with God and to encounter God.

Think of prayer like a two-sided coin. There are two purposes to prayer: to converse with God and to encounter God.

When you read the gospels, praying with power is what the disciples wanted to learn most from Jesus. After following Jesus around for three years, they saw Him in every imaginable situation. But they never asked Jesus for lessons on how to preach or how to heal people. Instead, the disciples came to Him and said, *"Lord, teach us to pray."*

I think there must have been something about the prayer life of Jesus that was so impressive, so moving, so meaningful, and so essential to them that they understood that if they were going to be what God wanted them to be, they were going to have to learn what it is to pray.

Of course, there isn't anyone who has a PhD in prayer. All of us are in kindergarten when it comes to this subject. But that reminds me of something I heard a pastor named Jerry Vines say: "I've been preaching the Gospel for over fifty years. Occasionally people say to me, 'What would you do if you had to do it over in your life and in your ministry?' Without fail, I always say, 'I wish I had prayed more.'"

Arm Wrestling God?

Sometimes I think people have this false perception of what prayer really is. They think that prayer is trying to convince God to do something that He ordinarily wouldn't do. Some people think that prayer is like arm wrestling with God. They think that if they will just pray hard enough and get serious enough about it they can just cause God to cry "Uncle" and get their will done.

No. When we pray it is not in order to twist God's will into our will. When we pray we do so in order that we might surrender our will to the will of God.

> "He was never long in prayer, but he was never long without prayer."

Prayer is simply talking to God. I don't know if you kneel or not, but I like to kneel in prayer. Sometimes the posture of my body helps the condition of my heart. But however you do it in the morning when you get ready to pray, just keep in mind that you are talking.

Powerful praying doesn't necessarily mean long praying either. It's interesting that Jesus never condemned short prayers. But you have more than one statement in the Bible where Jesus actually condemned long prayers. He told the Pharisees who were the hypocritical religious leaders of that day, *"You make long prayers."* In Matthew 6:8, Jesus said, *"Therefore do not be like them. For your Father knows the things you have need of before you ask Him."*

So we have on record that Jesus condemned pretentious, long prayers. Most of the prayers that Jesus prayed were short prayers and in a way, the shorter we pray, the bigger we make Him. We're saying, "It's not about us Lord, it's all about You." I want it to be said of me what was said of Dwight L. Moody: "He was never long in prayer, but he was never long without prayer." Think about it this way: When you pray, don't put a period on your prayers. Leave yourself open to still hear the voice of God speaking to you throughout the day.

Connecting Prayer with Faith

The prayer that moves the heart and hand of God is the prayer prayed in faith. There are really three simple steps to praying with bold faith.

STEP 1 - ASK.
Tell God your thoughts. Let Him know what it is you are asking Him to do. Pray specific prayers.

Earlier, I mentioned that David Yongi Cho, pastor of the world's largest church said, "God doesn't answer vague prayers." I think that statement is spot on. The Bible makes a clear case for this.

In Mark 11:24, Jesus says, *"I tell you, you can pray for anything, and if you believe that you've received it, it will be yours."*

The word "It" is a small word, but, "it," refers to something specific. When you pray, you don't pray for just anything, you pray for something: healing for a loved one, strength for yourself or a friend, wisdom for a decision, protection for your children, provision for a need, and the list goes on. Here is another example:

"But if you remain in me and my words remain in you, you may ask for anything you want, and it will be granted!" (John 15:7).

The reason why God doesn't want you to pray without specificity is because *vague prayers don't take faith*. Why do I need to be specific with my prayers? Is God nitpicky? No, we pray specifically because vague prayers don't take faith, and faith is the currency of heaven. What is faith? Faith simply means belief and trust.

It doesn't take any faith whatsoever to say, *"God, would you please give me anything?"* Or *"God, would you please bless Jimmy today."* Bless him with what? What is it that you are asking God to do in Jimmy's life? How do you know if and when the prayer has been answered if you don't even know what you are asking for? Do you even know what "blessing" means?

> The reason why God doesn't want you to pray without specificity is because vague prayers don't take faith.

But when you pray and say, *"God, I need help to finish my paper on time. Will you help me to study and write effectively?"* God says, "Of course, I can help you with that!"

"God, I need money to buy my books this semester. Can you provide for me?" That's something God can answer.

"God, I really need wisdom for my marriage. I don't know how to talk to my husband to bring up this sensitive issue. Can you give me wisdom to know what to say?" God says, "Why yes, I would love to help you with that and along the way, I will also give you humility so he will receive it well!"

Craig Groeschel once asked a thought-provoking question. He said, "If God were to answer all your prayer tomorrow, what would be different about the world?" Wow! When I first heard that I was cut to the core. Prayer isn't only about me and my needs; prayer is about a big God who wants to do big things; it's about our families, our friends, transformed cities and nations, revival, healing, justice, and the nations of the world. Do you really believe your prayers can affect change?

In Matthew 20, Jesus was walking through a town and there were two blind men on the side of the road. When they heard that Jesus was coming near them, they started shouting, *"Jesus, have mercy on us."*

The Bible says Jesus walked over to them and asked them a question: *"What is it that you are asking me to do for you?"*

> Faith is believing that something is so when it is not so so that it can become so because God said so.

At first, that seemed like a strange question. It was obvious that they were blind. It was pretty obvious what they needed. So why did Jesus say to them, *"What is it that you are asking me to do for you?"* He wanted to see what they were believing Him capable of doing. They could have said, "Jesus, we just need some help out here. We're blind. We just need a place to live. We just need some dinner."

If they were to have asked from a limited faith, they would have stayed in their limited situation. Instead, they asked *big*. They said, "Lord, we want to see. We want our eyes to be opened." They were saying, "We know you can do the impossible." When Jesus heard their request, He touched their eyes and they could instantly see.

God is asking you the same thing he asked those two blind men: "What is it that you want me to do for you?" And how you answer that question is going to have a great impact on what God does.

Don't just say, *"God, my family is so dysfunctional. Just help us to survive."*

Don't say, *"God, I don't like my job, just help me to endure it."*

That short-sighted mindset will limit what God is able to do in your life. So step one is simply to ask – be clear in your mind what it is that you're asking God for.

STEP 2 - BELIEVE.
I think of three stages in our partnership with God. First, God initiates what He wants by declaring it in His Word and stirring our hearts to believe for it.

Second, we respond in obedience with prayer, speaking God's will back to Him.

Third, God answers our prayer by releasing what we pray for.

Step two is believe. Believe that it's already yours. Have what I call unwavering faith. Faith is believing that something is so when it is not so so that it can become so because God said so.

STEP 3 - RECEIVE.
Over and over again, Jesus says that you must believe that you have already received the answer to your prayer.

Mark 11:24, *"Therefore I say to you, all things for which you pray and ask, <u>believe that you have received them</u>, and they will be granted you."*

If you place an order on Amazon, you relax knowing that you're going to receive what you asked for and you go on with your life.

Praying in faith means you are acting, thinking, and speaking as though you are receiving it now. You have to believe that you have it already.

For me, receiving means feeling the way I will feel once God answers my prayer. Exactly how it's going to happen and precisely how God is going to answer that prayer is not your concern and it's not your responsibility. When you spend all your time trying to figure out how God is going to do something, you're not believing that you have it already.

Think of a car driving through the night. The headlights only go a couple hundred feet in front of you. Still, you can make it all the way from New York to Los Angeles driving through the dark, because all you really need to see is just the next couple hundred feet. And that's how the will of God tends to unfold before us. If we just trust that the next two hundred feet will unfold, and the next two hundred feet will unfold after that, your life will keep unfolding. And God will eventually get you to the destination of what He wants to bring into your life. That's what it looks like to trust and believe and have faith. Dr. Martin Luther King, Jr. said, "Take the first step of faith. You don't have to see the whole staircase. Just take the first step."

Ten Prayer Promises That Fuel My Faith

In the flyleaf of my Bible, I've written these ten promises out by hand. When I pray, I keep returning to these promises over and over again as they truly do strengthen my faith to believe God for what only He can do. So here are my top ten prayer promises from Scripture:

1. John 15:7, *"If you abide in Me, and My words abide in you, ask whatever you wish, and it will be done for you."*
2. Mark 11:22-25, *"Then Jesus said to the disciples, "Have faith in God. I tell you the truth, you can say to this mountain, 'May you be lifted up and thrown into the sea,' and it will happen. But you must really believe it will happen and have no doubt in your heart. I tell you, you can pray for anything, and if you believe that you've received it, it will be yours. But when you are praying, first forgive anyone you are holding a grudge against, so that your Father in heaven will forgive your sins, too."*
3. John 14:13-14, *"Whatever you ask in My name, that will I do, so that the Father may be glorified in the Son. If you ask Me anything in My name, I will do it."*
4. 1 John 5:14-15, *"This is the confidence we have before him: If we ask anything according to his will, he hears us. And if we know that he hears whatever we ask, we know that we have what we have asked of him."*
5. Matthew 18:19, *"Again I say to you, that if two of you agree on earth about anything that they may ask, it shall be done for them by My Father who is in heaven."*
6. 1 John 3:22, *"And whatever we ask we receive from Him, because we keep His commandments and do the things that are pleasing in His sight."*
7. Jeremiah 33:3, *"Call to me and I will answer you and tell you great and incomprehensible things you do not know."*
8. John 16:23-24, *"Truly, truly, I say to you, if you ask the Father for anything in My name, He will give it to you. "Until now you have asked for nothing in My name; ask and you will receive, so that your joy may be made full."*
9. John 15:16, *"You did not choose Me but I chose you, and appointed you that you would go and bear fruit, and that your fruit would remain, so that whatever you ask of the Father in My name He may give to you."*
10. Matthew 7:7-11, *"Ask and it will be given to you; seek, and you will find; knock, and it will be opened to you. For everyone who asks receives, and he who seeks finds, and to him who knocks it will be opened. Or what man is there among you who, when his son asks for a loaf, will give him a stone? Or if he asks for a fish, he will not give him a snake, will he? "If you then, being evil, know how to give good gifts to your children, how much more will your Father who is in heaven give what is good to those who ask Him!"*

I heard about a man, who was sitting in a dark restaurant. He wanted to make conversation with the people around him so he said to the lady sitting next to him, "Would you like to hear a blonde joke?"

She said, "Well, before you tell me, you should know that I'm blonde, six feet tall, and a professional bodybuilder. The lady next to me is blonde, six foot two and a professional wrestler, and the lady next to her is blonde, six foot five and the women's kickboxing champion of the world. Now do you still want to tell me that blonde joke?"

He thought about it for a moment and said, "No, not if I'm going to have to explain it three times."

How many times does God have to keep explaining His promises on the power of prayer?

I used to worry, "I don't know if I can pray in faith about that because it might not be His will."

Listen: If it's not His will, don't worry about it, He's not going to allow that door to open anyway.

But when I ask for something that is in alignment with God's Will, He will open a door that no man can shut.

Tips to Effective Prayer

James 5:16 in the Living Bible says, *"The earnest prayer of a righteous man has great power and wonderful results."* I don't know about you, but that's the kind of prayer life I want to have. Here are a few tips for effective praying (Courtesy of Kent Murawski):[1]

Ask God to search your heart. Before you ask God for anything, ask Him to search your heart (see Psalm 139:23-34). Forgive anyone you need to forgive (Mark 11:25). Get your heart right with God so you can start from a place of holiness and a clean conscience.

Take time to seek God's will first. If you want to pray effectively, first take some time to seek God's will or desire. *"This is the confidence we have in approaching God: that if we ask anything according to his will, he hears us. And if we know that he hears us—whatever we ask— we know that we have what we asked of him"* (1 John 5:14-15). You may not get it right every time, but asking Him to reveal His will before you ask for anything else is a good start. First and foremost His will is His word. He also speaks to His children through His Spirit. That being said, His spirit will never speak contrary to His Word.

Start small. Maybe you are not ready to ask God to bring an end to the civil war in Syria. Ascertain your faith level and then ask for some things that stretch you a bit or are a little outside of your comfort zone.

Persevere. God answers some prayers quickly but others may take years. Abraham waited twenty-five years for God to answer the promise of a son. If you know it's God's will, hold on. At some point your prayers should go from asking to praising and thanking. You should get to a place where you know God has heard and answered your request and now you are just thanking Him and waiting for it to manifest!

Pray some big prayers. God does care about the little things, but remember, life isn't only about you and your world. He's the God of more than enough. He's the God who pulls down some kingdoms and builds up others. Big bold prayers take faith. Pray in such a way that it stretches your faith; in such a way that if God doesn't come through, it can't happen. Author Mark Batterson said it this way in his book *The Circle Maker*, "God isn't offended by your biggest dreams and boldest prayers. He is offended by anything less."

> We honor God by the magnitude of our faith and the size of our requests.

If you go through life only praying barely-get-by prayers, you will miss the fullness of what God wants for you. But when you comprehend in your spirit that the God who breathed life into you, the God who called you, set you apart, crowned you with favor, is a more-than-enough God, an abundant God, an overflowing God, then you will have the boldness to ask for big things. Prayer takes us well beyond human possibilities. When we pray, God hears more than we say, answers more than we ask, gives more than we imagine in His own time and in His own way.

The great French conqueror, Napoleon, in his quest to rule the world, was quite surprised on one occasion when he encountered unexpected resistance while attempting to capture an island in the Mediterranean. The fighting was fierce and he lost many good men in the battle before finally overcoming the enemy.

Napoleon and his generals were having a celebration feast when from out of nowhere, it seemed, a young officer approached him. Napoleon saw the young man and asked abruptly, "What do you want?"

The young man said, "Sir, please give me this island."

The generals were deeply offended at the brashness of the young man. But, suddenly, Napoleon asked for pen and ink, promptly writing out a deed to the island. He then signed it and gave it to the impetuous officer.

By this time the generals were astounded. They asked their leader, "How could you give away the island to that young man when so many of our men paid such a high price to obtain it?"

Napoleon responded, "He honored me by the magnitude of his request."

I think sometimes we simply pray too small. We pray prayers that might come to pass on their own because we're afraid to believe for the impossible. We pray safe prayers, for things that we can make happen on our own with hard work and perseverance. We pray for mud piles, but God wants us to pray for islands!

I believe the Lord is honored by those kinds of prayers. What's *your* island?[2] We honor God by the magnitude of our faith and the size of our requests.

NEXT STEPS

What are the top prayer promises that inspire your faith?

What is something big that you're praying and asking God for?

Discover Your Calling

"What we really want to do is what we are really meant to do. When we do what we are meant to do, money comes to us, doors open for us, we feel useful, and the work we do feels like play to us." — Julia Cameron

Life is never about "finding yourself." It's about discovering who God created you to be. Every person has a calling and a purpose in their life's work. Most people spend 40 to 60 hours at work each week and less than two hours on Sunday at church. Here are some alarming statistics:

- 90-97% of Christians have never been trained by their local church in how to apply biblical faith in their work life.
- 47% of people say that the teaching and Sunday morning preaching they receive is irrelevant to their daily lives. And it is least relevant where they spend most of their time: work and home.
- 50% of Christians polled have never heard a sermon on work. Never. Not one.
- 75% say they have never been taught a biblical view of work or vocation.

You might be reading this and you're retired. That's great, but God still has an assignment for you, and you are now more positioned than anybody to seize the opportunities God brings your way. Maybe you are a stay-at-home mom. In my opinion,

> **Think of prayer like a two-sided coin. There are two purposes to prayer: To converse with God and to encounter God.**

that's the highest calling one could ever have (and the most difficult job there is).

You don't need to be in full-time ministry in order to serve God full-time. I think that we sometimes forget that nearly all of the great heroes in the Bible had what some would refer to as a "secular" job.

- Abraham was a rancher
- Nehemiah was a cupbearer (butler)
- David was a shepherd and later a King
- Joseph was a governor of Egypt
- Ezra was a scribe (writer, professor)
- Joab and Jonathan were military generals
- Deborah was a judge
- Gideon was a farmer and later a judge
- Simon Peter, Andrew, James and John were all fishermen
- Luke was a medical doctor
- Matthew was a tax collector
- Lydia was a business woman with an entrepreneurial spirit
- Paul was a tentmaker
- Dorcas was a seamstress
- Jesus was a carpenter

The point is that God has designed and deployed each of us to represent Him in some workplace arena. And once we discover that sense of purpose and calling in our job, we experience a great joy and deep satisfaction living in that perspective.

Determine God's Calling on Your Life

It's been said that the two greatest days of your life are the day you were born and the day you find out the reason why. Without a clear vision of what our purpose is on this earth, we lose hope and eventually die on the inside. Without a mandate for our life, we lack direction. Some people aren't really living; they're just existing. Yet it was Jesus who said, *"I have come so that you might have life and have it more abundantly"* (John 10:10).

> You don't need to be in full-time ministry in order to serve God full-time.

People want to know that they have a purpose. *The Purpose Driven Life* is the bestselling non-fiction book of all time (outside of the Bible). Why has it sold so many copies? Because spiritual emptiness is a universal disease. I think at some point, we put our heads down on our pillow after a long day at work and think, "There's got to be more than this."

So how do we know what our calling in life is? The word "calling" comes from the Latin word evocare, and it means a call, a summons, or an invitation. It's the same word from which we get our English word "vocation."

Ephesians 2:10 says, *"For we are his workmanship, created in Christ Jesus for good works, which God prepared beforehand, that we should walk in them."* The word for "workmanship" is the Greek word *poiema* and it's where we get our English word "poem." Poiema or "workmanship" literally means that God put forth all His best efforts and creative powers to marvelously fashion you for a divine purpose. You are created in the image of God and He made you a workmanship that would be worthy to bear His name.

Sometimes people make this whole matter of finding God's calling or purpose for your life so complicated. It's really not that difficult to discern. Your purpose is found at the intersection of five different components. Think of this frame of reference like a Venn diagram.[1]

Your purpose is determined by the intersection of five criteria:
1. Your **Passion** (You love it.)
2. Your **Perception** (The world needs it.)
3. Your **Profitability** (You can be paid for it.)
4. Your **Proficiency** (You're good at it.)
5. Your **Past** (You've experienced it.)

So let's break each of these down and examine them more in depth:

Your PASSION: What You Love Doing

Your purpose is always linked to your passions. Your passions encompass what you love to do and what you care about most. There are certain subjects you feel passionate about and others you couldn't care less about. Some experiences turn you on and capture your attention while others turn you off and bore you to tears. These reveal the nature of your passions. Where did those passions come from? They came from God.

Passion is what sets you apart from others. It sets you above the crowd. A person with passion always stands out. This world is full of apathy. It's crowded with "average" and "mediocrity." But once you have a passion or a sense of urgency in your life, it distinguishes you and gives you a head start into finding and fulfilling your life purpose. Passion will take you where nothing else will ever take you.

> Passion is what sets you apart from others. It sets you above the crowd. A person with passion always stands out.

Scripture tells us over and over again to "serve the Lord with all your heart."[2] The calling of God on your life is appealing. It's something you really want to do in your heart of hearts. When you are operating out of what you're most passionate about, it drives you! No one has to motivate you, challenge you, or check up on you. You do it for the sheer enjoyment.

Ask yourself these questions:

- *What do you love?* What I love to do is often what I should do. God has created within us the capacity to enjoy certain things immensely. Many times that is an indication of what our life purpose ought to be about.
- *What do you really enjoy doing in your free time?*
- *What excites you the most?* Think about what it is that you look forward to. What ideas or subjects make you "come alive" when you think about them. If you're not excited about it, it's probably not the right path. Hunter S. Thompson said, "Anything that gets your blood racing is probably worth doing."
- *What energizes you the most?* Passion finds your purpose and purpose fuels your passion. Passion is the great energizer. Once you have passion, you have energy. There is no such thing as high energy people and low energy people. If you are a person who has a lot of energy, all that means is that you have a whole lot of passion! There are a lot of people kicking around these days who are already dead; they just haven't made it official yet! When we have a lot of passion, we love and are energized by what we're doing! As I'm writing this paragraph, I have been on a learning and writing frenzy this past week. I went to bed last night at 2 a.m. and I'm up and writing again at 5 a.m.! Ironically, I'm not tired (yet)! Why? Because following my passion and fulfilling my God-given purpose is what fuels my energy levels! I love what I do. Sometimes I love it too much and I get too excited, I can't go to sleep! I've had loving friends say to me, "Brandon, you're doing so much we want you to take it easy so that you don't burn out." I have a simple response: No one has ever suffered "burnout" living within the sweet spot of their passionate purpose. We become stressed when we take on other things that are outside the scope of what God's created us to do. Allow your passion to become your purpose, and one day it will become your profession.
- *What do you find yourself daydreaming about?*
- *What do you love learning about?* What websites do you frequent? What magazines do you subscribe to? What blogs do you read? What type of books do you peruse when you go to a bookstore? If you could go to a seminar on anything in the world – what would the topic(s) be?
- *What would you do if money weren't an issue?* There's no way you were born to just pay bills and die. If you want to be successful in this world, you have to follow your passion and not a paycheck. When you're passionate about something, you don't even think about it as work. You're just doing what you love to do. We've all heard people say, "I took a job I hate because I have to put food on the table

and pay the bills. But hopefully, I'll make a lot of money so I can someday quit and do what I love to do." That's a huge mistake. Don't waste your life in a job that doesn't express what you are most passionate about.

In the movie *Chariots of Fire*, Eric Liddell made a poignant statement about God and calling: "When I run, I feel His pleasure." One way to discover God's calling on your life is to ask yourself the question: "Where do I feel God's pleasure?"

James Michener said,
The master in the art of living makes little distinction between his work and his play, his labor and his leisure, his mind and his body, his information and his recreation, his love and his religion. He hardly knows which is which. He simply pursues his vision of excellence at whatever he does, leaving others to decide whether he is working or playing. To him he's always doing both.[3]

Passion is important but it's insufficient in itself. I have a passion for playing the guitar. But that has nothing to do with my purpose or God's calling on my life.

Your PERCEPTION: The World Needs It

Your calling is where your passion and abilities coincide with one of the world's greatest needs. We need to discover our purpose and then place ourselves in a position where we lose ourselves in something that is much bigger than us. Most people today are only looking out for themselves. "How am I going to advance? How am I going to achieve? How am I going to get to the next level?" Success is when I add value to myself, but significance is when I add value to others. When our *why* is bigger than us, it propels us into the sweet spot of God's calling on our lives. When you are bigger than your purpose, you have a career; when your purpose is bigger than you, you have a calling.

> When you are bigger than your purpose, you have a career; when your purpose is bigger than you, you have a calling.

So here are some questions to ask yourself:
- *What do you notice?* A salesman notices an uninspiring sales pitch. A hairdresser notices someone's hair is out of place. A mechanic hears something wrong with our car. A speaker notices an uninspiring speech.
- *What burdens you the most?* Many times the issues that burden and concern us the most are the very assignment God appointed us to have "for such a time as this." You can't fulfill your calling in your comfort zone. God has placed on your heart a special passion area where you feel a burning desire to do something. This is your calling!
- *What problem are you able to solve?* Your assignment is the specific problem that God wants you and created you to solve. Everything that God created solves some sort of problem. We needed to be able to hear, so God created ears. We needed to be able to see, so God created eyes. Solving problems, whether for God, your employer, or your city, raises the value of your influence capital and positions you to live out of the center of your purpose.
- *What change is needed in the lives of people today?* Adam Leipzig says that your life purpose can be determined by the following five criteria: 1.) Who you are, 2.) What you do, 3.) Who you do it for, 4.) What those people want or need, and 5.) How they change as a result. Notice when you look at those five criteria of determining your life purpose, only two of them are about you. The most

successful people in any field always focus most on the people they serve rather than how they are served themselves.[4]

Henry Blackaby said, "You never find God asking persons to dream up what they want to do for Him. When God starts to do something in the world, He takes the initiative to come and talk to somebody. For some divine reason, He has chosen to involve His people in accomplishing His purposes."

Your PROFICIENCY: You Are Great at It

Proficiency follows passion. Whenever you do what God has wired you to do, you get good at it. Romans 12:6 says, *"God has given each of us the ability to do certain things well."*[5]

When God wanted to create the Tabernacle and all the utensils for worship, he provided artists and craftsman who had *"skill, ability, and knowledge in all kinds of crafts to make artistic designs...and to engage in all kinds of craftsmanship"* (Exodus 31:3-5).

A lot of times, we fool ourselves into thinking that we don't have any abilities to offer. Nothing could be further from the truth. You have perhaps dozens, maybe even hundreds, of untapped, unrecognized, and unused abilities that are lying dormant inside of you. Many studies have revealed that the average person possesses anywhere between 500 and 700 different skills and abilities.[6] That's probably far more than you realize!

Here are some questions to ask:

- ***In what areas are you most proud of your work?*** When you step back and look at something you've accomplished, what is it that makes you feel a sense of pride (in the most pure sense of course)?
- ***What do my friends and family members say I'm good at?*** What do people compliment you on? What "fans" do you have? If no one enjoys your cooking, your calling is probably not to be a chef. It's possible to be passionate about something that you're not gifted in! If you need an example of this, just watch some of the auditions for *American Idol* or *America's Got Talent*. Some of these singers on there are just belting out badness. They are sincere. They are loving what they do. They're just passionately bad at it! Everyone in America is grabbing the remotes and hitting the mute button at the same time. Every time I see something like this on TV, I always have a question: where are their friends? We need to surround ourselves with people who will level with us and let us know what we're good at as well as what we're not good at.

    For the most part, the things we are really good at we take for granted. They're invisible to us a lot of the time and we tend to subconsciously think, "Everybody knows how to do this." Actually, not everybody does. You have a certain subset of strengths that is unique to you. Have a conversation with the friends who know you the best and ask them what they think you're good at? Their answers might surprise you.
- ***Where do I feel the most strong?*** When you are serving in the area of your giftedness, you'll have the capacity to develop those gifts. You'll really start getting good. Working hard for something we don't care about is called stress. Working hard for something we love is called passion. When you are operating in the area of your weaknesses, you get tired. When you're operating in the area of your strengths, you get energized.

- ***What opportunity is before me?*** When God gives you an assignment, not only will you be good at it – but you will have an opportunity to use it. He's not going to give you a gift and then not give you the opportunity to use that gift.

Once again, just your passion alone or your proficiency alone is not sufficient enough to discover your life purpose. One of my first jobs was working at a Christian Bookstore. I was really good at it. I got promoted to a management position pretty quickly. But I left that position to pursue what I felt was the calling of God on my life at that time: to be a pastor. Just the fact that you are very proficient at something doesn't necessarily mean that it's your calling. Remember, it's the intersection of all five of these areas.

Your PROFITABILITY: You Can Be Paid for It

Is there a market for what you are passionate about doing, what you're proficient at, and what the world needs. So the question is, "Can you make a living doing it?" Now I know what some of you are thinking, "Brandon, you're talking about money and that doesn't sound very spiritual." No, it's extremely spiritual because to the Christian, everything is spiritual.

It says in 1 Timothy 5:8, *"But if anyone does not provide for his own, and especially for those of his household, he has denied the faith and is worse than an unbeliever."*

Then 2 Thessalonians 3:10 adds, *"If anyone will not work, neither shall he eat."*

Moses told the Israelites: *"Remember the Lord your God, for it is He who gives you the ability to produce wealth"* (Deuteronomy 8:18).

You need profitability. If all you have is passion and proficiency – you don't have a calling, you have a hobby. So based on the other three criteria, here are some questions to gauge the profitability:

- ***Can I garner employment doing this?*** Would someone hire me to do this? Or if I'm self-employed, would someone pay me to offer these products and services? This question is tricky, because chances are, it lies outside of the realm of your knowledge. It's going to take both the favor of God, a good measure of patience, and your investigative research to find the answer.
- ***Is this something I feel comfortable charging for?*** Charging people for our products or services feels very uncomfortable for those of us who have giving hearts. Yet the reality is when you establish a price for what you do, it has a two-fold effect on your client or customer: 1.) It actually increases your product's value in the eyes of the person considering purchasing and 2.) it increases their commitment to it when they invest.[7]
- ***How might I live out my purpose in my current job?*** This chapter isn't meant for you to start freshening up your resume and start looking for another job. The median length of time that employees have been with their current employer is

> If all you have is passion and proficiency – you don't have a calling, you have a hobby.

> Our greatest life messages come out of our weaknesses, not our strengths.

4.6 years. Why not first think in terms of what it would look like if you were to live out of this new awareness of your calling in your current work environment? Why not have a conversation with your boss in regards to where you might meet bigger needs and add more value to your company through the fulfillment of your life's passions and purpose? I don't know of any supervisor who's going to squawk over an employee wanting to add more value and serve the needs of their client base in a greater capacity. If God does not open up a door of opportunity for you to fulfill that purpose in your current job, then wait for Him to open up the door somewhere else.

Your PAST: What You Have Experienced

God has given each of us experiences in life: the good, the bad, and the ugly. Every experience you've had can be used for God's glory whether it is to allow Him to maximize your past blessings or redeem your past mistakes. Paul knew this full well. He said, *"Now I want you to know, brothers, that what has happened to me has really served to advance the gospel"* (Philippians 1:12). Since our greatest life messages come out of our weaknesses, not our strengths, we should pay close attention to what we've learned in the "school of hard knocks."

In 2 Corinthians 1:3-4 we read, *"Blessed be the God and Father of our Lord Jesus Christ, the Father of mercies and God of all comfort, who comforts us in all our affliction, so that we may be able to comfort those who are in any affliction, with the comfort with which we ourselves are comforted by God."* Paul knew that God never wastes a hurt. The best person to counsel someone who has lost a child is another person who has lost a child. He wants you to be open to ministering to people who are going through what you've experienced.

Edwin Korver writes: "Everything we experience, can potentially define us or confine us. It is from those experiences that we tell our stories. These stories can be used to serve others and to act as a catalyst for change." Consider these questions:
- ***What has been the biggest challenge you've been able to overcome?*** God often uses our deepest pain as the launching pad of our greatest calling.
- ***What has caused you to grow the most?*** Usually, the most meaningful work for you is work that helps others in ways that you've needed help.
- ***In what areas have you experienced some success?*** Where you have been fruitful in the past may be a huge indicator of what you were wired to do with your life.

There is something that you were made to do that only you can do in exactly the way you might do it. You might be thinking, "Now Brandon, don't over exaggerate. My life is not that unique." Perhaps, but your experiences are. Your unique mix of spiritual gifts, passions, abilities, personality, and experiences add up to make you unique. Just like a snowflake, there has never been and never will be another person quite like you.

Lay Down Your Staff

In Exodus 4:2-5 we read,
The Lord said to him, "What is that in your hand?" He said, "A staff." And he said, "Throw it on the ground." So he threw it on the ground, and it became a serpent, and Moses ran

from it. But the Lord said to Moses, "Put out your hand and catch it by the tail"—so he put out his hand and caught it, and it became a staff in his hand— "that they may believe that the Lord, the God of their fathers, the God of Abraham, the God of Isaac, and the God of Jacob, has appeared to you."

In the book of Exodus, we have a fascinating story. When God called Moses to return to Egypt and free His people, He first speaks to him through the burning bush. But when Moses doubted his own ability to do what God was asking him to do, the Lord posed a peculiar question. God said, *"What is in your hand?"* Moses responded very simply. It was a staff, a shepherd's staff. God told Moses to throw it down before Him. If you've seen the movie *The Ten Commandments*, you'll remember what happened next. When he threw it down, the staff became a living snake. Then God said, "Pick it up." And when Moses picked it up by the tail, it became a staff again. What is all of this about?

First of all, God never does a miracle just to show off. Throughout Scripture, there's a message behind the miracle. Secondly, if God ever asks someone a question in the Bible, it's not because He doesn't know the answer. When God asks a question, it's not for His benefit but for yours. God asked Moses, "What is that in your hand?" The reason for that question is powerful. The shepherd's staff in Moses' hand represented three things about Moses' life.

First, it represented his **identity**. Moses was a shepherd. He had been tending sheep for the last forty years. It was a symbol of his occupation, career, job--his identity.

Secondly, it was a symbol of his **income**. All of Moses' assets at that time were tied up in sheep! In those days, nobody had checking accounts, hedge funds, or American Express cards. All of his assets were tied up in his flock of sheep. So the staff symbolized his identity and his income, but that's not all.

Thirdly, it was a picture of his **influence**. What do you do with a shepherd's staff? You move sheep from point A to point B. Either by hook or by crook, you either pull the sheep or poke the sheep to keep them moving in the right direction.

So what was God really asking Moses when He asked him to throw down what was in His hand? God was saying, "Moses, what is in your hand? You've got to lay down your identity, you've got to lay down your income, you've got to lay down your influence. And once you lay it down before Me, I will make it come alive. I'll do some things that you could never imagined would be possible."[8]

When you read the Book of Exodus, you find that God did all of these miracles – from the plagues in Egypt to the parting of the Red Sea – all through Moses' staff. What could God do through your life and your workplace if you laid your identity, income, and influence before Him?

D.L. Moody said, "The first forty years of Moses' life, he thought he was a somebody; the second forty years of his life, he thought he was a nobody; the last forty years of his life-- Moses discovered what God can do with a nobody!"

> What could God do through your life and your workplace if you laid your identity, income, and influence before Him?

It's one thing to read through this material; but it's another thing to actually sit down and take the time to thoughtfully answer each of these important questions. It's only when you walk through these exercises that your purpose becomes clear and you start getting excited about living it out.

Occasionally the question is raised: "Can you have a calling today that becomes something completely different five or ten years from now?" Of course that's certainly possible. The calling of God for your life may only be for a season. You are not called to serve in a place; you are called to serve in place of the Savior. I do believe there are certain qualities and abilities within us that are hardwired in and are immutable, but there are a myriad of other variables that could cause God's calling on our lives to pivot into a new direction. It's been said that the greatest challenge in life is discovering who you are. The second greatest is being happy with what you find. Even if God doesn't have a new assigment for you, be happy where you are and bloom where you're planted.

When you find your why you find your way. Everything changes at that time. An old Roman proverb says, "When the pilot does not know for what port he is headed, no wind is the right wind." But if you know where you're going, and you can catch the wind in your sails, then not even the storms can deter you.

NEXT STEPS

Carve out some time and begin journaling your answers to these critical questions that will help you decipher your calling:

Your PASSION: What You Love Doing

What do you love?

What do you really enjoy doing in your free time?

What excites you the most?

What energizes you the most?

Your PERCEPTION: The world needs it

What do you notice?

What burdens you the most?

What problem are you able to solve?

What change is needed in the lives of people today?

Your PROFICIENCY: You are great at it

In what areas are you most proud of your work?

What do my friends and family members say I'm good at?

Where do I feel the most strong?

What opportunity is before me?

Your PROFITABILITY: You can be paid for it

Can I garner employment doing this? How much of an income might I possibly make?

Is this something I feel comfortable charging for?

How might I live out my purpose in my current job?

Your PAST: What you have experienced

What has been the biggest challenge you've been able to overcome?

What has caused you to grow the most?

In what areas have you experienced some success?

Increasing Your Faith

"Faith and fear both demand you believe in something you cannot see. You choose!" — Bob Proctor

Faith is so vital to the our life that Scripture tells us that without it, it is impossible to please God **(Hebrews 11:6).** Faith does not make things easy. It makes them possible (Luke 1:37). Faith is like Wi-Fi. It's invisible, but it has the power to connect you to what you need. Stress makes you believe that everything has to happen right now. Faith reassures you that everything will happen in God's timing. Faith is seeing light with your heart when all your eyes see is darkness.

In Luke 17:5, the disciples made a request of Jesus: *"Increase our faith."* They wanted Jesus to help them believe more because it was obvious to them that they weren't believing enough. The disciples felt that much of what the Lord was asking them to do just didn't seem normal or natural. In effect, they were saying, "Lord if you're asking us to do that, you're going to have to give us more faith than what we already have."

> **Faith is like Wi-Fi. It's invisible, but it has the power to connect you to what you need.**

Isn't it true that much of what God asks us seems out of our reach? It seems beyond what we're able to do with the faith we have. We know what God wants us to do, but sometimes it just doesn't seem practical. We feel like we don't have the patience or the power to carry it out.

Our Faith Grows When We Walk with God Through Difficulty

Faith is like a roll of film: it develops best in the dark. When I was a little kid growing up in Port St. Lucie, Florida, we lived near a convenience store. Around the age of nine, I remember asking my dad for permission to ride my bike down to the other end of the neighborhood, where our convenience store was, to buy some candy. I was shocked when my dad said, "Yes." I felt so grown up and independent riding my bicycle that far away from home. Just recently, I brought that up with my dad and said that I couldn't believe he would let me ride my bike that far away from home all by myself at such a young age. My dad started laughing and said, "You really thought you were alone when you went to that convenience store?" He said, "I followed you the entire time. I walked along behind you and stayed behind the trees so you couldn't see me. The entire time you were in that convenience store, my eyes were on you. You thought you were alone. But you were never alone."

Isn't that like our relationship with God? There are times when we feel alone and isolated. We feel like God may have even forgotten about us. If only we would remind ourselves that His presence has been with us the entire time and His watchful eye has never left us.

There are ten scriptural references to the promise that God will never abandon us. For example, Hebrews 13:5 says, *"I will never leave you; nor forsake you."* Sometimes, we're tempted to think, "Lord, why have you left me alone? Why is your hand not on me? Are you really aware of what is going on in my life? Do you really care?"

And all along, God is saying, "When you thought I wasn't there, I was walking right behind you. When you thought I wasn't aware of what was going on, my eyes never left you. When you thought that I didn't care, I was behind the scenes working in your life." Faith is trusting God even when you don't understand His plan.

The only way that God can show us He's in control is to put us in situations we can't control. God doesn't give us what we can handle; God helps us handle what we've been given.

Our Faith Grows When We Remember God's Faithfulness in the Past

Faith believes in spite of the circumstances and acts in spite of the consequences. I saw a sign once that gave this acrostic of F.A.I.T.H.: Forwarding All Issues To Heaven. We learn in 1 John 5:4, *"This is the victory that has overcome the world – our faith."* On the cross of Jesus Christ, all the sin (past, present, and future) of the entire world along with its consequences were nailed to Jesus Christ. If Jesus was able to overcome those sins and resurrect in victory over them and then to be seated at the right hand of God, His indwelling presence can surely overcome any destructive force you're facing right now.

If a weight lifter can bench press 500 pounds, is he going to have any problem carrying 25 pounds of groceries for you? Your part is to believe that Jesus can enable you to overcome, and then you act on that belief. God has never asked you to do anything that He is not absolutely certain you can do through Him.

When you read biblical examples of audacious faith, it ought to cause your own spiritual circuit board to light up! And when you look back on your own life at how God has been faithful to you, it should increase your faith. Every miracle in the Bible first started as a problem.

We must never allow our feelings to get in the way of our faith. Faith is not equal to feelings. To allow your feelings to guide your faith is like a truck driver being controlled by the cargo in his truck rather than by the wheel he is steering. It is the wheel that controls the cargo, not the cargo that controls the wheel.

Our Faith Grows When We Mature in Our Understanding of Who God Is

The reason that God honors faith is that faith honors God. Hebrews 11:1 says, *"Now faith is the substance of things hoped for, the evidence of things not seen."* Faith has to have substance. If after a child has lost a tooth, their parent goes to bed saying, "I am trusting in the tooth fairy to put a dollar under my son's pillow," that's just wasted conversation. There's no substance. In order for faith to do something, it must be based on something. We are told to have faith in our God and His Word.

In a message one Sunday, I picked a couple out of the crowd and asked them how long they had been married. The husband said they had been married for 29 years. My next question was, "Would you say that you love your wife more now than you did when you first got married?" He said, "Yes!"(Good answer, by the way!) I then asked him if he loved his wife with 100% of his heart on their wedding day? He said, "Yes!" (Another good answer!) So what happened? You can't love someone more than 100%, right? I'll tell you what happened. Their capacity to love grew over time. They weathered some difficulties, went through some storms together, and experienced fights requiring them to forgive one another. Their love became more seasoned over the years, which has increased their ability to grow in love for each other. That's how our faith grows as well. The more faith you have, the more ability you have to grow in your faith.

After hearing the story of Jonah and the whale, a little boy asked, "Dad, how could a fish swallow Jonah?" His dad said, "Well, if God can make the world simply by speaking the word, then surely He could speak the word and make a fish large enough to swallow a man." The little boy said, "Well, I didn't know you were going to bring God into it." When you bring God into the equation of faith, you don't need a lot of faith. You just need a lot of Him! You don't need more faith. What you need is the right kind of faith.

When Jesus was in His hometown of Nazareth, the Bible says that Jesus could do no mighty works there because of their unbelief (Matthew 13:58). Even though Jesus was fully God, He was limited because of the people's unbelief. It was their lack of faith that kept Him from doing some mighty works in their lives. Remember, Jesus taught us, *"According to your faith, be it unto you"* (Matthew 9:29).

> God has never asked you to do anything that He is not absolutely certain you can do through Him.

Some people say that *"faith moves mountains."* That is not true. It is God that moves mountains. Jesus told us in Mark 11:22 to *"have faith in God."* Your faith is no better than its object. Faith in faith is just positive thinking, and that's a recipe to get discouraged. You must place your faith in God. It's not the size of your faith, but the object of your faith that really counts.

When you look through the Bible, almost everyone who received a blessing from God was an individual with weak faith! There were a few who had very strong faith in Jesus, but most of them didn't. There was a man whose son was demon possessed, and he came

> The way we grow in our faith is by growing in our understanding of God's Word and the promises He makes to us.

to Jesus saying, *"If you can do anything for my son, please do it."* Jesus said, *"If you believe--all things are possible to him that believes."* The man said, *"Lord, I believe, but help my unbelief"* (Mark 9:24). Have you ever been there? "Lord, I believe. I have a modicum of faith. But Lord, help my unbelief." That's what God is looking for as a starting point. Remember this: God still demonstrates His power and supplies His provision in direct proportion to the faith of His children.

The size of our faith isn't determined by who God is, but by who you believe God is and whether you have the courage to respond accordingly.

Our Faith Grows When We Believe in God's Promises

One of the simplest definitions I've heard on this subject is that "Faith is acting as if God is telling the truth." Faith simply means you believe God will do what He said He will do. God's promises are not mottos to hang on the wall; they are checks to take to the bank. Faith is taking God at His Word. Romans 10:17 says, *"So faith comes from hearing, and hearing through the Word of Christ."* That means that faith comes from outside of you; you don't generate faith. The way we grow in our faith is by growing in our understanding of God's Word and the promises He makes to us.

In Luke 17:6, Jesus said, *"If you have faith as small as a mustard seed, you can say to this mulberry tree, 'Be uprooted and planted in the sea,' and it will obey you."* Notice that Jesus says, "If you have faith as small as a mustard seed." A mustard seed is extraordinarily small. It's not gargantuan. It's tiny. It's not much bigger than the period at the end of this sentence. Weak faith in the right object is better than misplaced faith in any object. Weak faith in God is better than strong faith in anything else. Jesus is saying that mustard seed faith is really all you need. While a mustard seed is really small, it packs a lot of life. When you plant a mustard seed, it gives you a tree that grows up to fifteen feet tall.

Jesus told his disciples what that mustard seed faith could do. He said you could speak to a mulberry tree to be uprooted and planted in the sea, and it will obey you. That may not sound like much to you, but to the disciples, this was a staggering statement due to the nature of the mulberry tree. A mulberry tree (or a sycamore tree) has an in-depth root system that not only goes way down into the ground but intertwines itself with its roots and anything else in the neighborhood. It was said of a mulberry tree that once it's planted, you might as well leave it alone, because you'll never be able to uproot it. They could live for up to 600 years! That's how solid and deep their roots went. Yet Jesus said that if you have faith as small as a mustard seed, you could say to it, "Get up and get out," and it will go!

Some of the problems you have in your life are like mulberry trees. Those roots run deep. They've been hanging around a long time. And try as we may, we've been unable to untangle them. It just keeps on, year after year, producing new problems in our lives.

Let's look at another instance when Jesus talks about mustard seed faith. When the disciples came back discouraged because they were unable to drive out an evil spirit in a demon-possessed boy, they asked Jesus why they could not drive it out. Jesus responded: *"Because of your little faith. For truly, I say to you, if you have faith like a grain of mustard seed, you will say to this mountain, 'Move from here to there,' and it will move, and nothing will be impossible for you"* (Matthew 17:20).

A mountain was something too high to get over. It was an obstacle too great for you to climb. It represents something too big for you to handle.

Jesus says, "Don't allow the magnitude of that obstacle to intimidate you. A mustard seed faith will do."

Notice that in both of those Scripture passages, Jesus tells us to demonstrate our faith by speaking to the mulberry tree or to the mountain. In the Bible, whenever God wanted something to take place, He would just speak it. (See Psalm 33:9; Hebrews 11:3.) When Jesus was on this earth and He wanted something to happen, He would simply speak and things changed. The Bible says that life and death are in the power of the tongue (Proverbs 18:21).

Faith is the medium of exchange in Heaven. If you need an answer to prayer, spend a little faith. That's why Jesus said, *"According to your faith, be it unto you"* (Matthew 9:29). One man put it this way: "Pray and doubt; you'll do without. Pray and believe; you will receive."

Our Faith Grows When We Step Outside Our Comfort Zones

Peter was the only disciple who walked on water, but he was also the only one willing to get out of the boat. You will never walk on water and reach your full potential unless you have the courage and the boldness to take a step of faith and do what God has put in your heart. God made you and He knows what you're capable of. Throughout your life, He's going to present you with opportunities that, in the natural sense, you may not think you can handle. You'll be tempted to shrink back with fear. But God will empower you to do His will. Anything God orders, He will pay the bill for.

Too many people are living in the safe zone, but God wants you to step out into the faith zone. Have some courage and boldness to pursue what God has put in your heart. Your faith is like a muscle. You need to stretch it to build it up and work it for it to grow.

> You will never walk on water and reach your full potential unless you have the courage and the boldness to take a step of faith...

Growing up, I was extremely shy. I had a speech impediment and a severe stuttering problem. Being a communicator and megachurch pastor would have been the last thing my parents could see me doing when I grew up. However, when I stepped out and got beyond my own natural ability, that is when God stepped in and gave His supernatural ability. He brought gifts out of me that I never even knew I had. You too have incredible things on the inside of you that you probably never knew you had!

Many times we say, "God, if you'll just show me the blueprint ... if you'll just give me the details, then I'll be a whole lot more comfortable." No. If God did that, it wouldn't require any faith on your part. You sometimes have to take a step of faith and then God will lead you and show you the next step.

God told Abraham, *"Leave the place where you are and I will show you where I am sending you"* (Genesis 12:1). We think just the opposite: "God you show me and I'll go!" Instead God says, "You go and I'll show you." In other words, God wants us to take the first step of faith. It's interesting that when God parted the Jordan River for the children of Israel to cross, the Bible says that the waters did not open up until the priests first put their feet in the waters (Joshua 3:13). Don't you know that it took faith to go out there walking in the water expecting God to open it up? We think to ourselves, "God, if you part the seas in my life, I'll go running through them!" No, God says, "You get out there and get your feet wet and watch me do supernatural things in your life." Faith is directly tied to an action done in response to a revealed truth.

Our God is a progressive God. Once you reach a certain level, He might leave you there for a little while, but He's not going to let you stay that way too long. He's going to push you. He doesn't want you to stay stagnant, mediocre, or comfortable for too long because your spiritual growth will come to a screeching halt.

Maybe you have an opportunity right now in which God is calling you to take a step of faith. Or maybe God is preparing you today to have faith for whatever future opportunities may await. When you step out in faith and take God up on His Word, you will live a life of worship and honor the God for whom you serve.

NEXT STEPS

Has there ever been a time in your life when your faith hit a low point? What led to your loss of faith, and what helped you regain it again?

Today you read five ways God grows our faith. Which one has made the biggest difference in your confidence in God? Why?

An Attitude of Gratitude

"The worst moment for an atheist is when he is really thankful and has no one to thank." — G.K. Chesterton

Rudyard Kipling, the British author who wrote *The Jungle Book*, made a great deal of money on his work before he died. One day a newspaper reporter asked him, "Mr. Kipling, I read that somebody calculated that the money you make from your writings averages a hundred dollars per word."

In Luke 17:5, the disciples made a request of Jesus: *"Increase our faith."* They wanted Jesus to help them believe more because it was obvious to them that they weren't believing enough. The disciples felt that much of what the Lord was asking them to do just didn't seem normal or natural. In effect, they were saying, "Lord if you're asking us to do that, you're going to have to give us more faith than what we already have."

Isn't it true that much of what God asks us seems out of our reach? It seems beyond what we're able to do with the faith we have. We know what God wants us to do, but sometimes

Mr. Kipling said, "Really? I wasn't aware of that."

The reporter cynically reached into his pocket and pulled out a $100 dollar bill and said, "Mr. Kipling, here is a hundred dollar bill, now can you give me one of your hundred dollar words?"

He took it, folded it, put it in his pocket, and said "thanks" before walking away.

> One of the enemy's plans for your life is to keep your mind off of the blessings of God.

The word "thanks" truly is a hundred-dollar word, perhaps even a million-dollar word. Having an attitude of gratitude adjusts your mind to focus on the positive. As a result, you'll see, discover, and create more of the same, experiencing more abundance, well-being, love, joy, and happiness.

There may be no greater sin on the face of the earth than the sin of ingratitude. Shakespeare once described ingratitude as a "marble-hearted fiend." In other words, an ungrateful person has a heart as hard as marble. He also said, "How sharper than a serpent's tooth it is to have a thankless child."

Sometimes we can become so focused on the goal ahead that we don't even see what we already have beside us. Cicero said, "Gratitude is not only the greatest of all virtues, it is the parent of all others."

A family had twin boys whose only resemblance to each other was their looks. If one felt it was too hot, the other thought it was too cold. If one said the TV was too loud, the other claimed the volume needed to be turned up. Opposite in every way, one was an eternal optimist, the other a doom and gloom pessimist.

Just to see what would happen, on the twins' birthday their father loaded the pessimist's room with every imaginable toy and game. The optimist's room he loaded with horse manure. That night the father passed by the pessimist's room and found him sitting amid his new gifts crying bitterly. "Why are you crying?" the father asked.

"Because my friends will be jealous, and I'll have to read all these instructions before I can do anything with this stuff. I'll constantly need batteries, and my toys will eventually get broken," answered the pessimist twin.

Passing the optimist twin's room, the father found him dancing for joy in the pile of manure. "What are you so happy about?" he asked. His optimistic son said, "Because with all this horse manure, there's got to be a pony in here somewhere!"

That story illustrates an important truth: We are either the master or the victim of our attitudes. It is a matter of personal choice. Gratitude is an act of the will. We choose to be thankful for something regardless of the circumstances.

Scripture tells us, *"in everything we are to give thanks."* Notice the Bible says be thankful "in" everything, not necessarily "for" everything. We are not necessarily to be thankful for trouble, but we are to be thankful in the midst of trouble.

The Neurological Effects of Gratitude

Maybe like me, you occasionally struggle with bouts of depression. I used to take antidepressants daily, until I began fostering the habit of gratitude. It's been proven that the discipline of mentally listing out ten different things you are grateful for each day has the same affect on you neurologically as taking an antidepressant. I'm not your doctor so I can't say that it will have the same effect for you, but it is what worked for me. Emily

Fletcher explains why: "When we take the time to ask what we are grateful for, certain neural circuits are activated. Production of dopamine and serotonin increases, and these neurotransmitters then travel neural pathways to the 'bliss' center of the brain—similar to the mechanisms of many antidepressants. Practicing gratitude, therefore, can be a way to naturally create the same effects of medications and create feelings of contentment."

Being grateful is not only good for your spirit; it's also good for your brain. Did you know that you can literally "rewire" your brain to be happy by simply recalling three things you're grateful for every day for twenty-one days. The more you stimulate this new habit of gratitude, the stronger and more automatic the neural pathways become. It's an example of Hebb's Law which states "neurons that fire together, wire together." Think of it as if you're forging a new path in the woods for the first time. The first trip is the most challenging as you have to be deliberate. But the more times the path is traveled, the more defined it becomes and the easier it is to follow. Your brain works the exact same way. The more you practice the discipline of being grateful for every little thing you notice in life, the more times a certain neural pathway is actived (neurons firing together), the less effort it takes to stimulate the next time (neurons wiring together).[1] After several weeks of discipline, you will have established a new habit pattern that will make your attitude of gratitude only grow and expand each time it's used.

One thing that God has taught me is that the seeds of discouragement will not grow in the soil of a thankful heart. When I find myself getting discouraged and depressed, it's usually in direct correlation to a lack of intentional gratitude on my part.

Don't Be Like a Leper

In Luke 17, we have a fascinating story of Jesus healing a group of lepers. In Bible times, leprosy was pretty much the worst disease you could imagine. Not only was it a horrible and painful sickness, but there was a terrible social stigma that followed you everywhere you went. You were not fit to worship in the temple, could no longer live with your family and friends, and were required to be exiled to live outside of the city. The law also required that the lepers' faces be covered and they were to shout out loud, "Unclean!" anytime someone came close to them. In fact, they were ordered to stand at least 100 steps away from anyone else.

These lepers *"stood at a distance"* and cried out saying, *"Jesus, Master, have mercy on us."* This was all they could do. They were completely helpless to this deadly disease and Jesus was their only hope. Verse 14 says that Jesus had compassion on them and told them to present themselves to the priests as they were healed. Once the priests inspected them and gave them a clean bill of health, they would be allowed to return to their families.

Why did Jesus tell them to start walking towards the priests before they were healed? Why didn't He just say, "Be healed!" and cure them on the spot? I think there are two reasons for this:

1. Because an act of faith is always required of a person before God intervenes. They went on walking by faith and as they did they were healed. God's power is not released into our lives until we step out in faith.

2. I believe Jesus was testing them to see how many would return to thank Him. Out of those ten lepers that were healed, how many came back to thank Jesus for what He did?

Only one. What happened to the other nine? They got so preoccupied and excited with the *blessing* that they forgot to thank the *Blesser*. Only one leper was reminded of just how far God had brought him and he returned to offer his gratitude.

Isn't that a picture of our lives too? For every ten blessings that God gives us daily, we might be lucky if we remember even one of them to offer a prayer of thanksgiving back to God out of grateful hearts.

Luke 17:15-16 says, *"One of them, when he saw he was healed, came back, praising God in a loud voice. He threw himself at Jesus' feet and thanked him."* Notice that it says he praised God in a "loud voice." With the same loudness and intensity he cried for help, he intensely glorified God! Most of the time, our problem is that we cry loud for help and low with praise.

If we get in a serious automobile accident and come out alive, we typically thank God for sparing our lives. But do you ever just thank God for saving your life as you drive home from work without an accident? Isn't that even better? I heard a story that poignantly illustrates this. There was a family who heard that a person in their church gave a significant love offering to the memory of their son who died on the battlefield. On the way home, the wife asked her husband, "Why don't we give an offering for our son?" He said, "Why? Our son wasn't killed." She said, "Don't you think that's a good reason?"

Isn't it a shame how we don't really know and appreciate what we have until it's gone? Our power is shut off, and suddenly we become thankful for electricity. A good friend dies, and suddenly we discover how much he meant to us. Our water becomes too polluted to drink, suddenly causing us to appreciate having good water. Why is it that we take for granted the uncounted blessings of life until they are removed from us?

Gratitude will make you sensitive to the power of God at work in your life. One of the enemy's plans for your life is to keep your mind off of the blessings of God. He will constantly try to tell you just how bad you have it. He will try to convince you that everything is wrong in your life. The devil knows that once you begin to recognize how much you have in the Lord, your heart will grow to be thankful. And when you are thankful, your heart will abound with a greater love for God and others. The degree to which you are thankful is a sure index of your spiritual health. Max Lucado wrote, "The devil doesn't have to steal anything from you, all he has to do is make you take it for granted."

Remember the Onion

When my wife and I first got married, we were fresh out of college and dirt poor. I was pastoring a small country church in Virginia and on this particular week, we were completely out of groceries. It was Saturday night and I wouldn't get a paycheck until the next day. But we did have one grocery item left in the cupboard. It was a big vidalia onion. And that evening, Carrie chopped it up and sauteed it in the frying pan and that was our dinner. We prayed over our "dinner" that evening and thanked God for what we had and surprisingly, it filled us up.

Carrie and I have been able to enjoy much success and prosperity since that day, but we often reflect back on that meager meal in our little apartment. Every once in a while, we tell each other, "Remember the onion" as a reminder of just how far God has brought us.

So how do you turn thanksgiving into thanksliving? I think one word sums it all up: *Thinking*. Did you know that *thankfulness* is actually an old Anglo Saxon word that means "thinkfulness"? The more you stop to think and recognize God's blessings in your life, the more this attitude of gratitude will well up inside of you. That's why David prayed in Psalm 103:2, *"Bless the Lord, O my soul, and forget not all of His benefits."*

Psalm 69:18 says, *"Blessed be the Lord, who daily loads us with benefits."* Every day, God gives a new fresh load of blessing. That's why you should never pray without thanking God. Some of us should probably pull out some groans in our prayers and shove in some hallelujahs!

Thanking God in Advance

Here's one last thought I want you to contemplate: The greatest expression of faith is thanking God for an answer to prayer that you have not yet received. A grateful heart is a magnet for miracles.

We have a couple in our church that recently had a baby girl, yet for years they were unable to conceive a child. Since they were in our life group, we prayed and prayed that God would give them a baby. But years went by and nothing happened. Then one day after hearing a teaching I did on gratitude and thanking God in advance, CJ began to change his prayer. He said instead of praying and asking God for a baby, he would thank God in advance for the child that they would someday have. Just a couple of weeks ago, I had the privilege of dedicating, Caradyn, their new baby girl! God loves to answer prayers prayed in gratitude by faith.

> The greatest expression of faith is thanking God for an answer to prayer that you have not yet received.

In 2 Chronicles 20, Jehoshaphat, King of Israel was faced with a very serious problem. There were three enemy nations that were plotting together to overtake the nation of Israel. Jehoshaphat was afraid because he was facing what seemed to be a hopeless situation. He looked to God and prayed, *"We do not know what to do, but our eyes are upon You"* (2 Chronicles 20:12). The King asked the entire nation to fast and pray as they sought the Lord for help. But notice how God responded to their prayer: *"Do not be afraid or discouraged because of this vast army. For the battle is not yours, but God's."* The reason why you don't have to be afraid of your problems is because God has promised to fight the battle *for* us and *with* us. They fully believed that God was going to answer their prayer and they began thanking Him in advance for the answer. How do we know that? Because on the day of battle, Jehoshaphat appointed a choir to be on the front lines of the battlefield thanking God for His faithfulness to them. Can you imagine a military today having a church choir lead their troops to battle? That's exactly what Israel did.

Over and over again, the choir sang, *"Give thanks to the LORD, for his faithful love endures forever...Give thanks to the LORD, for his faithful love endures forever."*[2] They kept praising God and thanking Him for the victory before they even stepped into battle. So what happened? Scripture says that the three enemies that were coming against Israel got confused and they ended up killing each other! By the time the Israelites had showed up, the battleground was littered with so many bodies that it took them three days to gather up the spoil to take back home with them. That's what happens when God fights your battles for you and you thank Him in advance.

Thanksgiving is an act of faith. Faith allows us to obey God even when life is difficult or doesn't make sense. When you have a thankful heart, you enable yourself to rest in God's presence and wait for Him to move in your life.

A boy named James was not a believer, and in fact was anti-Christian. One day his mother bought him a Bible, laid it on his desk and said, "Here, son, is your new Bible." James replied, "What's that for?"

His mother answered, "You don't know it yet, but you're about to become a Christian."

James replied, "No I'm not. I'm going to play football and go to hell."

His mother stood up in church that night and said, "My son is about to become a Christian.

He doesn't know it yet, but I'm thanking God in advance."

So James's friends began to walk up to him on the street and say, "I heard you became a Christian."

"No it's just my crazy mother. I'm going to play football and go to hell."

But his mother even told her pastor, "I want you to save 20 minutes on Saturday night for my son to give his testimony."

The Friday night before that Saturday, James was playing football when he suddenly felt the presence of God right there on the playing field. He got down on his knees and prayed right in front of everybody: "God, I really need you in my life. If you can make a difference, come in and change me. Save me, whatever it takes. Make me born again."

James ran off the field in his uniform, down the street, and up the stairs into his house. He hugged his mother and said, "Mom, I just became a Christian."

She said, "Of course you did…I've been telling you that for three weeks!"

That is a true story of thanking God in advance. There is power in thankfulness. This morning would you be willing to pray, "Lord, I know I have problems, but I thank you in advance because there is no situation that you can't take care of."

NEXT STEPS

In your own words, why should you thank God in advance for answers to prayer not yet received.

Practice this new gratitude habit today by jotting down the first ten things you can think of to be grateful for. Offer to God a prayer of thanksgiving for what He has blessed you with.

Five Things God Does Not Know

"Because Jesus walked such a long, lonely path utterly alone, we do not have to do so." — Jeffrey R. Holland

This book is organized around Five Essentials to improving your life. We have journeyed together from the least to the most important of these. This chapter, then, focuses on the most essential part of the most important of the Five Essentials. A person might excel with the first four and seem to make strides in the fifth essential, but if they fail to take seriously the lesson of this chapter, all their efforts amount to little. In Mark 8:36, Jesus says, *"For what does it benefit a man to gain the whole world yet lose his life?"* With that in mind, let's explore five things God does not know.

That statement might surprise you. Maybe you're thinking, "I thought God knew everything?" That's true. God is omniscient, meaning He is all-knowing. In fact, God already knows everything about you. He knows when you went to bed last night, how many hairs are on your head, and even the number of heartbeats you have left. But it may surprise you to learn that there are five things God does not know:

#1 – God Does Not Know How to Love You More than He Already Does

True love is always sacrificial. If you want to know whether somebody really loves you, find out what he or she is willing to sacrifice for you.

A father and son were traveling down a country road one afternoon in the spring when suddenly a bee flew in the window. Being deathly allergic to bee stings, the boy began to panic as the bee buzzed all around inside the car. Seeing the look of horror on his child's face, the father reached out and caught the bee in his hand. Soon, he opened his hand, and the bee began to buzz around once again. The boy began to panic. The father reached over to his son and opened his hand showing him the stinger, which was now lodged in his palm. He said, "Relax son, I took the sting for you. The bee can't hurt you anymore."

Through His death and resurrection, Jesus took the penalty of sin, death, and hell away from those who believe in Him. That's why Paul said, *"Where, O death, is your victory? Where, O death, is your sting?"* (1 Corinthians 15:55).

One man said, "I asked Jesus how much He loved me. He answered 'this much.' Then He stretched out His arms and died for me." Jesus stretched out His arms so that wicked people could nail Him to the cross. That's how much He loves us. He stretched out His arms to take the sins of the entire world. That's how much He loves us. He stretched out His arms to take away our penalty of death. That's how much He loves us. The cross of Jesus Christ is the clearest, loudest, most powerful "I love you!" ever proclaimed. It doesn't matter what you may have done in this life or where you are today. It doesn't even matter if you believe in God or not! The God you say you don't believe in died on the cross for your sins. Romans 5:8 says, *"God demonstrates His own love for us in this: While we were still sinners, Christ died for us."* You are loved more than you will ever know by Someone who died to know you.

> The cross of Jesus Christ is the clearest, loudest, most powerful "I love you!" ever proclaimed.

A soldier had just been discharged for his years of wartime military service. He called his parents and informed them that he would be coming home, and they were thrilled knowing that they would see him soon. But in that conversation, this man said to his parents, "Mom, Dad, I'll be home in a week, but I'm bringing a friend to live with me. He's not in good shape. He's a little different. He's been greatly hurt in the war. My friend has one eye out. He has one arm shot off, and a leg that is completely blown off as well. He is crippled and confined to a wheelchair. But he doesn't have anywhere to go, and I wanted to know if you would receive somebody like that."

And the mother said, "Oh son, I'm so sorry to hear about your friend; but please don't bring him home with you. We just can't take care of someone in that kind of condition. It would just be too much of an inconvenience."

A few days later, a body was found along with a suicide note. It was the body of that young man from the war. When they brought the young man's body home and the parents looked inside the casket, that mother looked down at the body of her son and saw that he had one eye missing, plus one arm and one leg gone. Then she remembered just a few days before saying not to bring someone like that home.

I'm so grateful to know that my God is not like that. Two thousand years ago, Jesus looked at your soul so scarred with sin, so crippled by your own mistakes. He looked at your life so imperfect but He loved you anyway. And He wasn't like that mother. His message to you today is simple: "Come home to Me. I want you to have a relationship with me through Jesus Christ."

#2 – God Does Not Know How to Ignore Sin

A story goes that everyone sitting in the courtroom had their eyes on the judge. After hearing the case, he looked up and slowly pronounced his judgment upon a young woman who was found guilty. He said, "I find you guilty and hereby fine you the maximum fine possible: $10,000." The courtroom gasped in astonishment. The judge then got up, took off his robe and walked to the front of the bench. Taking out his checkbook, he wrote a check for the full amount. Turning to the courtroom, the judge said, "This is my daughter, and even though I love her, I cannot overlook what she has done. Her actions still have repercussions, but I'm going to pay the penalty for those consequences."

I want you to think of the most horrendous sin you have ever committed. Do you have it? Do you remember it? Now, I want you to understand that it was that sin that God the Father saw when He looked down from Heaven and saw Jesus take your sin upon Himself. It was all of the sins, both large and small, that you and I have committed that Jesus took into His perfect body when He was dying on the cross.

Maybe you don't know what sin is. Sin is any thought, action, or attitude that goes against God and His standard of morality. Not only were we born with a sin nature (e.g. you never have to teach a toddler how to throw a temper tantrum), but also throughout our lives, we have all deliberately committed sinful acts. Scripture says, *"All have sinned and fallen short of the glory of God"* (Romans 3:23). All sins are serious and have serious consequences. It doesn't matter if you've committed one sin or committed a million. God's judgment of us will not be based on how we compare to other people; rather, it will be based on how we compare to His standard.

> God's judgment of us will not be based on how we compare to other people; rather, it will be based on how we compare to His standard.

Even though God loves us, He cannot overlook the fact that we have sinned. The penalty for our sin must be paid in full. This is what happened when Jesus was on the cross. He took the full punishment for our sins.

Someone has to pay for your sin. Either Jesus pays or you do. If we personally accept His offer of complete payment for our sins, we will not be required to pay the penalty ourselves.

#3 – God Does Not Know How to Turn Away Anyone Who Comes to Him with Repentance and Faith

"God couldn't love me. I'm not good enough." Have you ever thought that? God isn't in the business of saving good people--just people who are truly repentant. God promised that *"if you confess with your mouth, 'Jesus is Lord,' and believe in your heart that God raised him from the dead, you will be saved"* (Romans 10:9-10).

It's important for us to understand that when Jesus died on the cross, He didn't die alone. He died in between two thieves who were being crucified because of crimes they had committed. One of the criminals railed at Jesus, saying, *"Are you not the Christ? Save yourself and us!"* The other thief watched how Jesus responded and put his faith and belief in Him, and to that man, Jesus said, *"Today you will be with me in Paradise"* (Luke 23:43).

On that day, one man died on the wrong side of Jesus and another man died on the right side of Jesus. The way he got right is the way that we must get right. That second thief saw something about himself in those last minutes of his life. He saw his own sinfulness, and he placed his faith in the One who was dying next to him. Those two men are a representation of the decision that every person in this world has to make: Will I choose to receive Jesus or will I choose to reject Him? To not make any decision is a decision to reject Him. We will be judged not for the sins that we have committed but for the Light we have rejected.

Notice that the thief who believed had nothing to offer. There was nothing he could do to earn God's favor. This man didn't receive salvation because of his good works. He didn't have any. He wasn't saved because of church membership. He never joined one. He wasn't saved because he was baptized. He didn't have time. All he had was his faith and God's grace.

> **Salvation is not in the merit of man; it's in the mercy of God.**

Ephesians 2:8-9 says, *"For by grace you have been saved through faith, and that not of yourselves, it is the gift of God, not of works, lest anyone should boast."* There is nothing you can do to earn your salvation. Salvation is not in the merit of man; it's in the mercy of God. It's not in the goodness of man; it's in the grace of God. Salvation is not a reward for the righteous; it's a gift for the guilty.

God has given His word that if you will come to Him in faith with a repentant heart, He will save you so you can spend eternity with Him in Heaven. There is no person so good that they need not be saved, but there is no person so bad that they cannot be saved.

#4 – God Does Not Know Another Way to Be Saved but Through Jesus

Jesus is our way to God and God's way to us. Christianity is not a code, a cause, or a creed, but Christ. Jesus put it this way: *"I am the way, the truth, and the life. No one comes to the Father except through me"* (John 14:6).

God has chosen to redeem mankind and save you through Jesus Christ. In 1 Timothy 2:5 we read, *"There is one God, and there is one mediator between God and men, the man Christ Jesus."* How many mediators? Just one, and His name is Jesus.

If you could get to Heaven by being a good person, why would Jesus have to die? You may be a moral person with wholesome values. You may be a good citizen who abides by the golden rule. But those things, while they are good, will not save you from your sins. Only Jesus can do that. *"Salvation is found in no one else, for there is no other name under heaven given to men by which we must be saved"* (Acts 4:12).

#5 – God Does Not Know a Better Time to Make This Decision than Right Now

In 2 Corinthians 6:2, Paul says, *"Behold, now is the favorable time; behold, now is the day of salvation."* If you sense God working in your heart today and drawing you to Him, you need to make this decision today. There is a danger that you may harden your heart to the point that you don't sense God drawing you to Him again. There is a danger that you may die before you get another opportunity to respond to Christ. You are living on borrowed time. Everyone faces death. Only a fool would go through life unprepared for something he knows is inevitable.

In 1829, a man named George Wilson attacked and robbed a mail carrier. He was sentenced to die, but received a pardon from the President of the United States. But to the shock of the White House, Wilson rejected the pardon. The President of the United States had set him free, but George Wilson said, "No." The case went to the Supreme Court, and the issue was simply this: If the President gives you a pardon, aren't you pardoned? Can you reject a pardon given by a Sovereign? Chief Justice Marshall rendered the decision: "A pardon rejected is no pardon at all. Unless the recipient of the pardon accepts the pardon, then the pardon cannot be applied."

> If you could get to Heaven by being a good person, why would Jesus have to die?

Because of Jesus' death, burial, and resurrection, you have been offered a pardon. But in order for the pardon to be effective, you must choose to believe and receive.

Are You Certain of Your Salvation?

John 3:16 says, "For God so loved the world, that He gave His only begotten Son, that whosoever should believe in Him, shall not perish but have eternal life."
If you are not certain of your salvation and you would like to respond to the gospel in believing and receiving Jesus as your personal Lord and Savior, I want to encourage you to pray and make that decision. Praying a prayer doesn't save you. Salvation is an act of your will to respond to what God is doing in your heart.

> *"Dear Jesus,*
> *I know I am a sinner. I know I cannot save myself. I believe in who You are and what You came to this earth to do. I do not want to die in my sins. I want You to save me. Come into my life and make me a new person. I turn away from how I've been living, and for the rest of my days, I want to live for You. Thank you for giving me salvation and eternal life.*
> *In Jesus' name, AMEN!"*

If you prayed that prayer, you just made the greatest decision you'll ever make in your life! Trusting Christ is the most essential step of the most important of these Five Essentials. This is the first step on an exciting new journey! I want to encourage you to send me an email to brandon@brandonpark.org. I'd love to celebrate this decision with you and share with you personally some next steps you can take on your faith journey!

Crafting Your
GROWTH PLAN

Get Motivated

"The man on top of the mountain didn't fall there." — Vince Lombardi

You write goals, but then you procrastinate. You make plans, but you don't follow through. Sound familiar? Why is it that motivation seems like such a limited resource? It turns out, there are certain things you can do that are scientifically proven to increase it. The next time you think you can't simply motivate yourself to study, hit the gym, or work on your projects, ask yourself: "Have I laid the proper motivational groundwork?"

It's not that we can't motivate ourselves to do something. It's that we haven't yet set up the systems that create that motivation. Plus, we haven't overcome the myriad of internal factors that can stymie our motivation like self-doubt, distractions, or complacency.

Let's face it, it's not a matter of not having enough time to do what we want to do; it's about not having the right priorities. 84% of people watch between five and 20 hours of TV each week, while only 32% say they invest time each week to work on something they are passionate about. If you really want to do something, you'll find a way. If you don't, you'll find an excuse. Almost every successful person begins with two beliefs: the future can be better than the present, and I have the power to make it so.

> If you really want to do something, you'll find a way. If you don't, you'll find an excuse.

So here are a few tips that can get you motivated:

Put yourself in the right environment. Are you in a place where you are continually challenged to grow in your calling? If you want to grow spiritually, you can't do that effectively until you join a good church. If you want to be fit physically, group fitness classes are actually one of the most motivating things you can do as being in that environment will push you further than you would ever push yourself.

Surround yourself with others who challenge you. Remember the rule of five — that your character, thinking patterns, and even your motivation level will be a composite of the five people you spend the most time with. If you're at the head of the class, you're in the wrong class. Find a group of others you can glean knowledge from who are further down the road than you are.

Don't wait until you feel like you're ready. Hugh Laurie said, "It's a terrible thing, I think, in life to wait until you're ready. I have this feeling that actually no one is ever ready to do anything. There is almost no such thing as ready. There is only now."

Focus on progress, not perfection. This is hard for me because I am a perfectionist. My tendency is not to do something until I know for a fact that I can do it right with the highest level of excellence. However, perfection is the enemy of progress. It is action today which produces the fruit of tomorrow.

Set mini-milestones along the way. The only way this book got written was that I set out to write 2,000 words per day. Once I hit that target, I got a little dopamine rush when I could check that item off my to-do list and it gave me maybe just an additional 1% of willpower to tackle the next day's writing assignment with full force. 1% may not seem like much, but after fifty days of consistent action, you've got 50% more willpower than you did before you started! Motivation is something that accrues when we choose to do the hard things.

Keep pressing on ahead. Be like the snail who was slowly working his way up an apple tree. As he was starting to go up, a worm came out from a crevice and said, "No need to go up there... there aren't any apples in this tree yet." The snail said, "There will be by the time I get there." Day by day, just keep on keeping on. John Maxwell, "Successful and unsuccessful people do not vary greatly in their abilities. They vary in their desires to reach their potential."

Our willpower is sort of like a muscle. The more you actively go out of your way to use it to do something that isn't already a habit, the stronger your willpower muscle will become. This means that you'll have more willpower and more strength over the long run to use for other hard tasks. Put simply, you receive additional motivation when you force yourself to do whatever it is you "don't feel like doing" in the moment.

Remember that the greatest things you'll ever experience in life will never come from your comfort zone.

Your only limit is your mind. Be stronger than your excuses. Push yourself because no one else is going to do it for you. Sure, growth can be painful. Change is painful. But nothing is as painful as staying stuck somewhere you don't belong. The three C's in Life are Choice, Chance, and Change. You must make the choice, to take the chance, if you want anything in life to change.

Dwayne "The Rock" Johnson said, "Success at anything will always come down to this: Focus and Effort. And we control both."

You will never just "always be motivated;" so you must learn to be disciplined.

Jim Rohn often repeated, "Successful people do what unsuccessful people are not willing to do. Don't wish it were easier, wish you were better. If you want something you never had; you have to do something you've never done."

Know Your Why

In the Andes Mountains, there were two warring tribes that not-so-peacefully existed. One of them lived in the lowlands and the other lived high in the mountains. One day, the mountain people invaded the lowlanders, plundered them, and even kidnapped one of the babies from that village. The lowlanders were pushed to action at the disappearance of one of their own, but they didn't know any of the trails that the mountain people used. They didn't know where to find the mountain people or how to track them in that steep terrain. Even so, they sent out their best brigade of warriors to climb the mountains and bring that baby home.

The men tried one method after another to climb those mountains. They tried one trail and then another. After several days of effort, they had only climbed a few hundred feet. Feeling hopeless and helpless, these lowlander warriors returned home deciding that the cause was lost.

As they were packing their gear for descent, they saw the baby's mother walking toward them. They realized that *she* was coming down the mountain that they hadn't figured out how to climb. They saw that she had a baby strapped to her back.

One man greeted her in amazement and said, "We couldn't climb this mountain. How did you do this when we, the strongest in our village, were unable to?"

She looked intently at them and said, *"It wasn't your baby."*[1]

When you know your "why" with crystal clarity, it gives you the power to push through all the obstacles. All of the *hows* in the world are meaningless until your whys are meaningful. If your "Why Power"—your driving desire—isn't strong enough, then any new endeavor will be just as effective as setting a New Year's resolution, only to have forgotten about it by the first of February. Darren Hardy says, "The person with a clear, compelling and white-hot burning reason *why* will always defeat the best of the best at doing the *how*." Nietzsche said, "He who has a why to live for can bear almost any how." There will be times when you feel like quitting. That's when you need to think about why you started in the first place.

Remember that the greatest things you'll ever experience in life will never come from your comfort zones. Whatever you do, always give it 100% (unless you're donating blood.) Set a goal that makes you want to jump out of bed in the morning.

You Will Never Grow by Accident

We have to realize that growth is not automatic. If you don't do the work, then you won't get the results. There are many successful people who haven't reached half their potential because they quit growing. There's something called "Destination Disease" that comes when we reach a certain goal, be it earning or degree, getting a certain position at work, or getting the house paid off. We just kick back and put our mind in neutral and begin to coast off of what we've already learned. Sure, we might make a little more progress here and there, but we're really not expanding and growing like we used to.

One of the reasons for this is the way we were trained. As little kids, we grew automatically. We got bigger physically. We had teachers and parents and coaches that challenged us to grow. Early on, growth was automatic. It was just a part of our lives. The problem is, when we get out of school, that growth is no longer automatic. If we're going to continue to grow, we have to take responsibility for our own growth. We have to have the attitude, "How can I improve? What can I do to make myself better?" We should have a goal to grow in some way every single day. I've witnessed countless individuals work so hard to earn their degree and soak in information like a sponge, only to graduate and never pick up another book again. Jim Rohn said, "Formal education will make you a living; self-education will make you a fortune."

Jim Rohn said in one of his seminars, "All life forms strive to reach its maximum potential except human beings." You'll find that to be true when you give some thought to it. Think about it: How tall will a tree grow? As tall as it possibly can. You never hear about a tree growing half the height that it could. A tree will always drive its roots as deep as it can, reach as high as it can, and bear as much fruit as it can. Every life form strives to the max except human beings. What makes us different? God gave us the dignity of choice. You're not a robot. You don't have to make this year a repeat of last year. We have to decide, do we want be *part* of all we were meant to be or *fully* who God wants us to be."

Your happiness and contentment is not something that you postpone for the future; it's something that you design for the present. So we're going to help you do that and come up with a plan for personal growth and development. As Les Brown said, "You don't have to be great to get started, but you have to get started to be great."

NEXT STEPS

What was the most surprising or thought-provoking thing you take from this chapter.

In which of the Five Essentials do you most often lack motivation for improvement?

A Blueprint for Life

"An extraordinary life is all about daily, continuous improvements in the areas that matter most." — Robin Sharma

No builder would break ground on a new construction project without having a detailed blueprint ahead of time. No one would make a long distance trip to a place they've never been without consulting a map or GPS. Why is it we understand this concept in every other area of life except for the most vital area of all, actually making a blueprint for our future of personal growth and development.

A lot of men and women do this for their job. It's required in some lines of work to have goals and key performance indicators. But I want to encourage you that before you build your business plan, build your life plan. Figure out what kind of life you want to have first. Make your business plan fit your life plan, not the other way around. Most of us do just the exact opposite. We build our business plan first, set up our goals, and dedicate our lives towards executing them. Only then do we figure out how to fit our life around that (usually to the detriment of our Spiritual and Relational Essentials).

Jesus put it this way in Luke 14:28-30, *"For which of you, desiring to build a tower, does not first sit down and count the cost, whether he has enough to complete it? Otherwise, when he has laid a foundation and is not able to finish, all who see it begin to mock him, saying, 'This man began to build and was not able to finish.'"*

Jesus said as you're building your life, you had better have a plan. Otherwise, you'll get halfway up and be unable to finish!

You wouldn't build a house without a blueprint, would you? Suppose you were wanting to build your dream home and you hired a contractor to construct your house and he laid out a paper bag on the back of his pickup truck and sketched out the blueprint. You'd probably say, "No way, Jose! *Next!*" You wouldn't hire that contractor because his lack of diligent planning gives you a lack of confidence.

> "Success is something you attract by the person you become."

If you wouldn't hire someone like that to build your house, then don't commit the same mistake when trying to build your life plan. You must begin with the blueprints. Remember: "Success is something you attract by the person you become."

I've partnered with *Trailhead Planners* in developing a specialized planner for this book. I want to encourage you to purchase this planner so you can get the most out of what you just read. You can find *The Five Essentials of Life Planner* on Amazon.

STEP 1 - Your Statements of Faith

The first step to setting goals is to dream big. In essence, a goal is a statement of faith. It's believing that God could do something through you by a certain period of time.

I want to encourage you to come up with a list of statements of faith, the dreams that you are building for your future. Pray and ask God to help you dream bigger. If you can think it, it's already too small in the eyes of God, for Scripture says, *"No eye has seen, no ear has heard, and no mind has imagined what God has prepared for those who love him"* (1 Corinthians 2:9).

And I want to encourage you to take this list and not just read it. Instead, recite it out loud. We live in a day of voice-activated devices like Amazon Alexa or Siri, but did you know that our faith is also voice activated? To be clear, I'm *not* talking about what is known as "word of faith" doctrine where some believe you can have whatever you say. This is not some "name it and claim it" or "blab it and grab it" doctrine. Our words do not have more power than God's plan. He is the all-sovereign, all-knowing, all-powerful God. But when Jesus taught us about having "mountain-moving faith," He taught us to literally "*speak*" to our mountain. A mountain is a symbol for anything that is a barrier to you completing God's will for your life. Incredible power is released when we speak to our mountains. But too many times, we talk to God about how big our mountains are when we should be talking to our mountains about how big our God is.

The words you speak become the house you live in. It's the repetition of affirmations that leads to belief. And once that belief becomes a deep conviction, it begins to change who you are, how you see the world, and the goals you attract. Affirmations enable you to design and develop the mindset (thoughts, beliefs, focus) that you need to take any area of your life to the next level.

I read that 80% of women have self-deprecating thoughts about themselves (body image, job performance, other people's opinion of them, etc.) throughout the day. I'm sure men do as well, although it may be to a lesser extent.[1] Those negative thoughts can lead to negative outcomes, but similarly, positive thoughts can lead to good results.

Try speaking your statements of faith out loud. They may not feel true at first, but you keep saying them until they do become true to you. In order for God to change you, in order for God to lead you into the person He wants you to become, there must first be a change in the way you think. When you declare something over and over again, you might just get to the place where you start to believe it.

If you don't have a strong "why" like we looked at previously, if you don't keep this image of the person you're going to become in front of you, you might succeed in your goals for a little while. However, you're likely to return right back to where you started in the first place. This is why someone might make a goal of losing weight. They reach their goal targeted weight loss and then fluctuate right back to the same weight or more than when they got started. They may have temporarily lost the weight, but they didn't change their "set point." When you write out your statements of faith, these become your true north; the compass point that enables you to navigate with confidence.

I want to encourage you to sit down and write out on a piece of paper what you would like to see God do in your life. Write it in the present tense. Start by saying, "I am happy and blessed now that..." And then explain how you want your life to be, in every area. I want to encourage you to do this in each of the *Five Essentials*: Spiritual, Relational, Intellectual, Physical, and Financial. Write out a description of what you want your life to look like in each of these areas by listing at least five statements of faith (your dreams in this area of your life):

FINANCIAL: "I am so happy and blessed now that..."

- _____
- _____
- _____
- _____
- _____

PHYSICAL : "I am so happy and blessed now that..."

- _____
- _____
- _____
- _____
- _____

INTELLECTUAL: "I am so happy and blessed now that…"

- _____
- _____
- _____
- _____
- _____

RELATIONAL: "I am so happy and blessed now that…"

- _____
- _____
- _____
- _____
- _____

SPIRITUAL: "I am so happy and blessed now that…"

- _____
- _____
- _____
- _____
- _____

STEP 2 - Set Three SMARTER Goals for Each Essential

Socrates said, "The secret of change is to focus all of your energy not to fight the old, but to build the new." You will never make progress if all your focus is merely on "fixing" what you think is broken in your life. Setting goals is what enables you to build the new instead of fighting the old.

You need goals that will inspire you and motivate you to push forward. Set some goals that will stretch you in these five areas. Someone once told me not to bite off more than I could chew. I said I'd rather choke on greatness than nibble on mediocrity.

So look at your list of statements of faith that you just did. Now here's what I want you to do: **Set three goals that align with your statement of faith in each of the Five Essentials.** If you need help setting goals, refer back to the previous chapter under the Intellectual Essential heading. In that chapter, I talked about the importance of setting SMARTER goals. Do you remember what SMARTER is an acrostic for? To make goals that really work, they need to be:

S - Specific
M - Measurable
A - Actionable
R - Realistic
T - Time-Sensitive
E - Exciting
R - Relevant

Gary Ryan Blair says, "A goal is created three times. First as a mental picture. Second, when written down to add clarity and dimension. And third, when you take action towards its achievement."

Sometimes, it helps us to see other people's goals and that gives us ideas and inspiration towards writing our own. In his eBook, The Powerful Goals Playbook, Michael Hyatt gives 120 proven goal-setting templates to jumpstart your progress. So here are some suggestions for each of the Five Essentials:

FINANCIAL Goal Ideas:
- Improve net worth $___/___% by ___.
- Pay off the remainder of car loan in the amount of $___ by ___.
- Create a monthly income and expense budget by ___ and forecast the next 6/12/18/24 months.
- Reduce eating out to ___ meals each ___ beginning ___.
- Pay down $___ in credit card debt by ___.
- Give $___ each month/year to my church/charity.
- Save an additional $___/___% from each paycheck for an emergency fund starting ___.
- Plan for my next house/car/major project by saving $___ each ___ beginning ___.
- Increase my monthly 401k/retirement savings by $___/___% starting ___.
- Get taxes done early this year: Assemble all necessary paperwork by ___ and complete forms by ___.
- Start working on my next "side hustle." I want to earn $___ extra per month starting ___.
- Launch a new product/service by ___.
- Write a new business/proposal plan for ___ by ___.
- Quit job and launch a new business by ___.

PHYSICAL Goal Ideas:
- Lose ___ pounds by ___.
- Bring down my blood pressure ___ points by ___.
- Research and hire a nutritionist to complete a personalized meal plan by ___.
- Run/walk ___ minutes/miles each day, ___ days a week at ___ a.m./p.m.
- Research and hire a fitness coach to craft a personalized workout regimen by ___.

- Do strength training at gym ___ minutes/hours, ___ days a week starting ___.
- Lift ___ pounds at ___ exercise by ___ date.
- Improve my deadlift/bench press, etc. By ___ pounds by ___.
- Cut LDL cholesterol ___ points by ___.
- Finish my first 5k race/half marathon by ___.
- Complete a five-day juice fast by ___.
- Start intermittent fasting by fasting ___ hours a day from ___ time to ___ time.
- Choose a regular bedtime and get ___ hours of sleep per night for the next ___ days beginning ___.
- Wake up at ___ each day.
- Download a health-tracker app (e.g. MyFitnessPal) and begin inputting my daily calories immediately after each meal or snack.

INTELLECTUAL Goal Ideas:
- Read ___ books per month/quarter, starting ___.
- Audit a college class on the subject of ___ during the ___ quarter/semester.
- Select ___ conferences to attend and register by ___.
- Go back to school in ___ and get my Bachelors/Masters/Doctorate.
- Look for an online web course in ___ to grow in and calendar ___ minutes/hours per day to take the course.
- Read ___ minutes each morning/night at ___ a.m./p.m.
- Buy a foreign language program and learn ___ by ___.
- Participate in educational trip to the state/country of ___ by ___.
- Research and write my own book on ___ by ___.
- Research the best five business or self-help books in my area of expertise and the five best across the board and read ___ each ___ beginning ___.
- Get certified in ___ by ___.

RELATIONAL Goal Ideas:
- Plan ___ regular dates each month with my spouse and get them on the calendar by ___.
- Create a date night profile on Netflix and load up our favorites for a weekly date beginning ___.
- Attend the ___ marriage conference on ___.
- Write a list of my spouse's favorite qualities. Read it once daily, and pick one to focus on for the day for ___ days.
- Pick out ___ books (fiction or nonfiction) to read together.
- Pray with my spouse. Set aside a regular time each ___ beginning ___.
- Handwrite a note to someone every ___ (day of the week), for 52 weeks, beginning on ___.
- Leave the office by ___ to have enough time for ___ with the kids starting ___.
- Interview kids about their dreams. Pick one to accomplish together by ___.
- Pick a board/card game with the kids and a regular time to play once a week by ___.
- Cook ___ meals at home each week beginning ___.
- Write the kids ___ letters each week/month expressing ___ beginning ___.
- Plan a girls' trip / guys' trip with ___ of your friends. Book it by ___.
- Schedule ___ lunches/coffee dates with ___ friends by ___.
- Host ___ families/friends at my home for dinner ___ night(s) each month.
- Invite friends over for weekly/monthly movie/game night beginning ___.

SPIRITUAL Goal Ideas:
- Set aside ___ minutes in the morning, ___ days a week for Bible reading and prayer starting ___.
- Find a yearly Bible reading plan and follow it each day beginning ___.
- Ask friends, pastor, etc. About their favorite spiritual books. Pick ___ and read one each ___ beginning ___.
- Read the Bible ___ chapters/minutes each ___ starting ___.
- Keep a daily prayer journal. Start by ___.
- Choose a mentor/counselor and meet with him/her ___ times per month.
- Find a retreat sponsored by my church and make plans to attend by ___.
- Find a small group to attend at my church and go ___ times a month, beginning ___.
- Start a gratitude journal and list ___ things I'm thankful for each day starting ___.
- Practice biblical meditation for ___ minutes each day, ___ days a week beginning ___.
- Journal at least ___ minutes at the end of each day starting ___.

Don't feel like you need to pick any of the goals in these suggestions. This is just meant to prime the pump and get your creative juices flowing. In writing your top three goals in each area, you can also refer back to the NEXT STEPS sections of each chapter in this book under that specific essential.

So what are your top three goals in each of these Five Essentials? Make sure you put a target date on it! A goal is a dream with a deadline. And also make sure that you have these goals someplace where you can review them daily — preferably every morning and every evening. You can write your rough draft here, but don't forget to transfer it to someplace where you can review it daily later.

MY TOP 3 FINANCIAL GOALS

1. _____
2. _____
3. _____

MY TOP 3 PHYSICAL GOALS

1. _____
2. _____
3. _____

MY TOP 3 INTELLECTUAL GOALS

1. _____
2. _____
3. _____

MY TOP 3 RELATIONAL GOALS

1. _____
2. _____
3. _____

MY TOP 3 SPIRITUAL GOALS

1. _____
2. _____
3. _____

STEP 3 - The Secret Sauce: Weekly Accountability Register

Life will only change when you become more committed to your dreams than you are to your comfort zone. And the way that you build that commitment is by developing a system that will keep you accountable and committed towards reaching those goals.

A dream written down with a date becomes a goal. A goal broken down into steps becomes a plan. A plan backed by action makes your dreams a reality.

So in *The Five Essentials of Life Planner*, we've provided for you a place to do the following three things at the beginning of each week:

1. Focus — what are the top three goals you want to focus on this week and what are the action steps you will take that will help you progress toward those goals?

FOCUS
Write down the goals you are focusing on this week and the intentional action steps you are planning on taking.

GOALS	ACTION STEPS I AM TAKING THIS WEEK TOWARD THESE GOALS
READ __ BOOK BY __	READ __ PAGES EVERY DAY
LOSE 10 LBS BY __	RUN ON TREADMILL 30 MINUTES EVERY DAY

2. Approach — This gives you your week-at-a glance. Go ahead and map out your schedule and plot out any daily action steps, projects, or even your weekly meal plan. This is a place to see your entire week at a glance.

APPROACH
Plot out any daily action steps, appointments, projects or even your weekly meal plan here. This is a place to see your week at a glance.

SUNDAY	MONDAY	TUESDAY	WEDNESDAY	THURSDAY	FRIDAY	SATURDAY
				RUN 30 MIN		RUN 30 MIN
			SHOPPING			

3. Accountability — How are you doing? Reflect each day and hold yourself accountable. Did you do what you said you would do? As you go through the week, check off each day that you accomplished that task.

ACCOUNTABILITY
How are you doing? Reflect on your week and hold yourself accountable. In the action write down what you are doing. For example, Morning Devotions with an S next to it or Work Out 30 minutes with a P next to it.

Examples: **P - Physical, I - Intellectual, R - Relational, F - Financial, S - Spiritual**

As you go through the week, check off each day that you accomplish that task.

	ACTION	SUN	MON	TUE	WED	THU	FRI	SAT
S	DEVOTIONS	X		X	X		X	
P	RUN ON TREADMILL 30 MINUTES		X	X		X	X	
F	CALL 3 PROSPECTS			X		X		
I	READ 10 PAGES							

Here is what a blank sample page from the planner looks like:

WEEK 1 — FOCUS

GOALS | ACTION STEPS I AM TAKING THIS WEEK TOWARD THESE GOALS

APPROACH

SUNDAY	MONDAY	TUESDAY	WEDNESDAY	THURSDAY	FRIDAY	SATURDAY

ACCOUNTABILITY

ACTION	SUN	MON	TUE	WED	THU	FRI	SAT

"Every time you look in the mirror remember that God created you and that everything He creates is beautiful and good!"
— JOYCE MEYER

STEP 4 - Schedule Your Goals on Your Daily Agenda

I used to do the old-fashioned to-do list; but what I discovered was that most of the items that I scheduled were piddly things that never really advanced my bigger goals in the Five Essentials. Most of us are already "slaves" to our calendar. I use iCal on my Mac to schedule all of my appointments. My entire life is already on my calendar. So why not take the time to actually schedule work on my goals?

What gets scheduled is what gets done.

This has been the number-one difference maker for me. On Sunday, I plan out my week before I live my week. And I put all of my "To-Do" list items in green. Let's say you have a goal to spend 30 minutes in Bible reading, prayer, and meditation each day. Then enter it in your calendar to make it part of your daily agenda. Do you want to get a 45-minute workout in four days this coming week? You're more likely to do it if it's on your calendar as an appointment for a specific time of day (making sure to allow time to commute to and from the gym). What gets scheduled is what gets done.

Mike Murdock says, "You will never change your life until you change something you do daily."

Here is a sample daily agenda page from *The Five Essentials of Life Planner*.

STEP 5 - Evaluate Your Progress

Before you plan your next week, evaluate your previous week. Take a look at your weekly accountability register again. Is there another one of the Five Essentials you need to emphasize more this week that was missing from the previous week?

You either evaluate or you stagnate. It's okay to make some pivots and shifts in your goals and trajectories from time to time. Tough times will come. Unexpected things happen. Be flexible enough to adjust accordingly. As John Maxwell states: "The pessimist complains about the wind. The optimist expects it to change. The leader adjusts the sails."

Wrapping it Up

Every next level of your life will demand a different version of you. That's why you've got to be committed to growth and expansion in these five areas that matter most.

Think of your life today like a seed. Every apple seed has an apple tree in it. And the potential success of that tree is held within that seed. That is exactly how God created you. Whatever you were born to do and become is within you now and the success of your life depends on you becoming all that is already trapped inside of you. So ask yourself this question: "How would the person I'd someday like to be, do the things I'm about to do?"

Proverbs 16:3 tells us to *"Commit your work to the LORD, and your plans will be established."* We are to commit our works to the Lord. Lay this personal growth plan before Him and seek His wisdom and input. Ask God if there is anything He wants you to add or change. The word "commit" in this verse means "to carry into action deliberately." *Commit* means to make it happen no matter what. Remember this the next time you have bacon and eggs for breakfast. The chicken was involved, but the pig was committed! When you decide that you're going to be committed no matter what, life changes for you. Perhaps that's why Socrates said, "The uncommitted life isn't worth living."

Do things the right way and you'll reap the results in the right time. God can bless anything but nothing; so give God something to bless.

And don't forget to help others along in your own journey. Life has no value and meaning apart from a life lived with God and others. Jack Welch said, "Before you are a leader, success is all about growing yourself. After you become a leader, success is all about growing others."

Jim Rohn once said, "If you want to have more...you have to BECOME more. Success is not a *doing* process; it is a *becoming* process. What you do, what you pursue, will elude you—it can be like chasing butterflies. Success is something you attract by the person you become. For things to improve, you have to improve. For things to get better, you have to get better. For things to change, you have to change. When you change, everything changes for you."

This is the precise reason why I wrote this book. The Five Essentials of Life aren't about arriving at a destination but about becoming the person God has made you to be along the way. I invite you on such a journey--the journey of continuous personal development in the areas that matter most.

NOTES

Understanding the Five Essentials

1. Hardy, Darren. *Living Your Best Year Ever* (Success Books, 2012), 28.
2. One study from 2010 can be found at http://content.time.com/time/magazine/article/0,9171,2019628,00.html.
3. See Matthew 6:19-34 for the whole context.
4. Matthew 6:33
5. Mike Breen, *Oikonomics* (3 Dimension, 2014), Digital.
6. Psalm 37:4

Achieving a Laser Focus

1. Philippians 3:13 NIV
2. https://www.inc.com/wanda-thibodeaux/new-survey-shows-70-%-of-workers-feel-distracted-heres-why.html (Accessed October 22, 2018).
3. https://www.livescience.com/2493-mind-limit-4.html (Accessed October 22, 2018).

Postponing Your Procrastination

1. This teaching of the gap between the imagined world and the realized world is from an emailed article by Bryan Ward, "Why Visionaries are the Worst Procrastinators."
2. Clark, James L. "6 Ways To Stop Procrastinating." James L. Clark (blog), September 8, 2018, http://www.jameslclark.org/6-ways-to-stop-procrastinating/.

The Wheel of Life

1. The questions in this assessment are adapted from Darren Hardy's book, *Living Your Best Year Ever*. He assesses eight life areas, whereas the focus of this book is only on the five essentials.

The Greatest Financial Principle

1. Geraci, Jonathan. *Wealth Building Secrets from the Bible* (Self-Published, 2017), 66.

A Bulletproof Budget Strategy

1. Geraci, Johnathan. *Wealth Building Secrets from the Bible* (Self-published, 2017), 67

Accelerate Your Debt Reduction
1. Proverbs 22:7
2. https://www.thesimpledollar.com/the-emotional-effects-of-debt/ retrieved October 18, 2018.
3. https://www.cnbc.com/2018/01/23/credit-card-debt-hits-record-high.html (Accessed October 26, 2018).
4. You can go to their website www.digit.co for more information.
5. Luke 18:27

Invest for Tomorrow
1. https://www.cnbc.com/2018/05/31/a-523-monthly-payment-is-the-new-standard-for-car-buyers.html (Accessed October 27, 2018).
2. Proverbs 21:20
3. This is according to Investopedia based on Bitcoins value on June 22, 2018. https://www.investopedia.com/articles/investing/123015/if-you-had-purchased-100-bitcoins-2011.asp (Accessed October 27, 2018).
4. https://smartasset.com/investing/pros-and-cons-of-using-a-robo-advisor-to-build-wealth (Accessed October 27th, 2018)
5. This statistic is taken from their website, www.betterment.com.
6. Adapted from this blog: https://singlemomsincome.com/how-to-get-started-investing-for-complete-beginners/ (Accessed October 27, 2018).
7. Ecclesiastes 11:2 from the New Living Translation.

What the Wealthy Do Different
1. https://www.boostmybudget.com/habits-of-millionaires-make-you-rich/ (Accessed October 28, 2018).

Nutrition: Eat This, Not That
1. https://www.littlethings.com/superfoods-body-parts/6 (Accessed October 31, 2018).

Your Guide to Health Supplements
1. https://holisticchristianlife.com/i-dont-believe-in-supplements/ (Accessed November 2, 2018).
2. To type the link directly into your browser: http://onnit.sjv.io/c/1297530/455688/5155

3. https://thetruthaboutcancer.com/5-cancer-fighting-healthy-fruits/ (Accessed November 2nd, 2018).
4. LEGAL DISCLAIMER: This book provides general information and discussions about health and related subjects. The information and other content provided in this book, or in any linked materials, are not intended and should not be construed as medical advice, nor is the information a substitute for professional medical expertise or treatment.

    If you or any other person has a medical concern, you should consult with your health care provider or seek other professional medical treatment. Never disregard professional medical advice or delay in seeking it because of something that have read in this book or in any linked materials. If you think you may have a medical emergency, call your doctor or emergency services immediately.

    The opinions and views expressed in this book have no relation to those of any academic, hospital, health practice or other institution.

Exercise: Your Fitness Challenge

1. https://www-m.cnn.com/2018/10/19/health/study-not-exercising-worse-than-smoking/index.html (Accessed October 20, 2018).
2. https://www.the-bodybuilding-blog.com/2016/03/27/the-9-best-exercises-for-muscle-growth/ (Accessed (November 4, 2018).

The Five Rules of Fat Loss

1. http://leancalories.com/6-simple-weight-loss-tips-to-lose-weight-very-fast/ (Accessed October 31, 2018).

The Benefits of Intermittent Fasting

1. https://jamanetwork.com/journals/jamaoncology/fullarticle/2506710
2. https://translational-medicine.biomedcentral.com/articles/10.1186/s12967-016-1044-0
3. https://www.karger.com/Article/Abstract/212538

Become an Early Riser

1. These five benefits are adapted from the following YouTube video: https://www.youtube.com/watch?v=5w4vOxOmK6U&feature=youtu.be (Accessed November 5, 2018).

2. https://www.entrepreneur.com/article/291907 (Accessed November 5, 2018).
3. Ray Williams, "Early Risers ar Happier, Healthier, and More Productive Than Night Owls." https://www.linkedin.com/pulse/20140808173331-1011572-early-risers-are-happier-healthier-and-more-productive-than-night-owls/ (Accessed November 5, 2018).

Invest in Yourself

1. Luke 2:49 NIV
2. The content for this section is adapted from an article by Stephen Blandino, "The Four Dimensions of Jesus' Personal Growth" https://stephenblandino.com/2015/03/four-dimensions-of-jesus-personal-growth.html (Accessed Nov. 6, 2018).

Develop a Clear Vision

1. Darren Hardy, *Living Your Best Year Ever* (Success Books, 2012) xi.
2. Mark Batterson, "10 Steps to Setting Life Goals" https://www.sermoncentral.com/scdownloads/10steps.pdf (Accessed November 10, 2018).
3. Clayton Mosher. *The Scientific American*. "How to Grow Stronger Without Lifting Weights." https://www.scientificamerican.com/article/how-to-grow-stronger-without-lifting-weights/ (Accessed November 10, 2018).
4. Ibid.
5. Hal Elrod. *The Miracle Morning* (Hal Elrod International, 2017). 73-74.
6. If you'd like detailed instructions on this process, Christian Kane has a blog on "How to Make a Vision Board" as well as a free eBook titled *The Complete Guide to Vision Boards*. www.ChristineKane.com.

Set Goals That Work For You

1. The SMARTER outline and much of the content in this section is adapted from Michael Hyatt's seminar. You can also access your own *5 Days to Your Best Year Ever!* seminar with Michael Hyatt by visiting: https://bestyearever.me/

Time Management

1. Check out the originator of the Pomodoro Technique by going to this website: francescocirillo.com.
2. Focus@Will offers both an app and a website: focusatwill.com

How to Rewire Your Brain

1. See the Book of Daniel chapter 10.
2. John 20:21-22, New King James Version
3. 1 John 4:4

Make Stress Your Friend, Not Your Enemy

1. Nature Builds Health, "Conquer (Chronic) Stress: The Ultimate Guide to Stress Relief. https://www.naturebuildshealth.com/blog/stress (Accessed November 12, 2018).
2. This illustration came from "Making Conversations Count," a lesson from The C12 Group. www.C12group.com
3. Alicia Carol. "Learn Something New to Overcome Stress." https://www.sproutandprosper.com/learn-something-new-overcome-stress/ (Accessed November 12, 2018).
4. Ibid.
5. You can access the full TED Talk by Kelly McGonigal by accessing this website: https://www.ted.com/talks/kelly_mcgonigal_how_to_make_stress_your_friend/up-next?referrer=playlist-talks_to_help_you_manage_stres

The Foundation of All Relationships

1. Matthew 22:37-39 (ESV)
2. The three dimensions of love is an outline I adapted from a sermon by James Merritt on love as a fruit of the spirit.
3. *The MacArthur New Testament Commentary on 1 Corinthians* by John MacArthur was used to learn the meaning of each of these 15 aspects of love in 1 Corinthians 13.

The Art of Listening

1. Science of People: "How to Read People Through Their Eye Movements and Uncover Hidden Emotions" https://www.scienceofpeople.com/read-people-eyes/ (Accessed November 13, 2018).
2. See 1 Kings 19.

Making and Keeping Friends

1. Medium.com, "Dunbar's number — the law of 150." https://medium.com/@social_archi/dunbars-number-1a8d75b94576 (Accessed November 15, 2018).
2. Proverbs 18:24, Good News Translation.
3. Billy Graham. *Just As I Am: The Autobiography of Billy Graham*. pp. 125-129.

The Science of Likability

Sources used in the development of this chapter:

The Science of Likability by Patrick King

11 Laws of Likability by Michelle Lederman

The Art of People by Dave Kerpen

Enchantment by Guy Kawasaki

ArtofLikability.com by Arel Moody

Working Your Networking

1. Minda Zetlin. "How to Network Like You Really Mean It."
2. https://www.inc.com/minda-zetlin/8-things-power-networkers-do-make-connections.html (Accessed November 13, 2018).
3. https://www.youtube.com/watch?v=reCX9LDQVKw (Accessed November 13, 2018).
4. Darren Hardy, "Winning Friends and Clients." https://www.youtube.com/watch?v=p5iv59YTP5o (Accessed November. 14, 2018).
5. Maya Elious, "How to Introduce Yourself at a Networking Event." http://www.mayaelious.com/how-to-introduce-yourself-at-a-networking-event/ (Accessed Nov 14, 2018).
6. Lisa Nichols, "The S.N.A.A.P. Technique: How to make an unforgettable impression in 60 seconds." https://www.youtube.com/watch?v=UzT2pYIMCyc (Accessed November 14, 2018).

Seek Him First

1. This outline of Frustration, Fatigue, and Fragmentation was adapted from a sermon by Kerry Shook, "The Center of Attention."
2. James Merritt's sermon: "The King and His Kingdom"

How to Pray with Power

1. Kent Murawski, "Does God Answer Vague Prayers?" http://kentmurawski.com/vague-prayers. (Accessed November 19, 2018).
2. Lee Bezotte. "Learning How to Pray from Napoleon Bonaparte." https://leebezotte.com/learning-how-to-pray-from-napolean-bonaparte/ (Accessed November 9, 2018).

Discover Your Calling

1. Venn diagram inspired by: *iCity Magazine*, Edwin Korver. "Storytelling on Purpose: The Missing Link"

2. Deuteronomy 11:13; 1 Samuel 12:20; Romans 1:9; Ephesians 6:6
3. Michael Hyatt, "How to Discern Your Calling" (Podcast S07E02) https://michaelhyatt.com/season-7-episode-02-how-to-discern-your-calling-podcast.html
4. Excerpt from Adam Leipzig's TED Talk: "How to know your life purpose in less than five minutes:" https://www.youtube.com/watch?v=vVsXO9brK7M
5. Quotation from the New Living Translation
6. Warren, Rick. *The Purpose Driven Life*. Pg. 242
7. Michael Hyatt, "How to Discern Your Calling" (Podcast S07E02) https://michaelhyatt.com/season-7-episode-02-how-to-discern-your-calling-podcast.html
8. https://www.ted.com/talks/rick_warren_on_a_life_of_purpose/transcript?language=en#t-1096180

An Attitude of Gratitude

1. Emily Fletcher. "The Neuroscience of Gratitude" https://zivameditation.com/zivablog/articles/the-neuroscience-of-gratitude (Accessed November 21, 2018).
2. 2 Chronicles 20:21

Get Motivated

1. Darren Hardy, *Living Your Best Year Ever* (Success Books, 2012), 3-4.

A Blueprint for Life

1. Hal Elrod, *The Miracle Morning*, pg. 63.

Made in the USA
Columbia, SC
20 December 2018